A YOUNG LOOK AT EUROPE

A YOUNG LOOK AT EUROPE

Theodore S. Voelkel

Edited by

Michael I. Eizenberg

The American Leadership Press

First published in 1971

Copyright © 1971 by Theodore S. Voelkel
The American Leadership Press, Worcester, Massachusetts 01602
Third Edition 1974

Library of Congress Catalog Card Number: 70-165117
International Standard Book Number: 0-87821-051-2
Printed and bound in the United States of America

CONTENTS

AUTHOR'S FOREWORD

This book is in three parts. The first part, "Getting to Know Europe," is designed to anticipate something of the sensation (even the shock) of going abroad and encountering firsthand the basic points of contrast between European life and our own. The second and major part of the book, "Day-by-Day through Europe," explains these differences in terms of the people, places, and events which have contributed to the shaping of modern Europe. It offers the reader a set of clues which can enliven his journey from one European country to another. The third part, consisting of "Orientation Essays," attempts to knit together the multitude of facts and details about Europe into a pattern of *ideas*, providing an intellectual background for the trip abroad and assisting the reader in retaining what he has experienced long after his return home.

A Young Look at Europe was written originally as a field manual for high school and college students participating in a program of overseas study and travel sponsored by The American Leadership Study Groups, Worcester, Massachusetts. It was intended to whet the young person's appetite for Europe. The author is pleased that the publication of this book makes it possible for him to share his own appetite for Europe with a wider audience.

PREFACE

In New Haven, during the early months of 1966, two students set about making plans. Both were avid Europhiles, and both were pursuing Ph.D.'s in philosophy. Their aim was to bring together their professional careers in education and their deep personal interest in European travel. They would do so by taking high school students to Europe as part of a new educational experiment.

Most young people who went to Europe, they observed, were given to *see* it without learning anything significant about it — without fixing the myriad sights and sounds to which they were exposed (and which they would soon forget) within a *framework* which would hold and unify them. Other students, not to be victimized in precisely *this* fashion, came all the way to Europe to hole up in a summer school for five weeks. These students, so it seemed, ended up seeing pitifully little of Western Europe, and learning, in most cases, what they could have learned in less time at home.

The two graduate students were confident that a course could be charted between the Scylla of empty tourism and the Charybdis of boring bookwork abroad, and seized upon a scheme whereby small groups of American students would spend three weeks of relatively concentrated study at the major university cities of London, Rome, and Paris, and two additional weeks of fairly brisk travel between these points. By traveling in small groups, it was hoped, the student could combine the best of travel on the one hand, and summer school on the other. A name was chosen for the groups. They would be called "The American Leadership Study Groups." The idea seemed to be a good one.

It was. Students and teachers responded to their ALSG-sponsored experience overseas by recommending it to their colleagues and best friends, who in many cases enrolled in subsequent summer sessions. As a result, the program grew. Teachers often became so enthused that they selected eight, ten, or fifteen of their best students to participate in the program under their guidance. The program grew even more. Eventually, the flattery of imitation was provided as well, with self-proclaimed "institutes" and "academies" of overseas study suddenly springing into existence with boasts of "academic tourism." All this was heartening to the two graduate students, whose original idea had been to take young Americans overseas in just this way, and with just this balance of study and travel. Their idea had fostered an organization — the ALSG — and this organization had been supported by an ever-growing constituency, and was now even being emulated.

Success mothered invention. It had always been a major tenet of ALSG educational philosophy that learning can proceed only against a background of *feeling*, and that a teacher's first job, even if not his last, is to create a context of personal involvement within which the student will *want* to remember facts, names, dates and the like. But with an ever-increasing number of young Americans enrolling in ALSG programs overseas, the articulation of this educational philosophy became much more difficult. Qualified staff are always limited in number, and possess only finite amounts of energy and enthusiasm. Thus, when teacher-student ratios tended to widen, the ALSG was presented with a crucial challenge. Fortunately, success was not allowed to ruin a good idea. Instead, every attempt was made to open new channels of communication with the student — channels which could provide more teaching leverage to the ALSG staff, and thus allow them to succeed at their original task with larger and larger numbers of students. Vigorous experimentation with media aids ensued, for the attempt was being made to explore every possible avenue by which the teacher-student relationship could be deepened and enhanced. A film was made one summer overseas, and shown to subsequent program enrollees as part of the pre-departure preparation. A series of educational cassette tapes was produced, and involved acoustical images as diverse as *The Rolling Stones*, a German band, and Debussy. Slide shows and drama found their way into the typical ALSG syllabus. "You and the City" encounter sessions were devised in an attempt to force a confrontation of student and foreign environment.

Also, a book was written. This book.

The book was first entitled *Field Manual: A Guide to the ALSG Experience Overseas*. Its purpose, like that of other media aids pressed into service by the ALSG, was to give the reader a *feel* for his adventure overseas — a feel which would make him want to learn about Europe. As such, the book is light on facts (although it does contain a fair number of them), and heavy on imagery, evocation, and the poetical dimensions of European travel. It is not to be read as a guidebook, though it has helped thousands of people to understand what they were about to see. Nor is it to be read as a sample itinerary, though many readers have planned exciting and successful excursions through Europe by taking their cues from it. Instead, it is to be enjoyed with a straightforward passion — the passion with which one anticipates an exciting experience, or thinks back on it afterwards. The book is nostalgic.

The author of *A Young Look at Europe* was one of the two students at whose hands the ALSG evolved during the winter of 1966. His name is Theodore S. Voelkel, and he is presently an Associate Director of the ALSG, and an Assistant Professor of Philosophy at Southern Connecticut State College. The other of the two — who has long since become a fast friend of the first — now takes this opportunity to thank the author on his own personal behalf, on behalf of the organization which he and his friend helped to found, and on behalf of the members of that greater audience to whom the present volume is destined, for having written the book that he did.

Gilbert Scott Markle
Executive Director
The American Leadership Study Groups

Assistant Professor of Philosophy
Clark University

ACKNOWLEDGEMENTS

The author wishes to express his thanks to the British Travel Association, German Tourist Information Center, Italian Government Travel Association, Swiss National Tourist Office, and French Government Tourist Office for their generous technical assistance; to Lewis Cetta, John Hyland and Robert Neslund for their many ideas and suggestions during the final preparation of the manuscript; to Mrs. Barbara Phelan, without whose ceaseless efforts at the typewriter there would have *been* no manuscript; to Michael Eizenberg, whose editorial rigor kept the author from making the fatal mistake of saying much more (though at times it *seemed* much less!) than he really meant to say; and in the last place — because in the first place — to his friend Gilbert Markle, who started it all by introducing the author to Europe during their student years together in graduate school.

GETTING TO KNOW EUROPE

GETTING TO KNOW EUROPE

It's surprising how easy it becomes to digest historical facts when walking around inside the Colosseum. Or to learn about the art of the Renaissance while viewing the *David* in Florence. Or to appreciate the importance of the Common Market by strolling about the center of Brussels, Europe's most international city. What was once a matter of dull and routine information comes to life as one is challenged day after day to assimilate a whole panorama of different faces, colors, sounds, and new ideas.

But there is a difficulty which a student traveling abroad often encounters. It's easy to get lost in an ocean of details; to become baffled and confused by the changing scenes, and to come away from the experience with only a blur or a vague feeling to show for it. The best way to avoid such problems is to have an idea of what to do beforehand — to plan a suitable itinerary, and stick to it. Europe is big, and very often things change dramatically in a matter of just fifty miles. It is impossible to cover it all thoroughly in one summer trip. The traveler has to select and concentrate on those cities and towns which are representative of each country, and which promise the most rewarding experience.

For example, a person could devote a whole lifetime getting to know Germany. An entire summer would only scratch the surface. But quite a lot can be accomplished in just a few days if the visitor knows what he's doing. There is Cologne, one of the most attractive and important cities in Europe, whose cathedral is among the most renowned of all Gothic monuments. Or Bonn, where the bustle and commotion immediately announce that you are in the capital city of the German Federal Republic. Or the enchanting university town of Heidelberg, a dream city all by itself, and the site of the most spectacular ruin in Germany. Or Munich, the city of Baroque churches and ultra-modern department stores, the "beer capital" of the world and an important electronics center as well. Or Aachen, a small town on the way to Cologne, where the Emperor Charlemagne held court back in 800 A.D., and which still houses one of the largest collections of medieval art. Nor would anyone want to miss an afternoon's boat trip up the Rhine River, so often celebrated in Wagner's operas, where reality blends with myth and folklore as the boat steams past the fairy-tale castles on the shore. Or take the lovely resort town of Garmisch, which straddles the highway between Munich and Innsbruck, Austria. Its gaily painted houses and ornate woodwork offer a fitting farewell to any trip through Germany. Cologne, Bonn, Heidelberg, Munich, Aachen, the Rhine River, and Garmisch: that's quite a bit for just a few days in Germany. But it can be done; it is simply a matter of intelligent and imaginative selection.

This same principle of selective concentration can be applied with fruitful results, not just to Germany, but to the whole of Europe. Our selective itinerary suggestions begin with a week or ten days in London, continue across the English Channel to Belgium, down the Rhine River to Heidelberg, east to Munich, south to Garmisch, and on to Innsbruck, Austria. The trip resumes again after a few days in the "Mountaineer's City," heading over the Brenner Pass to Venice and down the Apennine mountains to Florence. Then further south to Rome for another full week, including a day's trip to Capri. Then north again, but this time to Milan, and on over the Swiss Alps to Lucerne. The trip continues west to Paris for a final week or 10-day stay. The whole trip takes about five weeks, and can be done for less than $1000 by taking advantage of low student group and charter rates.

This itinerary has evolved from a summer program operated since 1966 by the American Leadership Study Groups. ALSG is an independent association of educators and students with offices at Airport Drive Road in Worcester, Massachusetts. Students and teachers in the program travel in groups of 35, following the route sketched above. The program avoids the "intellectual dizziness" which often accompanies a first trip overseas. There are two ways of doing it. The first has already been mentioned — namely, the principle of selective concentration. A second way is a series of multi-media presentations which suggest a few general ideas about the peoples and cultures of Europe. These ideas provide a broad, inclusive background for the students' sightseeing excursions in each city, and for visits to museums, art galleries, and musical performances. ALSG lectures focus on just such ideas. This book will outline a few of these ideas, especially in the Orientation Essays. It will also suggest some readable books which might be used in preparing for a first trip to Europe.

There is a positive philosophy behind the itinerary we have established. It's based on the conviction that Europe can be understood only against the general background of the Renaissance. The Renaissance was the period in which Western man came to a rediscovery of himself. By following our itinerary, and taking our suggestions along the way, a student can trace this rediscovery for himself through all the many activities and monuments in which it can be seen at work: in painting, sculpture, music, literature, social development, and philosophy. This theme can be seen in Memling's microscopically detailed paintings in Bruges, Belgium, in Michelangelo's *Moses* in Rome, or in a play at the Shakespeare Memorial Theatre in Stratford-on-Avon.

But man's rediscovery of man is by no means limited to the past. Europe is today. The rediscovery goes on. It's present in the Common Market, which promises a whole new kind of Europe in the future. It finds expression in the new trends in film and fashion. There's "mod" in London, a discotheque in Rome, or a hot debate among students in Paris on the future of the French University. There are new ideas developing about the relation of man to his environment. These too are worth exploring while tracing man's rediscovery of himself from Renaissance times to the present, to see what man *has* discovered about himself over the past 400 years or so. It's a fascinating story, just waiting to unfold before the visitor as he journeys from London to Rome to Paris.

First, however, a few remarks about some down-to-earth aspects of any summer overseas. Many Americans (especially adults) take out their maps of Europe and look them over in the following way.

> Hmm. England, France, Germany, Belgium. Looks pretty good. I think I'll try France this year. They say the weather's great in June, and my wife wants to go perfume shopping in Paris. And I've always wanted to see the Folies Bergères. Then maybe a short flight to London. KLM's offering a special husband-and-wife discount on a 9-day return basis. Right. That's exactly what we'll do.

To this man, Europe is flat. All the countries of this continent, with their complicated patchwork of languages, cultural traditions, and mannerisms, are all more or less on the same level — like cubbyholes in the Post Office. They number 1 to 100. Take your pick. If you don't like France, hop on a jet to London. If London's too wet and foggy, there's Brussels. And so on. Once our hypothetical traveler lands in Paris, he'll have his eyes wide open, but he won't see anything. Nor, in all probability, will his wife. If it's the Folies Bergères he wants to see, he can see it done better — and pay much less for it — in Las Vegas. His wife can buy all the French perfume she wants in New York City. And the weather's just as great in Oregon. Our travelers are missing the point about "being in Europe".

Although Europe is big – too big, in fact, to be taken in at a glance – it is made up of very small things. It's fascinating to watch Europeans in their day-to-day actions, for it is here that style comes out. "Seeing Europe" is seeing how a Frenchwoman buys a tablet of stationery in a bookstore. (It's quite a ritual, unless our visitor is too busy to notice.) In the U.S., the salesman smiles if the purchase is big, frowns if it is small. In Europe, there is an etiquette which almost every sales clerk follows. He says an elaborate "Thank you!", quite irrespective of the size of the purchase. The only exception, of course, is the harried salesman who has been jaded by U.S. tourists. "Seeing Europe" is seeing how a Londoner reads the morning newspaper. Or with what careful scrutiny the German *Hausfrau* selects her purchase of *Bratwurst* (sausage) at the local *Metzgerei* (meat store). Or the kinds of jokes that the different peoples of Europe enjoy.

Humor in Germany is a very different thing from what it is in France or in Britain. But European humor in general tends to be very different from its American counterpart. American humor, especially on TV or in the movies, is aimed at the instantaneous laugh. Think of the Johnny Carson show or the typical Phil Silvers stunt. The viewer roars with laughter, then waits for the next "gag". Five seconds later, he can't remember what it was that he found so funny. American humor tends to be a quantitative thing; the more outrageous the gag or the stunt, the funnier it is. The assumption is that if, instead of having one couple involved in a pie-fight, there are seven couples throwing pies at each other, the total effect must be seven times as funny. The European approach to humor is different. Europeans are more concerned with the quality of the joke – with its subtlety, complexity, and articulation – than with the quantity of instantaneous laughter it evokes. The point of a European joke often requires a great deal of thought to unravel. Europeans linger over a joke, repeating it often, recalling it fondly long after they have heard it the first time. Here is an example that will outdo any American joke for its sheer intellectuality:

French townspeople in a small provincial hamlet were laughing for days over a theater marquee which announced this film: "VOTRE FEMME NOUS TROMPE" ("Your Wife is Deceiving Us"). What's so funny about that? The verb "tromper" (deceive) is often used to indicate a wife's unfaithfulness to her spouse. In French literature and drama, one often encounters the expression "Votre femme *vous* trompe" ("Your wife is deceiving *you*"), as someone's friend lets him in on an unpleasant, but important, secret. Here, however, the one deceived is not the husband — or not *only* the husband — but a whole circle of his wife's paramours, who are apparently outraged that their mistress has turned to someone else. Hence the complaint, "Your wife is deceiving us."

The whole effect of this joke is created by a simple change of one letter: from *vous* to *nous*. This may not strike the American as being at all funny. In any case, the joke loses something in translation. But at least the point about European humor comes across. It is highly verbal, often intellectual, and in all cases much more subtle than the average Johnny Carson one-liner. In short, American humor, like everything else, tends to occur on a large scale; in Europe everything tends to be finer, smaller, more detailed.

Drinking is another way in which this difference can be seen. In America, people often sit and drink in silence, brooding over their home life, the unpaid bills, or the boss. That's what bars are commonly used for: the people inside drink to get "drunk". For them, drinking is a distraction from life. In Europe it's different. Drinking is a part of life, not a distraction from it. Europeans enjoy the experience of drinking itself — the conversation, the occasion, the details, the friends with whom they share a glass of cognac. In Germany, it is traditional for students to sit with their professor a whole evening, discussing philosophy, literature, or music. They usually reserve a back room in a tavern for the occasion. One mug of beer will last each of them the whole evening. The Swiss theologian, Karl Barth, spent many evenings this way with his students. The sidewalk cafés of Paris are another example. All sorts of people are clustered together — husbands, wives, even the kids — lingering over their glass of wine, taking it slowly, savoring the bouquet. In Bavaria, the farmers still have a bottle of beer with their breakfast.

It may not be too much to say that Europeans in general have a much greater love for the small things of life, the things which last, and it's these things that often go unnoticed by the tourist. But the love of small pleasures does not mean that Europeans are gullible. A few years ago, the Pepsi Cola Co. conducted an advertising campaign in France in exactly the same way it does in the U.S. The country was festooned with billboards exhorting everybody to "Think Young, Drink Pepsi." The campaign was a flop. French people simply laughed at such appeals; they weren't about to be "taken" that easily. Later, Pepsi caught on to the *French* approach to advertising. In Paris, for example, French companies announce their wares very simply and unpretentiously. Riding on the Paris métro (subway), one notices advertisements go by outside the window which simply give the name of their product, nothing more: "Cinzano", "Renault", etc. No appeal to repressed masculinity, no hint of a glamorous career awaiting the user of "Gauloises". However, some American firms have yet to wake up to the kind of advertising that appeals to Europeans. Esso still sprinkles the European countryside with the "Tiger in the Tank" motif. They can be seen all over France: "Mettez un tigre dans votre moteur"; in Germany: "Pack den Tiger in den Tank"; or in Italy: "Metti un tigre nel motore". Europeans smile and shrug their shoulders.

There are many other "small things" worth noticing in Europe. Americans are often frustrated in their first attempt to read a British newspaper. The arrangement of material is quite different than it is in one of our own. Often, an advertisement will appear on the front page, while the news items surrounding it will seem to be absurdly trivial: wool prices in Nottingham, a county fair in Halstead. What Americans don't realize is that a British newspaper is designed to be opened up to the center first, where the international news appears. Then the reader works his way to the front or the back depending on whether he's looking for racing schedules or art exhibits. Most "tourists" miss these things because they don't pause to look for the small items which distinguish European life from our own.

John Gunther, in a burst of enthusiasm, once stated that "France is the most civilized country in the world." That might be overstating the case a little – the British, Germans, and Italians might want to qualify that statement. But Gunther's basic point about "civilization" is a valid and important one. Civilization means much more than a country's Gross National Product or its technological achievements. It is really a style and art of living that makes even the smallest act a ceremony. Life itself becomes a kind of ongoing dramatic experiment. To a European, it's not so much what one does, but how he does it. That's why the London Bobby seems excessively polite as he gives the visitor the directions he asked for. That is why the Frenchwoman makes the purchase of a tablet of stationery a minor ritual. For many Americans, life is not an art, but a business – a series of "problems" to be solved in the most efficient way. To a European, life is not a business but a style to be achieved. Both style and ceremony are often notoriously inefficient.

Civilization itself is a matter of style. Whole nations may have distinctive styles, and each separate internal region may have its own peculiar style. Each individual in that region will have his own variation to make on that regional style. Many European wars over the past 300 years may be considered conflicts of style as well as of ideals or national interests. The writer, F. Scott Fitzgerald, was one of the few Americans to perceive the kind of passion which motivated the common foot soldiers in World War I. He saw the conflict, not just as a war between nations, governments, ideologies, or classes, but as a struggle between German beer and French wine or English roast beef. It was the little things that soldiers held dear which sustained them in combat. This is reflected in their songs: they are songs, not of lofty ideals or grand ambitions, but of home, family, friends, or the village parish.

There's something else worth noting. Europeans don't make such a fuss about the distinction between a person's public and private life. Americans tend to get "up tight" about any public discussion of one's private religious or political beliefs. These subjects, at least until recently, were taboo in ordinary conversation. It's different in Europe. People openly acknowledge their religious or political affiliations. They don't fret if a cathedral or local church has been renovated with public funds, because a cathedral belongs to the life of the community. A person's "public" and "private" lives are not as rigidly compartmentalized in Europe as they are in the U.S. And the public life of a European community is all the richer for it. Europeans take a relaxed view of the "separation of church and state", even in countries having a mixed religious constituency. This can lead to some amusing situations. In England, both Houses of Parliament must pass on any major changes in the Anglican Prayer Book. One can imagine Bertrand Russell sitting in the House of Lords, discussing and voting on fine points of the Anglican liturgy, even though he was an avowed agnostic. He didn't regard this as out of place, though he may have been less than enthusiastic about the issue. Similarly in France, where each church building is owned, not by the Vatican, but by the local village or city in which it is located. Communist delegates on city councils might vote to put a new stained glass window in the local parish church. Why would they do it? Because the local church or cathedral is regarded as a monument to the life of the town. Europeans take pride in all aspects of their community, whether it be the parish church, a statue in the village square, an old brewery (which may still be privately owned), or an art exhibit. Life is much less fragmented in Europe than in the U.S. Each country has an overall unity of style which tends to encompass personal differences in outlook, religious affiliation, or political persuasion.

Similarly, in Europe there isn't as large a gap between the "intellectual" (the writer, artist, or film director) and the ordinary citizen as there is in the U.S. The greatest authors write for the whole community, and the ordinary citizen tends to look to the writer or film director for personal ideals. A look inside the bookstores in London or Paris bears this out. A lot of middle-aged people from all walks of life are seen in there along with the students. Europeans take their reading more seriously than Americans do. Many of them even shape their lives on the basis of a philosophy which they've encountered in a novel or film. There is much more contact and respect between the educated and the uneducated in Europe, even though a smaller percentage of the people are able to attend a university.

Some Practical Details

There are a few important (and readable) books which give the serious traveler an enormous advantage over the breathless tourist. The Orientation Essays at the end of this book will be helpful too. For the present, a few books can be recommended as valuable preparatory material. Crane Brinton's *The Shaping of Modern Thought* is a well-written account of the major ideas behind the development of modern Europe, including the idea of humanism. Helen Gardner's *Art Through the Ages* is a comprehensive treatment of the history and theory of art; it should be read in fairly small doses. C. G. Black's *Our Western History* gives the high points of modern European history and is useful as a quick survey. In addition, Jean Ann Vincent's *History of Art* (College Outline Series) is a ready reference manual which can be brought overseas; it can be tucked into any flight bag along with camera film. For those interested in the concepts of the Renaissance, there is the extremely valuable collection of essays, *The Renaissance: Medieval or Modern?*, edited by Karl H. Dannenfeldt. Different writers offer their evaluation of this period of history in relation to the medieval world which preceded it. Linda Murray's *The High Renaissance* is full of color plates, and can be used with the other books above. Kenneth Clark's excellent new book *Civilisation,* based on his TV series, is also well worth using.

Of course, there are a great many other books worth consulting throughout the winter and spring, depending on one's area of concentration and background. The TIME/LIFE series on the different European countries is a useful and informal introduction to each country, people, and culture. It's often a good idea to bring a French, Italian, or German dictionary along. The Berlitz series of self-pronouncing phrase books and glossaries are perhaps the most practical, especially for a beginner in any of these languages. For those with more experience, a more comprehensive dictionary would be helpful, but it should be a pocket-sized edition. Otherwise, it will sit in a bureau drawer or at the bottom of a suitcase the whole time.

Only two documents are required for travel abroad: a passport and a recent vaccination certificate. The former is obtainable from the nearest Passport Office or State or Federal Court upon the presentation of proof of citizenship (a birth certificate or a family passport), proof of identity (a driver's license), and two recent wallet-sized photos. A passport is valid for five years. The only inoculation required is a recent smallpox vaccination, and this must be dated within three years of one's return to the United States. The Passport Office provides the form which must be signed by a physician and then certified by the local Board of Health. Other shots are not necessary, but might be taken on the recommendation of a physician, provided they are administered well in advance of one's departure for Europe.

DAY BY DAY ITINERARY

DAY-BY-DAY ITINERARY

New York to London at 30,000 Feet

The actual clock-time of the flight from New York to London is less than seven hours. But the five-hour zone difference stretches the time out to twelve hours. Service on board most flights is a sheer delight. Passengers are served a meal about an hour into the flight, and breakfast some five hours later. In between, there are soft drinks, assorted "munchables", and plenty of anticipation.

But even the snacks, the conversation, and the general excitement are as nothing compared to the sunrise that greets the passenger at about 30,000 feet. It begins about three hours into the flight and lasts almost an hour. Since the plane is above the clouds, we can guarantee a spectacular sunrise no matter what the weather's doing below. All that can be seen at first is a soft glow on the horizon. All around it, the sky is a rich, dark blue. The glow becomes more and more intense, stretching all across the horizon, from left to right as far as the eye can see. Then almost at once, a gigantic sunburst rips through the darkness, as if an unseen hand had turned on a celestial strobe light. The whole sky explodes into color. Gradually, the orange light separates itself from the horizon and rises slowly into the sky.

Touchdown occurs a few hours later. Most of London's airports are located about twenty miles from the center of the city. But it's worth the slight inconvenience, for one is invariably struck by how quiet and peaceful everything is outside the London traffic scene. London Airport is nothing at all like JFK. It's far out in the country, and all around the airport there is pastureland: brown-and-white spotted cows asleep on a field of soft green. It is usually quite cool out here in the summertime — much cooler than in New York. In the morning especially, it can fall to the lower 50's, with a nip in the air. And the air itself is fresh and clear.

Check-in is usually simple and quick. A few brief formalities, and one is standing out by the buses, or browsing around the duty-free shops in the lounge. Then it may happen, and quite suddenly. If it's a first trip abroad, the feeling may be a bit strange. Everything looks pretty much the same as it does back home, and yet there are little differences, and these little differences have a way of adding up. The buses taking the passengers into London don't look quite like Greyhound buses. They may have two front wheels on each side, one behind the other. The bus will drive down the "wrong" side of the road; many Americans have experienced something close to heart failure the first time the bus passed an oncoming car. The street signs do not look quite the same. The towns through which the bus passes may have funny-looking names, like "Hattleswitch" or "Hoddesdon" and "Chipping Ongar". It seems like a wholly different world.

This experience has surprised and even puzzled many a first visitor, especially those who assumed that Britain would be more or less like the U.S. After all, the same language is spoken in both countries. But it's worth recalling what George Bernard Shaw once said: "America and Britain are two countries separated by the same language." It's our common language that deceives us into believing that the British way of life is just like the American way of life. For this reason, many Americans tend to travel through Britain with their eyes closed. We mention all this only to prepare the visitor for what all too many people dismiss as homesickness, but which is more accurately described as "culture shock". It's the sudden jolt he feels at finding himself thrust into a strange environment, where the "little things" he is used to at home are abruptly exchanged for a set of "little things" that the British are used to. But it's all a part of the experience of going abroad. Soon, culture shock gives way to curiosity, curiosity to excitement, and one is happily in the swing of things in a few days. In fact, the American traveler is surprised at his reaction when returning to the U.S. He has to get used to things all over again. For the first time, he can catch a

glimpse of American life as he has never seen it before — as a European sees it. This can be one of the most valuable aspects of any trip overseas.

The bus trip from the airport into London begins on a broad highway but soon switches onto a fairly narrow country road which passes through tiny hamlets and towns, many of them with Elizabethan-style cottages. It's hard to get over the picture-book nature of the landscape: little cottages with their colorful window boxes and small garden plots blending with the old-fashioned looking inns and shops.

As the bus approaches London, the scenery changes gradually from Elizabethan countryside to industrial suburb. The succession of towns grows more frequent, and then they begin to merge with each other into a continuous urban stretch. There are long blocks of row-houses, one after another, most of them gray stucco. Many of the houses were put up in the 1850's, 60's and 70's, during the heyday of the Industrial Revolution, and it becomes easier to understand the living conditions of the factory workers which Charles Dickens described in his novels. "Urban stretch" now gives way to "urban sprawl", as the traveler finds himself nearing the center of Europe's largest city.

Before long, the bus cruises down one of the major traffic arteries of London. Black taxicabs begin to swarm around it. The taxis all look pretty much the same, and not surprisingly, since they're all made by the same company. During his stay in London, the visitor is bound to walk past one of them from time to time as it stands idling at an intersection. Notice the strange rasping sound their engines give off. It's caused by the diesel engines they use. The fares, by the way, are remarkably cheap; a mile ride costs just over a dollar.

Great Britain: Some Facts and Figures

It may seem strange, but one of the most puzzling things about Britain is learning just what to call it. Is it England? Great Britain? Britain? The United Kingdom? What's the difference? The visitor who calls someone coming from Scotland or Wales an Englishman will have an argument on his hands, if not something worse. The official name of the country is "The United Kingdom of Great Britain and Northern Ireland". It is made up of the island of Great Britain and the counties of Northern Ireland. The island of Great Britain itself is composed of England, Scotland, and Wales. The "British Isles" is just a geographical expression, not a country, and it refers to the island of Great Britain, to

Northern Ireland, and to the independent republic of Ireland (or "Eire"). In short, speaking geographically, there is the island of Great Britain, the island of Ireland, and several smaller islands, namely the Hebrides, the Shetlands, the Orkneys, the Isle of Man, Anglesey, and the Isle of Wight. Speaking politically about the nations involved, there are two countries: the Republic of Ireland, and the United Kingdom. The United Kingdom includes England, Scotland, Wales and Northern Ireland (the scene of recent disturbances between Protestants and Catholics). Generally speaking, the best thing is to refer to the country as "Britain". That's what the British themselves do.

Since this book is concerned only with England and Wales, the following figures pertain solely to these two members of the United Kingdom. The total area is a little over 58,000 square miles, Wales taking up about 7,000. The length of the country from north to south is just over 400 miles and its greatest width from east to west is about 300. Most of the English countryside is made up of low, undulating hills and forests. The climate is quite mild, ranging from a 35° average temperature in January to a comfortable 60°–65° in the summer. The weather is proverbially unpredictable. It may rain in the morning, turn sunny in the afternoon, then cloud over in the evening. In fact, it's most often cloudy, though a sunny day here and there is not unknown. Then there's the "London fog", about which one hardly needs to be reminded. Nearly everybody has an umbrella with him at all times. It's not a sign of cynicism, but of long experience.

England and Wales together have a population of some 46 million, with an average density of 790 per square mile – the highest in Europe, except Holland, which has about 830. The population is spread very unevenly, however. Around the larger ports and industrial centers, the population is especially dense, and the towns are closely packed together. But in the country, particularly around the less fertile hills and woods, the population is very thinly spread. On the way to Stratford, for example, the towns are rather widely spaced, and there's a good deal of open pastureland. Thus, in spite of the heavy population it is possible to "get away from it all" by going a few miles out of town.

Some 40% of the people in England and Wales are employed in industry. British automobiles are famous, of course, as is the British textile industry, known for its excellent wools. About 20% of the British people are in administrative or clerical work. Another 15% are in business. Transport and communications account for another 10% or so, and the construction and building trades, 5%. Agriculture ranks rather low, accounting for only 10% of the population. This indicates how dependent Britain is on food imports, which come mainly from Denmark and the Netherlands, Canada, Australia, and New Zealand. Livestock is about the only food industry in which Britain is self-sufficient. British roast beef can more than hold its own on any gourmet's checklist. But most other staples must be imported.

About half the population belongs to the Church of England, of which the American Episcopal Church is an affiliate. The Archbishop of Canterbury is the chief clerical figure in the Anglican Church, but Queen Elizabeth is the nominal head of the church. The Anglican Church is the officially established denomination in Britain, and is supported by the state. Major liturgical and doctrinal revisions must be voted on by Parliament. Since the church has always been tolerant, few British people mind this arrangement. The other large denominations include the Roman Catholic Church, the Methodist Church, and the Baptist Church, as well as various minor sects. Witchcraft is quite a big thing in some of the back-country towns; from time to time the newspapers carry stories about strange goings-on: voodoo, Devil worship, magic, and so on. There's room for everything in British religious life.

The British educational system differs in several respects from our own, as well as from the educational systems of the Continent. Examinations and testing generally are less important than a balanced diet of books, sports, hobbies, and sound common sense. School is compulsory up to age 15. There are many state-supported schools, but those who can afford it will send their children to "public schools" (actually private prep schools), many of them having long and prestigious histories. Eton and Harrow are the best known. Oxford and Cambridge are the oldest and most renowned of the universities, but the University of London has grown in esteem over the past 10 years. Oxford and Cambridge have always been known for their broad, liberal-arts approach to education. But many of the newer universities are much more specialized, especially in the professions, in business, and in industry.

The biggest universities do not function quite the way Yale or Harvard do. There is no one central building or master curriculum. Instead there are many different "colleges" (at Oxford: Magdalen, Christchurch, All Souls, etc.), each of which has its own residence halls and meeting rooms. Much of the teaching is done by "fellows" and "tutors" (or "dons", as they are popularly known) on a tutorial basis, that is, through private consultations and research projects. Examinations, however, are given by the university as a whole, which also grants the degrees.

The British parliamentary system is unique, and reflects the distinctive qualities of the British character. The system that works so well in Britain became a disaster in France until the French adopted the American system of a directly elected chief executive or president. Queen Elizabeth is the nominal head of the British state (as well as of the church), but her power is largely ceremonial and confined to personal influence. Parliament, or the nation's legislative assembly, actually does the governing, just as Congress passes all the laws in our country. (The term "parliament" goes back to medieval times, and comes from the French word, *parler,* to speak. Parliament was first established as a council where members "spoke" or debated about public issues.) The difference between Parliament and the U.S. Congress is that Parliament selects the chief executive or prime minister, who then chooses the personnel of his cabinet. In the U.S. by contrast, the President is chosen by direct popular election, or more precisely, by the popular election of an Electoral College, which then votes for the President. Because the British Prime Minister is chosen by Parliament rather than by direct popular election, it is almost impossible for the Prime Minister to be from one party while the opposing party holds most of the seats in Parliament. In the U.S., it happens occasionally that the president is from one party while the other party holds a majority of the seats in Congress. Each system has its own advantages and disadvantages, which political scientists often debate. But on the whole, both systems work pretty well. There are seldom any insurmountable deadlocks, and each system is able to furnish long-range political stability.

In Britain, major political upheavals have been avoided by a traditional two-party system, and even more importantly, by certain national traits which make for the success of the parliamentary system as a whole. The British simply don't care that much about party politics. They vote pretty much for the man rather than the party. British politics tend to be fairly low-keyed and unemotional – at least by U. S. and, especially, by French standards. Thus, a prime minister can ride out a period of low popularity quite handily. If the same situation existed in France, the voters would be clamoring for his head. In the U.S., pollsters would be predicting imminent doom.

The major British parties are the Labour Party (sometimes called the

Socialist party) and the Conservative (or Tory) Party. The Labour Party is more or less the modern descendant of the earlier (19th century) Whig Party, the Conservative of the 19th century Tory Party. Parliamentary elections must be held at least every five years, but an election can take place any time the prime minister calls for one.

Where to Find it in London

The following list is intended to help one find those little essentials so often taken for granted in the U.S., but which can be devilishly difficult to track down in Europe.

As elsewhere in Europe, the post office in Britain is an important center for all kinds of services. In some countries, people pick up their welfare checks at the post office. It's also the best place – indeed the only place – to send a telegram or make a long distance telephone call.

Pay telephones in Britain work as follows: First, dial the number. Don't put in any coins right away. If the number rings and there is no answer, just hang up. If there is an answer, some quick beeps will sound just as the other party says "Hello". Insert a coin in the proper slot, and quickly. Otherwise, you'll be cut off. There is no point in trying to insert the coin before the beeps start, since the slot is blocked until someone answers the phone. Sometimes it's necessary to wait awhile for the dial tone, or even to re-dial the number if nothing happens the first time.

London probably has the best public transportation system in the world. The red double-decker buses go everywhere, even to the suburbs on the edge of town. One seldom has to wait more than a few minutes for a bus to come along. The signs at the bus stop indicate the route or destination of the buses. Once inside, the passenger announces his destination to the conductor, who tells him what the fare is; the fare varies with the distance traveled.

The Underground is not to be confused with what the British call a "subway". A subway in Britain is just a passageway for pedestrians that runs underneath busy intersections. The Underground or tube has various crisscrossing "lines", which are easy to get to know. They have such names as "Central", "Metropolitan", "Bakerloo", "Piccadilly" and others. One of the first things to do is to get an Underground map. Any station will have one; they're free. They are indispensable for planning routes and transfers. Tickets can be purchased either at the station booth or from one of the automatic machines. (It's a good idea to have a variety of British coins at all times.) Since the cost of a ticket depends on the destination, the passenger must decide in advance what station he's headed for. Tickets should be retained, since they're often collected as the passenger leaves the station; one must pay twice if he loses it. In fact, this is typical of most European cities. Europeans take their tickets seriously. One is always well advised to hold onto any tickets he may collect until back at home. There is no way of telling who may want that ticket back again. Incidentally, smoking is allowed on the London Underground. If a seat is available, it will most likely be an elegant upholstered one.

Banks are found everywhere in London, but they close in mid-after noon and on weekends. British money is called "sterling". The whol system has finally been put on a decimal basis, but there are still som confusing traces of the old duodecimal system. A pound is worth $2.4C It's divided into 100 pence, each worth 2.4¢. A dollar is about equal t 42 pence. The main British coins besides the penny are the half-penny the two-pence, the five pence (formerly called the shilling officially, stil known as such unofficially), the ten pence, and the fifty pence. The latter is something like a silver dollar to the British, and is worth $1.20

Suggested Activities in London

London is so diversified and so spread out that the visitor can't expect to explore too much in a few days — even if he has nothing else to do. Realistically, one can expect to see a few of the most famous spots, to get a general idea of the layout of the city, and (perhaps more important) to get some "feel" of the place by watching its people and listening to its sounds. One way to do this is to see at least one sight connected with each period of London's history, and to try to understand that sight against the background of its history. Otherwise one simply ends up looking at quaint antiquities.

The first thing is to get an overall view of London, and the best place to get it is from the observation deck of the Post Office Tower. Often the ascent involves waiting, so ample time should be allowed. (Hours: 9:30 a.m. to 9:30 p.m.; Sundays included. Fare: about 20 new pence.) On a clear day — well, you can't see forever, but you can see as far west as Windsor Castle; and there's quite a view when London's lights go on.

A closer-to-ground survey can be gotten from a bus: the second level is rather like a moving grandstand. The great Gladstone once gave the following advice to some American visitors, and it still holds: "The way to see London is from the top of a bus — the *top* of a bus, gentlemen." The cost is but a few pence. Perhaps the best place to start from is

Hyde Park Corner. Sunday afternoon is the time to go, when the corner is clustered with speakers of every possible persuasion. Few people actually ascend the soapbox themselves, but most join in on heckling a would-be messiah or two. (To get there: Piccadilly tube from Leicester Square and get off at the third stop – you're at Hyde Park.)

Not far from Hyde Park are several other possibilities: (a) Oxford St., one of London's busiest shopping streets; runs west from the base of Tottenham Court Road. (b) The British Museum is just a few blocks northeast – close to London University. (c) Charing Cross Road boasts bookshops in abundance, including Foyle's (at 119: one of the world's largest) and E. Joseph (at 48A: a great assortment of used books). A bookstore, by the way, is a good place to watch Londoners spend a noon hour. Or (d) Soho, London's exciting "foreign quarter", just to the southwest.

Americans are used to streets that run for miles crosstown (21st St., or Broadway) – all arranged in a neat gridiron. London is not set out that way. One thoroughfare is usually a whole series of "streets". For example, stretching east from Marble Arch (at the northeast corner of Hyde Park): Bayswater Road becomes in turn Oxford, New Oxford, High Holborn, Holborn, New Gate, Cheapside, Poultry, Cornhill, and Leadenhall – and all in about three miles. It's not illogical really; there are good historical reasons why. The names are fascinating, and tell what was happening on that street hundreds of years ago. For example: Jewry Lane and Poultry are names which go back to Norman times. Most street names are more interesting than those in the U.S. Londoners commonly have addresses like 21 Houndsditch St. or 86 Petticoat Lane or 315 Birdcage Walk.

Following are some places well worth seeing. It's best to pick a few of the more interesting places and do them well.

(1) *Westminster Abbey* and the *Houses of Parliament* are, except for the Tower of London, two institutions with more "history" packed into them than anything else in the city. (Tube: District line west from Charing Cross; the first stop is Westminster.) The Houses of Parliament are open to the public only at certain times. (Saturdays, 10 a.m. – 4:30 p.m. are the best bet; admission is free. The main entrance is at Victoria Tower – at the south end, not to be confused with Big Ben.) There are guides, but the visitor can explore on his own too. Parliament isn't much more than a hundred years old, despite its Gothic appearance.

Any superlatives of ours are inadequate to describe Westminster Abbey and what it means. Some of its architecture is without equal in Britain, and it is the national burial place for the most honored dead.

The Abbey deserves a few hours of attention; it takes time to appreciate such places. Fortunately, the Abbey is probably in better physical repair than any ancient church in Britain, and recently the stonework has been painstakingly cleaned and the vaulting regilded. Parts of the present church date back more than 900 years, to just before the Norman conquest — to King-and-Saint Edward the Confessor; and it was as the burial shrine of Edward that the church gained its importance in the Middle Ages. None of the jeweled splendor of his tomb has survived — only a battered stone box in his chapel behind the high altar. The abbey soon became the royal mausoleum, though several kings and queens were buried there without monuments at all. And there almost seems to be a law at work: the lesser the personage commemorated, the gaudier the tomb — with exceptions, though. One of the most moving is the plain tablet in the floor near the great west door; its only words: "Remember Winston Churchill."

(2) *Changing of the Guard.* At 11:00 a.m., the Horseguards change at Whitehall. "Whitehall" is actually a short street which begins at Trafalgar Square. It is the political and administrative hub of the British Commonwealth. The Admiralty, War Office, and Foreign Ministry, as well as the quarters of the Horseguards are all on this street. Westminster Abbey and the Houses of Parliament are nearby. To get to Whitehall, simply take the Underground to Westminster. To see the changing of the Footguards at Buckingham Palace (11:30 a.m.), stay on the Underground for two more stops, and get off at Victoria Station. From there, walk up Buckingham Palace Road (or follow the crowd) to Buckingham Palace. Of the two events, the changing of the guard at Buckingham is the more popular. One can try to race from Whitehall to Buckingham, but it's not recommended. In any case, it's best to be there one-half hour early. On Sunday, the Horseguards change at Whitehall at 10 a.m. Buckingham Palace itself has been the official residence of the British sovereigns since 1837, when Queen Victoria began her reign. It was built in 1825, but was refronted in 1912. Whenever the queen is in residence, her standard flies from the flagpole, and the Footguards begin changing at 10:30 instead of 11:30. They are accompanied by a band.

(3) *Parliament in Session.* It is possible to see the House of Lords and the House of Commons on Saturday, before 3:30 p.m. The buildings were constructed between 1840 and 1850 on the site of the old Palace of Westminster, which was destroyed by fire, except for Westminster Hall, the latter having been incorporated into the newer buildings. To get there, take the Underground to Whitehall.

(4) *The British Museum,* in the words of *London Spy,* "is not the place for half an hour's stroll, but for a week's gaping." It's necessary, of course, to be realistic, and fortunately the museum has just the place for harried visitors — King Edward VII's Gallery. The gallery is meant to be representative of the whole collection; it gives the visitor an inkling of what could be seen in a week. If possible, see the Manuscript Saloon, which features the *Anglo-Saxon Chronicle, Beowulf* (in Case T), Venerable Bede's *Ecclesiastical History,* and the original *Alice in Wonderland* (Case X). And in the room to the right: two of the four extant copies of the Magna Carta, numerous ancient Bibles, and a mortgage bearing the almost indecipherable signature of William Shakespeare. (Open from 10 a.m. to 5 p.m., Sundays, 2:30 to 6 p.m. Free.) The best way to King Edward VII's Gallery is via the back door in Montague Place.

(5) *The National Gallery* is, quite simply, one of the richest collections of great art anywhere in the world — in the same class with the Uffizi Gallery in Florence. (Tube: at Charing Cross transfer to the Bakerloo line, getting off at Trafalgar; the gallery overlooks the northwest corner of Trafalgar Square. Hours: 10 a.m. to 6 p.m., and note: Tuesdays and Thursdays until 9 p.m. Admission is free.) Most of the 4500 paintings are Italian, Dutch, French — late Gothic through Impressionism. A sampling: Dürer, Hogarth (satirical), Hieronymus Bosch (hellish), da Vinci, Vermeer, Rubens, Goya, Van Gogh, and many others. Rembrandt has all of Room XII to himself.

(6) *The National Portrait Gallery* often gets confused with the above, but the Portrait Gallery is the place to see the panorama of British history, literature, and science, represented by the portraits of giants in these fields. (It's located right next to the National Gallery. Hours: 10 a.m. to 6 p.m. Free.) Even some 20th-century portraits are there, but not yet those of the Beatles or the Rolling Stones.

(7) *The Tate Museum* is a must because it's different from most of the other art museums in Europe. Various periods and styles are represented, but the emphasis is on modern art. Some examples: Englishmen Francis Bacon (grotesque), Ben Nicholson, Henry Moore, and Graham Sutherland; and Continentals Klee, Chagall, Kokoschka, and — it goes without saying — Picasso. (Tube: Circle line west from Charing Cross and get off at Westminster; the Tate's a bit far up river, so it might be a good idea to catch bus 77. Otherwise, it's a 3/4 mile hike along the Thames — which is not a bad idea if the weather's nice. Since there are mostly classics elsewhere, concentrate here on moderns: especially galleries 14, 27-30, and 34.)

(8) The *Jewish Museum* is very close at hand, at Woburn House in Upper Woburn Place, just above Tavistock Square, east of London University. (Hours: 2:30-5:00 p.m.)

(9) Try the *Soane Museum* − if the off-beat appeals to you. Never has a more eclectic menagerie been displayed more haphazardly. (Tube: Central line east from Tottenham Court at Holborn; it's at 13 Lincoln's Inn's Fields − and the Old Curiosity Shop is just across the pasture.) In the words of *London Spy,* "fantastic and a little spooky."

(10) *Madame Tussaud's Wax Museum* and the *Planetarium* are perhaps even spookier. The Wax Museum features a Chamber of Horrors and "Heroes − Live!" There's also a revealing exhibition on the Royal Family. Everything is in wax, but with alarming realism. Next door is the Planetarium, which advertises itself as "something between a spacecraft and a time machine." Save a few pence by buying a combined ticket (about 50 new pence, or $1.20). An extraordinary place. (Tube: Central line west from Tottenham Court to Oxford Circus, transfer to the northbound Bakerloo line, and get off at Baker St. − shades of Sherlock Holmes. Hours: 10 a.m.-6:30 p.m.

(11) *H.M.S. Discovery.* This doughty old vessel is still outfitted with many artifacts, records, and mementos from Scott's Antarctic voyages. (Tube: Temple Station. From there it is a short walk down to the river, to where the good ship *Discovery* still lies at anchor.) Also down there are the *Wellington*, the *President*, and the *Chrysanthemum* − three other vessels whose days at sea ended long ago.

(12) *Thames Cruise.* Cruises originate at Westminster Pier (hard right by the Westminster tube station), beginning about 10:30 in the morning, and go down the Thames to Greenwich every half hour or so. Fare: about 40 new pence (96 cents). (To get there from the *Discovery,* return to Charing Cross and take the Circle line west one stop.) Greenwich is renowned for its observatory and for the "Greenwich Meridian" (zero longitude) which runs through it. The *Cutty Sark,* last and most famous of the clippers, is docked near Greenwich Pier; below deck is a collection of figureheads and other antique maritime curiosities.

(13) *Evening cruises on the Thames* originate at Charing Cross Pier (next to Charing Cross tube station). Excursions go to Greenwich, the Tower of London, and points along the way. Two hours' worth costs about 50 new pence ($1.20).

(14) *Soho* is one part of London most Americans have heard about. It's London's "foreign quarter" and definitely a must. Expect bookshops, cabarets, coffee bars, multilingual sidewalk scenes − and some of

the choicest little restaurants anywhere. Greenwich Village is pale by comparison. Soho's inhabitants have become considerably more respectable since Dickens described them over a hundred years ago in *Bleak House.*

> Many of them are not early risers at the brightest of times, being birds of night who roost when the sun is high, and are wide awake and keen for prey when the stars shine out. Behind dingy blind and curtain, in upper storey and garret, skulking more or less under false names, false jewelry, and false histories, they are a colony of brigands.

Dickens at his best. Soho's no longer dangerous, but it's just as exotic. Soho Fair, by the way, adds further color during July.

(15) *"Old Bailey"* is for those who would like some local color of the judicial sort. Consider sitting in on a half-hour or so of a trial at Central Criminal Court — one of the best free shows in London. The action begins at 10:15 and 1:45, Mondays through Fridays, except in August. (Tube: Central line east from Tottenham Court to St. Paul's station; walk northeast up Newgate.) On opening days, the judges carry bouquets, and sweet smelling herbs are strewn about the courtrooms, reminiscent of a time when the stench of Newgate Prison next door had to be mitigated, lest the honor of the court be compromised. Sheer British courtroom drama, wigs included.

(16) *Petticoat Lane Market* provides more local color, and can be for the visitor a needed change of pace. Not all of London is hip or aristocratic. Petticoat Lane (really Middlesex St.) is off Bishopsgate. (Tube: Take the Central line east from Tottenham Court to Liverpool St.) Just about anything can be found at Petticoat, and many memorable characters can be seen as well. But above all, listen! Sunday morning's the time.

(17) Speaking of Sunday mornings and listening: anywhere in London, but especially in the City, the bells are tremendous — all at once, about 10:30 or 11:00 a.m. The cacophony is delicious.

(18) *London Zoo* is located at the north end of Regent's Park. Allow at least two hours. (Tube: north to Camden Town station, the second stop north of Euston; then bus 74, or a half-mile hike through the park.) Admission: about 40 new pence (or 96¢). Two hours can give a hurried once over. There are more than 4800 inhabitants. Most interesting, perhaps, is the new Clore Pavilion for Small Animals. Widely acclaimed for its architecture, the pavilion's plan was based on a two-year study of various animals' natural habits —burrowing, etc. There is a special nocturnal section called "The Moonlight World", where the

day/night cycle has been reversed so that "night" animals are at their most active state during visiting hours (9 a.m.–7 p.m.).

(19) *Windsor Castle,* about 20 miles west of London and built by William the Conqueror, is the largest inhabited castle in the world. Admission to much of it is free. The train takes less than an hour, but it takes far more than that to absorb the splendors of the place. These include: the State Apartments (15 new pence), the Round Tower, the Old Masters Drawing collection (10 new pence), Queen Mary's Doll House (10 new pence), and the magnificent St. George's Chapel. (Connections: British Rail from Waterloo Station).

(20) *Shopping.* Harrod's motto, *Omnia Omnibus Ubique,* sums up London's shopping scene: "Everything for everybody everywhere." It wasn't for nothing that somebody called London the "clearinghouse of the world" or that Napoleon dubbed Britain *une nation de boutiquiers,* "a nation of shopkeepers". Most people will want to start with Carnaby St. – but it may take them by surprise. Carnaby is somewhat grimy, and only a couple of blocks long, on the outer fringes of Soho. It's almost back-to-back with expensive Regent Street. (Tube: Central line west from Tottenham Court to Oxford Circus; take Argyll St. south, cross Great Marlborough bearing east, and you'll run into Carnaby.) Three of the best known spots are Male One West, Lady Jane, and Foale and Tuffin. See Carnaby for the experience, but don't overlook some other possibilities. Numerous shops in Oxford Street and in King's Road are less expensive and equally avant-garde.

Farther west (at 87–135 Brompton Road) is the famed Harrod's – one of the greatest stores in the world; its more than 200 departments cover thirteen acres. Formerly staid, it's begun to swing. Nonetheless the clerks in some of the more posh departments confirm the outdated clichés about British superiority. Its "Way In" shop (on the 4th floor, close to the color TV and funeral departments) is definitely worth checking. Girls will find more than 30 fashion departments on the second floor, among them "Eighteen Plus". (Tube: Piccadilly line west from Leicester Square to Knightsbridge station.) Ask for an elephant and Harrod's could doubtless oblige with several varieties. Also in Kensington, for girls: "Biba's", at the lower end of High Street, and Scotch House (Knightsbridge) for those with Scottish ancestors.

King's Road, in Chelsea, has a plethora of hip shops, including "Mates", "Top Gear", and for young men, "Hung on You"; the last named, actually in Cale St., has perhaps the wildest toggery in town, but is rather expensive. Anyway, it's at least worth looking at. (Tube to

King's Road: take the District line west from Charing Cross to Sloane Square.)

About taxes: many of the larger stores have "Personal Export Schemes" which enable foreigners to purchase certain goods (clothing included) free of the Purchase Tax. To be exempted, one must show a passport; the goods are then sent either to a home address abroad or to a port of disembarkation. The first alternative, of course, is much simpler. Stores that offer this service display a notice in their windows.

(21) *Tea.* Britons brew almost half a billion pounds of tea a year — which averages out to about 200 per capita per annum of the cups "that cheer but do not inebriate." Clearly tea is an institution. It's also a ritual, a kind of sacrament, a mystical link among the "civilized". And it's a ceremony worth trying at least once. Watch closely; it's very revealing of the English. For those who want to do it up really right, take tea at Brown's Hotel in Dover St. (west of Piccadilly Circus). For tea in a more casual setting, there is the Ceylon Tea Centre (22 Lower Regent St. — at the corner of Regent and Jermyn, just south of Piccadilly Circus); their blends are nothing like Lipton's. Tea proletarian style is served at any lower-priced restaurant or café. About 4 p.m. is the time.

(22) *Pubs.*

> Gallants, lads, boys, hearts of gold, all the titles of good fellowship
> come to you! What, shall we be merry? ... Give me a cup o' sack!

There's probably no tippler in literature wittier than Sir John Falstaff; and at Boar's Head he was at his wittiest. The Boar's Head has vanished, together with the Mermaid and the Tabard. The Cheshire Cheese still flourishes, though. Rebuilt in 1667, right after the Great Fire, it stands on the site of the original pub that (it is said) dated from 1350. At last count, London had over 6000 pubs, but here are a few to check out. Nearly all will have a darts game going on.

The Printer's Devil is very traditional, and a rendezvous for newspapermen (98 Fetter Lane, an alley off Fleet St., right across from the Mitre Lane entrance to the Temple.) Especially interesting is the new *Sherlock Holmes* (just off Northumberland Avenue, near Charing Cross tube station.) Quips *Punch:* it "houses as fine a collection of Holmesiana as one can get, considering that he never existed!" (Upstairs is a reconstruction of Holmes' fictional room in Baker St.) For the strong of stomach there's *Old Dirty Dicks's,* a cobwebbed cellar decorated with assorted remains in varying states of preservation — definitely worth seeing. Despite the name, it's quite respectable. (Tube: Central line east from Tottenham Court to Liverpool St.; walk east into Bishopsgate.) For swingers, there's King's Road, Chelsea, and most notably the *Chelsea Potter.* The *Duke of York*, near the British Museum on Rathbon St., has a built-in museum of its own, replete with assorted odds and ends. "Wild!" exclaims *London Spy.* Like tea-time, the pub is one of Britain's most durable institutions. Hours: 11 a.m.–3 p.m. and 5:30 p.m.–11 p.m.; Sundays, noon-2 p.m. and 7–10 p.m.

   (23) Finally, if none of the foregoing seems worthwhile, call Tele-tourist at 246-8041 for a recorded message about what's going on in London on any particular day.

The Week in London

   A week or ten days may not seem like much back home. But overseas it's possible to pack a month's excitement into this period of time without getting exhausted. It all depends on how it's done.

   The best way to spend the first full day in London is to take a city sightseeing tour. It's not really as corny as it sounds; there's just no other way to see how the city is laid out. Getting to know it all in the company of a local Londoner is an experience in itself. The guides are always proud of their city and will want to show the visitor an intriguing variety of places, some of them conventional, some out-of-the-way. The morning tour usually includes the fashionable West Kensington district of London, Hyde Park Corner, the Albert Memorial, and Carnaby Street, which is decked out with psychedelic banners. Then there are the Houses of Parliament, Westminster Abbey and Grosvenor Square, called "Little America" because of its many American associations; John Adams, the first American ambassador to Great Britain and the second U.S. President, had a house there, near the present site of the U.S. Embassy. The afternoon tour usually heads east, passing through Fleet St., in the heart of the publishing district of London; includes an inside visit to St. Paul's Cathedral; and then continues further east to the Tower of London. Inside the Tower grounds, the guide points out the spot where many famous heads rolled, including those of St. Thomas More, Anne Boleyn, and Sir Walter Raleigh. Also pointed out is the place where the Little Princes are said to have been murdered and the gate where the condemned were led to their doom. At the conclusion of the day's sightseeing, the visitor is prepared to explore London on his own.

   There is as much going on in London as in any city in the world –

perhaps more so. In any case, it's an impossible place to be bored in. London is deservedly famous for its theatres. It has both Broadway-type fare as well as "underground" and classical theatre. Some typical mid-summer plays are *The Rivals,* an amusing comedy of manners by the 18th century English playwright Richard Sheridan; Agatha Christie's *The Mousetrap*, a thriller so perfect it has been running in London for 17 years; or the musical comedy *The Boy Friend*, in which Julie Andrews made her debut back in the early fifties.

The Cheshire Cheese can always be counted on for an interesting evening. This was the pub most often frequented by the lion of 18th century English letters, Dr. Samuel Johnson. He lived almost next door to the place, and would spend most of his waking (and some of his sleeping) hours inside, surrounded by his friends and admirers, including the redoubtable James Boswell. As Johnson downed one mug of "pale ale" after another, his opinions would grow more violent, and he would begin a declamation on everything from Scottish porridge to women to the Anglican Church, pounding the table with his fist to drive home each point.

This, then, is the week in London. A little of everything: a broad spectrum of sightseeing, evening excursions, a field trip to Oxford and Stratford-on-Avon, and free time simply to take it all in. One thing stays in the mind above all else: London is in many ways the most conservative-looking city in Europe, with black taxicabs, archaic place-names like "Blackfriars", reserved but courteous people, the pomp and circumstance of royalty, and above all, the traditions which have kept Britain on an even keel for centuries. But London is also brand-new, as new as Jodrell Bank's breakthroughs in astrophysics, the Rolling Stones, 840-line color TV (as against the old-fashioned 619-line color TV we have in the U.S.), "mod", and Barbara Hepworth's abstract sculpture. It has the oldest of the old and the newest of the new. There isn't another city like London in the world.

Oxford-Stratford-on-Avon Field Trip

This excursion is the high point of any stay in London. The visitor really feels that he has come to know Shakespeare a little better after looking around the town where he was born, grew up, and to which he returned after making a name and fortune for himself in London. The town of Oxford is on the way, and is also well worth seeing – particularly because the oldest and most renowned of European universities is located here.

To get to Oxford and Stratford, take British Railways from Paddington Station. The train leaves London by the northwest, and before long the soft green countryside so typical of England comes into view. Twenty yards away from the train, cows are grazing lazily in the pasture. There are tiny cottages with chickens out back. Things don't change too much there. People out here probably haven't heard the latest records, and the proprietor of a local inn won't be in a mod jacket or a polka-dot tie. In fact, his Midlands dialect may seem a bit heavy at first. In the distance, Windsor Castle gleams in the morning sun — like something from the set of *Camelot*. Pretty soon we're far out in the country, passing through "Maidenhead Forest". There aren't too many towns along the route from London to Oxford. We can therefore say quite accurately that the scenes outside the train window are almost exactly what young Will Shakespeare saw as he traveled from Stratford to London for the first time. In fact, this is the only world he had known before he was 20 or so. It's hard to imagine the experience of exploding into London for the first time. It must have been over-whelming, and enough to give a young playwright ideas for a lifetime.

Before long, Oxford appears up ahead. It's a bustling little city in its own right — quite apart from the University. Any of the colleges is worth a visit, but that of Christchurch is especially lovely. It's not quite like Harvard or Yale or Princeton. The buildings aren't 1930's Gothic. They're real Gothic: old and crumbly. There is no central heating in the winter, only portable stoves. Oxford was old even in Shakespeare's time — several hundred years old.

Oxford is more than just a university town. It's a city of 100,000 people, and the county seat of Oxfordshire. It has one of the largest automobile assembly plants in Europe, the MG factory. The two biggest streets in Oxford are High St. (called "the High" for short) and Cornmarket St. ("the Corn"). On either side of High Street are the different colleges of Oxford: Oriel College, University College, Brasenose College, All Souls College, Queen's College, and others. It's a busy city, even in the summertime. There are flowers everywhere: in window boxes, in garden plots around professors' homes, and in the town squares. On either side of town are large parks. Oxford is the loveliest university town on our itinerary, with the possible exception of Heidelberg.

An hour or two is enough time in Oxford, and then on to Stratford-on-Avon. The route takes us through the rich green countryside again, and it is fascinating to see the big oak trees in the wooded patches along the way. Many of them are gnarled and twisted into the most bizarre shapes. The route runs past Blenheim Palace, the home of the Dukes of Marlborough — that's Churchill's family. On through such towns as "Chipping Norton" and "Shipston on Stour" until the train reaches Stratford. There are some fine little restaurants in which to have lunch. The "Thatch" next to Anne Hathaway's cottage is especially good. Afterwards, one may look through some of the cottages and other buildings that formed an important part of Shakespear's early life. Anne Hathaway's cottage is by far the loveliest. It was damaged recently by fire, but has been repaired. Inside, a guide points out the huge fireplace where Mrs. Hathaway (Anne's mother) prepared the family's meals with the help of her servants, and the bench on which young Will probably courted Anne with some of his early attempts at poetry. There are the bedrooms upstairs, with furniture that may appear uncomfortable to us, but was quite a luxury in Shakespeare's day. There is the dairy, the bakery, the spinning room, the servants' quarters — all under the same thatched roof. The whole house looks pretty humble, but it was one of the better homes in Stratford when the Hathaways lived there. It's not really in town, but on the outskirts. There's pastureland around with vegetables and flower gardens. Each household of any size raised its own crops and milked its own cows. It was a self-sufficient operation, and not dependent upon the outside world except for manufactured goods.

Near the center of Stratford is the building in which Will's father carried on his glovemaking trade. The visitor can walk through the various rooms used for curing the hides, cutting and sewing the leather into gloves, and the salesrooms where the old John Shakespeare must have driven many a hard bargain.

There are other parts of Stratford worth seeing (Harvard House, the site of "New Place," which Shakespeare bought in 1597; Holy Trinity Church, where Shakespeare is buried; and the old schoolhouse — still in use), and the rest of the afternoon might well be invested in a visit to any one of them. After browsing around the town a few hours, a rest break is in order. Any one of the little inns serves scones with jam and Devonshire cream. There's really nothing like this available in the U.S. The Treasure House (9 Chapel Street) is especially recommended.

After supper, a performance at the Royal Shakespeare Theatre is well worth the time and expense. Depending on the date, it's likely to be *As You Like It, A Midsummer-Night's Dream,* or even Marlowe's *Doctor Faustus* (an unbelievable performance, unequalled anywhere else.) Whatever play it is, it will provide an ideal conclusion to the day and to the week in Great Britain.

Taking off for the Continent: London-Brussels

The trip from London to Brussels is as big an event as the trip from New York to London. But there will be this difference. After a week overseas, the visitor has begun to acquire his "sea legs", and is ready for strange sights and a little more "culture shock". He really feels abroad once he finds himself surrounded by a new language, and some unfamiliar customs.

There is still plenty of traveling to do in England itself, and through some of the loveliest countryside of all. It's best to be off fairly early in the morning. Heading southeast, our route passes through Canterbury on the way to Dover, and crosses the English Channel to Ostend, Belgium. Then we go from Ostend to Bruges, and finally into Brussels for supper and overnight.

After a last look at Tottenham Court Road, the Houses of Parliament, Big Ben, and the Thames, we're off through the industrial suburbs of south London. This is a rather seedy area of town, but for thousands of factory workers it's the only London there is. Before feeling too bad, however, take a look at the roofs of most of those gray stucco row-houses. They're plastered with TV antennas. In fact, when the movie *Sons and Lovers* was being filmed in some of the Midland mining towns, it was necessary to take all the TV antennas down.

Out in the country to the east, the scenery brightens up a great deal. The auto route runs parallel to the Thames a couple of miles to the north. This is pretty much the route the pilgrims followed as they traveled by foot or horseback to Thomas à Becket's shrine in Canterbury. From time to time, the sign "Dual Carriageway" pops up. It's the British way of saying "Divided Highway."

Fifteen miles out, the "Dual Carriageway" passes through a small industrial center, Dartford (pop. 45,000), and about 10 miles further, a sign points to Cobham, a charming village to the south. The highway continues eastward on the main route, but in this village stands a Swiss chalet where Charles Dickens wrote many of his novels. About 15 miles further, the highway runs through the heart of the county of Kent (county seat: Maidstone, some 10 miles to the south). Poets have called this the "garden of England" for its soft, languorous countryside and indolent beauty. Spring fever grows on trees here, no matter what the season.

Ten more miles and the highway bypasses Canterbury. An hour's visit to the town and Cathedral is well worth the time. Signs point the way into town. Ever since the 6th century, it's been the seat of the

Archbishop of Canterbury, Anglican Primate of all England. It is to Anglicans and Episcopalians what Rome is to Catholics. Canterbury Cathedral has been a mecca for pilgrims ever since 1170, when the pro-Saxon Archbishop Thomas à Becket was murdered by partisans of the Norman King Henry II. Anyone who saw the film *Becket* will remember the details of that famous struggle between church and state. Soon after his death, Becket was declared a saint, and mysterious powers, especially for healing, were attributed to him. Pilgrims came to Canterbury from all over England for his feast day and Chaucer describes several of them in his classic *Canterbury Tales.* Many students have memorized the first part of the Prologue in Chaucer's original Middle English, but for moderns, a few lines from a current translation may suffice:

> When the sweet showers of April have pierced to the root the dryness of March, and bathed every vein in moisture whose quickening brings forth the flowers ... then folk long to go on pilgrimage to renowned shrines in sundry distant lands, and palmers to seek strange shores. And especially from every shire's end in England they go their way to Canterbury, to seek the holy blessed martyr who helped them when they were sick. (*The Complete Poetical Works of Geoffrey Chaucer*, trans. John Tatlock and Percy MacKaye. New York, 1940.)

Canterbury Cathedral is one of the greatest architectural and historical treasures of England. It was built in the 12th century, and its tower reaches over 200 feet. Nearby is the Church of St. Martin in Canterbury, the first church built in England; it was begun in the 4th century, when the Romans still ruled the country.

Leaving Canterbury, the road crosses the bridge over the Little Stour river and heads straight for Dover, some 15 miles southeast. The visitor knows he's there when he spots the Channel and the unforgettable "white cliffs of Dover" on the right. Dover is still a bustling commercial harbor of 40,000 people, known as the "Gateway to the Continent". It's the best haven for ships on the English Channel. While pulling into the dock area, look behind and up at the hill. On top is Dover Castle, dating back to Norman times (11th century). Looking straight out to sea, it might be possible to see the coast of France if the weather is clear. In any case, an indescribable view of the town, the harbor, and the cliffs awaits the passenger from the ship as it heads out to sea.

The ship itself is a Belgian vessel, operated by burly Flemish sailors who have spent their lives on the choppy waters of the Channel.

Luncheon is usually served soon after sailing time. The dining salon's huge bay windows afford a view of Dover's chalky cliffs that the visitor won't be likely to forget for some time.

For the seasick-prone, it is an excellent idea to have some Dramamine or Bonamine tablets along. The pills should be taken before the ship sails. Also, it's best to be judicious at lunchtime. Frankly, the Flemish are great eaters, and they ply their passengers generously with food. But don't let them; effort is often required to keep both head and stomach intact, so be restrained. Not that the water is that rough. But the choppiness of the Channel is legendary, and even these heavy ships will feel the effect. For those who get a bit woozy, a brief nap will pick them up in no time. The men's or women's staterooms below deck provide just the place for one.

A few hours later, land comes into view again. This time it's the coast of Belgium. The port of Ostend begins to rise in the distance. It is an important shipping and fishing port of 50,000 people, with a drydock and over 300 large fishing vessels. It also has a popular resort beach. Nearby are the famous oyster beds, started in 1766. Actually, the oysters are caught off the coast of England, then brought to Ostend for fattening.

Debarking passengers are directed along the quay and into the Immigration Lounge. The first-time visitor is invariably struck by the trilingual signs: English, French, and Flemish (identical to Dutch). Flemish itself is a rather peculiar language: very guttural, raspy, even harsh. For example: *Uitgang* = exit; *stoomboot* = steamboat; *vertrek* = departure. The traveler can count on getting a good dose of it before he's out of Belgium.

The highway from Ostend to Brussels is modern and fast. Since the trip takes less than two hours, there should be time to stop off in Bruges on the way. It's about 15 miles inland, and one of the loveliest towns in all of Belgium. It's a page out of medieval Europe: a city of canals, art treasures, and Gothic towers and fortifications. No other town in Europe can match it for the sense it gives the visitor of being put down in Europe some 600 or 700 years ago.

The best thing is to stop for a while in the center of town, which in the summer is decked out with colorful banners representing the different counties and towns of Flanders. Flanders itself is a part of Belgium dating back to medieval times. It was an independent country, ruled by the Counts of Flanders, who later made their capital in Brussels. The name Bruges (in Flemish: Brugge) goes back to the old

Norse world *Bryggia,* meaning "landing" or "dock." Bruges was originally just that, a dock on an inlet of the North Sea, called the "Zwin."
Norse seafarers would navigate the Zwin as far inland as they could, and
there they built Bruges as a transit point for commerce going overland
to the east and south. The town is mentioned for the first time in 892.
Later, the Counts of Flanders built fortifications around Bruges to
defend it against Viking raiders from the sea. Protected from the sea,
the town became a flourishing trading center, and by the 13th century
it was the greatest market city in Western Europe. Goods from Italy,
England, the Balkan countries, and Russia all flowed through it. About
1350 or so, the town had grown to 35,000 people, a huge city by
medieval standards. (Its population today is around 50,000). With economic prosperity came artistic and cultural activity. The name of Hans
Memling (whose painting "Adoration of the Magi" appeared on the
U. S. Christmas stamp for 1968) and Jan Van Eyck ("Portrait of the
Artist's Wife") are intimately connected with the city. Several of Memling's paintings can be seen in Bruges.

Among the most important things to see in Bruges are the Market
Square (or *Markt* in Flemish), with its imposing Market Building (or
Halle) and Belfry. The latter is the huge tower that dominates the
square. It was begun in 1248 and is one of the purest examples of
Gothic civic architecture. It has a carillon of 49 bells, dating from the
1500's and weighing 28 tons in all. Look around the square at the
outdoor cafés with the colorful striped awnings. The Market Building
under the huge tower was used as a display center for goods, and
merchants from all over Europe came to buy and sell. Their goods were
exhibited in the arcades around the building. This, by the way, is
typical of the way business was carried on in the Middle Ages and even
into modern times. A merchant didn't "write orders" for so many head
of cattle or sheep or hides. He had to see them all himself, in person.
Hence the importance of market places and arcades as display centers.
They can be seen all over Europe, not just in Bruges. Imagine cattle,
leather goods, clothing, metalware, vegetables all piled into the narrow
arcades, and merchants shouting to anyone who would listen about the
virtues of their wares. It's been estimated that as many as 10,000
people would be packed into this square and its adjoining buildings on
any good market day.

In the center of the square are statues of Jan Breidel and Pieter de
Coninck, the heroes of the Battle of the Golden Spurs (July 11, 1302),
in which the people of Bruges defeated the army of Philip the Fair,
King of France, who had occupied the town for two years.

Since Bruges is often called the "city of art", a visit to the Hans Memling Museum, housed in the old St. John's Hospital (dating from the 13th-15th centuries), would be worth a good half-hour or so. Inside, a guide explains the fantastically detailed paintings by Memling, particularly the most famous one, the "Mystical Marriage of St. Catherine". On the way to the museum, the street runs past the Church of Our Lady, which has a white marble statue of the Virgin and Child by Michelangelo. It's the only piece of sculpture by Michelangelo in Belgium.

Then it's off to Brussels, the largest city and the capital of Belgium. Belgium itself is a small country, with an area of under 12,000 square miles. The population is dense: 9 million people. Belgium has a dual population. In the north and west, the people are of Nordic origin, and speak Flemish (or Dutch), a variant of German. They are known as the "Flemings" or the Flemish people. In the south and east, the people are of Celtic origin, and speak French. They are the "Walloons". Both, however, are Catholic. Though they agree on religion, they often disagree on other things. The French-speaking Walloons more or less control the business and industrial life of the country, as well as the universities. Although Brussels itself is in the Flemish portion of Belgium, most of the people of the city are Walloons. This makes for tension. Also, there is the fact that until recently the Walloons had a slight edge in the Belgian Parliament. From time to time, the newspapers report "race riots" between the Flemings and the Walloons. But things have been quiet for the past few years, and there is little danger that today's visitor will encounter a mob scene in Brussels.

Belgium is a constitutional monarchy. The present king is Baudoin I (French for "Baldwin"), and the queen is Fabiola, of Spanish descent. Like Queen Elizabeth, however, the king's position is basically that of a figurehead. His face and that of the queen appear on Belgian currency. The Belgian franc is worth about two cents; forty-seven make a dollar. For shopping after banking hours, or for buying an evening's coffee in the Grand' Place, about $10 or $20 worth of travelers checks can be changed in the lobby of the hotel. Hotels give about the same rate of exchange the banks would. $10 would come to 470 Belgian francs, give or take a few francs. There's an intriguing picture on the back of some Belgian banknotes. It's the "Atomium", a gigantic molecular model built for the 1958 Brussels World's Fair.

Belgium's major natural resource is coal, and it has plenty of it. Known as the "black bread" of the country, coal is produced at the rate of over 100,000 tons a day. Agriculture is next in importance, employing a fifth of the population. Belgium exports enormous amounts of iron and steel, most of it processed outside Liege, a large city which the highway skirts while on the way to Germany. Another big industry is diamond cutting, in which Belgium leads the world.

Just before entering Brussels, the highway circles around a huge church. It's the National Basilica of the Sacred Heart, begun in 1926. From its central altar radiate 10 chapels, dedicated to the 9 Belgian provinces and the (former) Belgian Congo.

There is only one thing to see during an evening in Brussels — an absolute "must". That's the Grand' Place. It's in the heart of the old town, just behind the *Bourse* (stock exchange). It has been preserved practically in its original condition. If Bruges was a "page out of medieval Europe" the Grand' Place is the text. It is impossible to describe. It has to be seen to be believed — all of it: the Town Hall, old Royal Palace, the residence of the Counts of Flanders, the office buildings of the old guilds, the coffee houses, cobblestones, old hitching posts, and about everything else associated with the Middle Ages. No wonder Victor Hugo insisted that it be called, not the "Grand" (great) Place, but the "Gigantesque" (gigantic) Place.

Through Eastern Belgium and along the Rhine: Brussels-Heidelberg

Our route continues east, through eastern Belgium to Germany. On the way out of the city, the visitor is bound to be struck by the difference between the Brussels that comes into view now and the Brussels he saw around the Grand' Place. This is the Brussels of the 20th century, Europe's most international city, the headquarters of the Common Market and the commercial center of Europe. Large glassy skyscrapers hover over the older streets and alleyways of centuries past. Brussels is a city of well over a million people. Greater Brussels has almost 2½ million. (In Flemish it's *Brussel*, in French, *Bruxelles*.)

About 25 miles out of Brussels is the city of Louvain (Flemish: *Leuven*), a city of 40,000 people and the capital of the old Duchy of Brabant. It's the center of Catholic intellectual life in Belgium, and possibly in all of Europe. Its university is renowned throughout the world. The original library of the university housed a priceless collection of ancient and medieval manuscripts, but was totally destroyed during the First World War. A new one was built with contributions from many colleges and universities in the U. S., and inaugurated by Prince Leopold in 1928. But in May 1940, it too was destroyed, along with a million books, when the Nazis swept through Belgium on their way to France. Reconstruction has begun again.

In spite of the ravages of war, Louvain continues to be one of the greatest centers of intellectual activity on this side of the Atlantic. Thousands of students from all over the world, including the U. S., come here to study with leading scholars in every field from folklore to phenomenology. Many of their research projects are published by the university press. The university itself dates from 1432, and was one of the largest in Europe by the 1500's, when it had more than 6000 students in 52 colleges.

The highway continues through Tienen (pop. 22,000) and other smaller towns, until it reaches Liège, the greatest industrial complex in Belgium. (In Flemish, it's called *Luik*.) It is a city of half a million people, most of them workers in the huge iron and steel refineries outside the city. (That's what all the smoke is about.) But it has its cultural associations too. The 19th century composer César Franck was born here, and its university (one of the two state universities in Belgium) offers some of the best science and engineering courses anywhere in Europe.

About 40 miles beyond Liège is the German border. Customs formalities are usually brief and uncomplicated. An official may ask to look over a passport, but they seldom inconvenience the visitor.

Aachen is the first notable city along the route through Germany. Aachen, or Aix-la-Chapelle as it was called during the Middle Ages (and still is, in French), was the capital of Charlemagne's empire in the 9th century. Charlemagne (Charles the Great) ruled over the first great Christian empire in the West. He brought together the Franks in the west (in what is now France), the Bavarians in the south, the Saxons in Northern and Central Europe, and welded them all into a powerful state which preserved what was left of classical learning after Rome fell to the barbarians. He patronized artists and scholars, including Alcuin, the greatest physician and scholar of his day. He even tried to teach himself a little Latin and Greek, but he overreached himself there. Though he brought about a cultural renaissance in northern Europe, Charlemagne himself never learned to read or write.

Today, Aachen is a great industrial center, busily refining coal and ore from nearby mines, and boasting some of the best technical schools in Europe, especially for electronics and engineering. It has a population of almost 200,000. It is famous for its health spa, which has one of the hottest springs (166°F.) in Europe.

A fast Autobahn, heading east, connects Aachen with Cologne. About 30 miles north is the greatest industrial area in Western Europe: the Ruhr Basin. (It's appropriately named. *Ruhr*, the name of a river running through the area, also means "commotion" in German.) It includes such cities as Düsseldorf, Essen, Dortmund, Duisburg, and others. It is here that the oil refineries, iron and steel mills, and chemical plants that kept Germany going for two world wars are to be found, including the famous Krupp armament works. Needless to say, it was all heavily bombed during the war, but has since come back to life and continues to be the power plant of the West Germany economy. Over 5 million people live and work in the Ruhr Basin, most of them in industry. Though the highway runs 20 or 30 miles south of all this, there are a few smokestacks here and there. Mostly, though, it's wheat and cattle raising that take up the land between Aachen and Cologne.

Pretty soon the highway approaches Cologne (in German: *Köln*), one of the most important cities in Germany. About the name "Cologne": the city wasn't named for the perfume. The perfume was named for the city. In 1709, an adventuresome Italian chemist named Giovanni-Maria Farina settled in the town, and invented a new type of lotion, which became known as *Kölnisches Wasser*, or "water from Cologne". In French it was called *Eau de Cologne,* and is still known by that title.

Cologne is a city of almost a million people, and a busy metallurgical and chemical center. Needless to say, "cologne" as well as chocolate and pharmaceuticals are manufactured here. But its real importance is cultural. It has one of the finest cathedrals in Europe, which took 600 years to build. In the Middle Ages, it was the largest city in Germany, with 40,000 people (compared with 35,000 in Bruges at that time). The Archbishops of Cologne were a powerful political force in Europe. Great scholars and preachers, including Albertus Magnus, came from all over Europe to preach in Cologne Cathedral. Cologne has always been a thriving commercial center. In the Middle Ages it held huge trading fairs, attracting merchants from hundreds of miles away. It was 90% destroyed by Allied bombs, but has since been rebuilt, and many of its artistic treasures have been recovered.

Cologne started out as a Roman army camp in 38 B.C. Later the Romans named it *Colonia Agrippinensis* (or "colony of Agrippina") in honor of the wife of Germanicus Caesar, who was leading a brief military campaign in Germany at the time. It has flourished ever since. It is particularly famous for its statues of the Madonna, which can be seen on many of the medieval churches. These "Beautiful Madonnas" as they are called, are known for their slender proportions and soft, beguiling smiles. They inspired a whole school of church sculpture that spread through Europe in the 1400's. But there's more to Cologne than madonnas, manufacturing, and cologne. It's a good idea to have lunch here, and a bit of rest.

Then off again, the route now heading south. Ahead lies Bonn, the capital of the German Federal Republic and a city of 150,000 people. Beethoven was born here in 1770. The town really wasn't prepared to become a capital city. It was always a quiet university town of narrow streets and gossipy marketplaces until it was chosen in 1949 to become the temporary capital of the Federal Republic. (Berlin is still the official capital of Germany, and will function as one if and when the two Germanys are ever reunited.) Because of its importance as a political capital, Bonn has bulged suddenly and awkwardly into a busy (not to say chaotic) metropolis. Foreign embassies stand next to open market stalls. Sleek black Mercedes carrying diplomats to conferences mingle with Volkswagens and Hondas in a downtown traffic nightmare. The local people – the inhabitants who are still sane – call this beehive of a city the "Federal Village". It simply isn't able to digest all the activity forced upon it by its status as a political and diplomatic crossroads.

Whenever there's congestion, look for fast, fast relief. And the best way to get it is to head further south, along the Rhine. The Rhine is to Germans, especially to Romantic poets and musicians, what the Seine is to Paris or the Mississippi to the Old South. It's not just a river, it's a national myth, the very image of what is quite essentially German. It is the river of Wagner, of the Rhine Maidens, of a hundred mossy and forboding castles. Practically every bend, every cliff, every village, every pebble at the bottom of the river has a story connected with it. A spectacular way to see the Rhine is from the deck of one of the steamers which ply the river in the summertime. It carries the passenger into a world apart, where folklore and legend reign supreme.

The best known of all the Rhine legends is that of the Nibelungen. Richard Wagner (1813-1883), whose house you will have a chance to see while in Lucerne, celebrated the myth of the Nibelungen in a series of four operas, known collectively as "The Ring of the Nibelungen" The four operas are *Das Rheingold* (or the "Gold of the Rhine"), *Die Walküre* (or "Valkyries", fierce she-warriors who collected the corpses of fallen heroes and brought them to Valhalla), *Siegfried* (the hero of the cycle, son of the god Wotan and the brother of Brünnhilde), and

Die Gotterdämmerung (the "Twilight of the Gods", in which Valhalla and all the gods go up in flames). The legend can be found in many different forms all through the Nordic countries. It comes from the Middle Ages, and is about a race of people, the Nibelungs, or "People from the Land of Mist." The German word for "mist" or "fog" is *Nebel* —hence the "Nibelungs". The Nibelung legend describes the various intrigues, plots, counterplots, murder, and treachery which take place as one person after another attempts to steal the gold.

Another legend tells of a rock, the "Lorelei", which actually exists on the banks of the Rhine. According to the legend, a gorgeous blonde siren, Lore, would sit on the rock combing her golden locks and singing in a hauntingly beautiful voice. Sailors on board passing ships, spellbound by this vision, would steer their ships toward her, unable to help themselves. The ships would crash on the reefs or sink in the whirlpools at the base of the rock, and the sailors would never be heard from again. Meanwhile, Lore would continue singing and combing. Lovely tale.

Unlike most rivers, the Rhine flows from south to north. It starts high up in the Swiss Alps and gradually makes its way to the north, across the plains of western Germany and through the industrial heartland of the Ruhr Basin. After several stretches of rough rapids and whirlpools, it evens out just before the portion used by the pleasure steamers, and continues placidly and lazily until it crosses into Holland. This stretch of the river is known as the Rhine Valley, one of the most serene and restful spots in all of Germany.

The Rhine is a great commercial waterway. Huge barges haul as much as 1500 tons of cargo at a time. German, Dutch, Belgian, French, and Swiss vessels carry everything from Ruhr coal and French fertilizers to Swiss printing presses and Italian automobiles.

Back on the highway, we head further south to Koblenz, where the Rhine joins the Mosel river. The valley of the Mosel, off to the left, is famous for its light, dry wines. The Autobahn continues further south, skirting Frankfurt (possibly the most important commercial center in Germany), past Mannheim (where the Rhine joins the Neckar river), and then east, following the Neckar into Heidelberg. Along the way are U.S. Army jeeps and base camps, a reminder that since 1945 Heidelberg has been the headquarters of all U.S. forces stationed in Germany.

If the Rhine is the river most often celebrated by Romantic poets and musicians, Heidelberg is the town where they felt most at home. It was the setting for the musical *The Student Prince,* and more American students come to study here than anywhere else in Europe. It's a fairly big city that looks like a small town — the exact opposite of Bonn, which is a village pumped up into a sprawling metropolis.

The first thing that comes into view is the Neckar river valley, and the soft green hills that line each side. The mammoth Heidelberg Castle dominates the hillside above the town. It's the most spectacular ruin in Germany, and is flood-lit at night. In fact, that's the best time to see Heidelberg, when the castle is bathed in a strange, pinkish glow, and the river reflects the twinkle of hundreds of city lights. It's hard to resist a stroll through the narrow streets and alleys or around the wooden inns and guest houses, and a walk over the old Karl-Theodor Bridge, which dates from the 16th century. The castle up on the hillside was built in various stages, beginning in the 1300's and continuing until about 1630. The most conspicuous part of it is the building in the center, the one with the many windows and the two gables on top. It has the best preserved façade, and is known as "Frederick's Wing". It was put up by Prince Frederick IV (1592-1610) in a mixture of Renaissance and Baroque styles.

As peaceful as Heidelberg may seem at night, it has a turbulent history. It was the capital of an independent state, called the Rhineland Palatinate. During the Reformation, the rulers, known as the "prince-electors", cast their lot with the Protestants, and Heidelberg has had a predominantly Protestant population ever since. But the Catholic states nearby didn't miss this opportunity for conquest, and they made incursions into the Palatinate under the pretext of religious crusades. The Protestant states of Germany did the same thing to the Catholic states in their area.

The most disastrous invasion of all came when King Louis XIV of France claimed the Palatinate for France by right of the marriage of his brother to Princess Elizabeth Charlotte. His army entered Heidelberg in 1689, destroyed much of the town, and plundered the castle. Large sections of it were blown up by the king's gunpowder experts. Four years later, in 1693, the town was ravaged by fire. Most of the buildings were of wood and simply couldn't be saved. Practically all of the buildings in present-day Heidelberg date from after that time. Occasionally one still comes across an old wall or a ruin which has an inscription in Latin and the date "1689" or "1693" on it. It's an apt historical reminder.

The university is located in the center of town, and its buildings are clustered around the Universitätsplatz or University Square. The university dates from 1386 and has always been one of the best in Germany. The noted existentialist philosopher, Karl Jaspers (1883-1968) taught here for many years. Over the centuries, the town has grown with the university to become a full-sized city of 130,000 people.

Germany, a House Divided

It is almost as difficult to say what "Germany" is as it is to explain the meaning of "Great Britain". At the moment, there is not one Germany, but two. There's the German Federal Republic, whose capital is Bonn, which is commonly called "West Germany". Then there is the "German Democratic Republic", that is, the Communist state which is known as "East Germany". The Federal Republic, or West Germany, came into existence on August 14, 1949, when the Western Allies (the U.S., Great Britain, and France) fused their zones of occupation. A general election was held, and representatives were selected for the *Bundestag* or Parliament. This pattern has continued ever since. A president is elected, but real executive authority is held by the Chancellor, who functions pretty much like the British prime minister or our president. Two major political parties have emerged, the Christian Democrats, who had a majority of the seats in the Bundestag until 1969 when Willy Brandt became Chancellor; and the Social Democratic party, which is much older as a party but was unable to achieve a majority in the Bundestag until 1969. There is a smaller third party, the Free Democrats, who have usually entered into a coalition with the Christian Democrats, but more recently switched to join the Social Democrats, thus giving the latter a majority in the Bundestag.

West Germany is divided into ten states, or *Länder* (lands). Our route takes us through five of them. The trip from Aachen to Cologne and down the Rhine passed through the state of North Rhine-Westphalia. Before leaving the steamer, however, we had crossed into the state of "Rhineland-Palatinate", whose old capital was Heidelberg; but Heidelberg is now in another state. When we skirted around Frankfurt, we were briefly in the state of "Hesse". (The "Hessians" of the American Revolution were from Hesse. They were hired as mercenaries by the British to fight the American revolutionaries.) Just before entering Heidelberg, we crossed into the state of Baden-Württemberg. Bavaria in the southeast is the fifth state along the way. Bavaria (in German, *Bayern*) is the largest state of all, and its capital is Munich. From Munich we head south to the Austrian border.

All these states used to be independent countries, though their borders were arranged and re-arranged many times as a result of wars, peace treaties, and royal inheritance. In fact, it is only recently that Germany became a unified country. Unification took place on the 18th of January, 1871, when Wilhelm I was proclaimed the first Emperor of Germany. His son, Wilhelm II, was the famous Kaiser who led Germany into the First World War. Many historians have explained Germany's military ambitions in the 20th century as a means of compensating for a kind of political inferiority complex which Germany had developed over the centuries. France, England, Spain, Poland, Russia, and other countries were all unified and powerful nations. But Germany was simply a collection of independent states, some of them large (like Prussia in the north, whose capital was Berlin), but most of them tiny. Any of the larger powers surrounding Germany could conquer this or that German state more or less at will. (The plunder of Heidelberg by Louis XIV of France in 1689 is one example.) It was natural that Germany should develop a feeling of hostility and suspicion toward the rest of Europe. She began to place more and more emphasis on military strength as a way of counteracting the threat of invasion from her neighbors. Once Germany became a single nation in 1871, she over-compensated for her previous status as a political inferior. By 1900, Germany was the greatest military power in the world. She had nothing to fear from without. But old habits die hard. German statesmen couldn't forget the age-old memory of being surrounded by hostile powers. A large army was maintained. Tough talk issued forth from the Kaiser. This attitude, plus a few other factors, led to the First World War. Then came the humiliation of the Versailles Peace Treaty in 1919, and a revival of the feeling of being threatened by more powerful neighbors. Hitler was able to exploit this sentiment with great success.

Today, German attitudes toward the outside world are practically the opposite of what they had traditionally been. For one thing, West Germany finds herself allied with the other powers of the West. She has developed strong economic, military, and psychological ties with the U.S. Since West Germany is the greatest economic and industrial power in Western Europe, she has little to fear from her closest neighbors.

But a major problem still remains for Germany. It is a house divided. An artificial line runs through the center of Germany, separating the Communist regime in the east from the pro-Western and democratic republic in the west. Families, geographical and cultural regions, even towns, have been split in half by this division. What are the prospects for future reunification? Who can say? It is an enormously complex

problem, and one which will probably remain unsolved for years to come.

West Germany itself has an area of 95,000 square miles, about the size of Great Britain and North Ireland combined. The country runs 500 miles north and south. Including West Berlin, the population comes to over 60 million. There are more than 50 cities having a population of 100,000. The portion of Germany covered by our itinerary consists for the most part of low hilly regions, large flat plateaus or basins, and small river valleys, such as the one running through Heidelberg. In the summer, the climate is fairly mild, usually between 70° and 80°, and it never gets too cold in the winter. Germany is predominately an industrial country. It is rich in coal (used by the countries of the Common Market), making it the world's fourth largest supplier of this energy source. It is third in steel production (after the U.S. and the U.S.S.R.), and fourth (behind Japan) in overall industrial output. Germany is one huge power plant.

Germany doesn't look like one, however, and that is what makes the difference between the Ruhr Basin and a city like Pittsburgh, Pennsylvania. Germans have always been romantic nature enthusiasts. Any major city, even a throbbing industrial town like Essen, will set aside large areas of land for parks, woods, lakes, even outdoor zoos. From a distance, it's hard to tell the Ruhr Basin from any other part of Germany. Tall trees blot out the smokestacks. Long ago, practically all of what is now Germany was covered by huge forests. Many place-names and even personal names in Germany end with the syllable *–wald* (woods), and this indicates their origin. For example: the town of Mittenwald (literally: "in the middle of the woods"); or even Wald-kirche ("forest church").

Hiking and camping are major sports in Germany, and more than "sports" in fact. Hiking has long been held to have a rejuvenating effect on the whole person, and no doubt rightly so. There is a very long tradition in Germany of the *Wanderlust* (literally: "joy in wandering"), especially among the students. They'll put on their *Lederhosen* (leather shorts), knapsacks, grab their carved walking sticks, and set off for the hills and forests. They might be away for a long weekend, or several weeks if it's during the summer. They do more than just walk and camp out. They often recite poetry, sing together, and discuss literature or philosophy far into the night. Often, farmers let the students sleep in their barns or stables. Thomas Mann describes these student treks and some of the involved conversations in his novel *Doctor Faustus*.

All this is connected with a very deep Romantic streak in the Germans. It comes out especially in German poetry and music. The students go out hiking in order to feel at one with the forest, to identify with something larger than themselves and to return to that mysterious source of all things from which they feel they have been estranged. It is a longing for a kind of Romantic rebirth. These themes are developed in a series of beautiful poems by the 18th century Romantic Heinrich Heine, called *Die Hartzreise* ("Journey through the Harz Forest"). But it's nowhere so well expressed as in German music, and particularly in the music of Richard Wagner. Even a short piece of his, like the "Siegfried Idyll", conveys a sense of oneness with nature which words, even the most beautiful words, can only hint at.

There is one other thing the visitor can't help noticing about the Germans, and that is their hospitality. The legendary efficiency and thoroughness of the Germans has not made them brusque or inconsiderate. They're usually willing to help in any situation, and a policeman, for example, will go out of his way to help a visitor find the exact place he is looking for. This is particularly true in the smaller towns. There are exceptions to every rule, of course, but the exceptions are fewer in Germany than in most other countries. Practically all Germans who have had a university education can speak at least passable English, and a great many of them are fluent in both English and French. In fact, more people speak English in Germany (and in Austria and the German portion of Switzerland) than in any other country of Western Europe, save England itself. Unlike the French, the Germans are not offended at the visitor's stumbling attempts to speak their language. They're flattered by it, and will help him along.

The basic unit of currency in Germany is the mark. One mark is worth a little more than 28¢. The one-mark coin is what the visitor becomes most familiar with. It's the size of a quarter, and looks like one. Just as our dollar is equal to 100 cents, so the German mark is divided into 100 "pfennig", a word which is related to our Anglo-Saxon word "penny". There are 5-pfennig, 10-pfennig, 20-pfennig, and 50-pfennig coins. To compute their value, simply divide the amount by four. 80 pfennig is worth 22¢. 20 *marks* is worth over $5.

South Germany and the Bavarian Alps: Heidelberg-Munich-Innsbruck

There is a great deal more of Germany to be seen as we continue our southward course toward Austria. The Autobahn begins just outside of Heidelberg and heads due south. As it nears Karlsruhe, it turns almost due east, heading towards Munich. The name of the city of Karlsruhe is instructive. It means "Karl's Rest" in German. It was built by Prince Karl Wilhelm, who ruled over the whole area when Louis XIV and his marauders descended on Heidelberg. So great was the devastation that he decided to abandon his castle at Heidelberg and build a new one in the middle of his favorite hunting grounds. He was sick of war and destruction, and wanted rest. Hence the name Karlsruhe: Karl's Rest. Today it is an important manufacturing and oil refining center. The Supreme Courts of the German Federal Republic are located here. A nuclear research center is being built outside the city. The physicist Heinrich Hertz, who discovered electro-magnetic waves in 1894, carried on his research at the Technological Institute in Karlsruhe.

The next big city is Stuttgart (pop. 650,000), the capital of the state of Baden-Württemberg. Stuttgart is one of the greatest printing and publishing centers in Germany, and has been so ever since the German Reformation. Two important figures in the automobile industry got their start here. They were Gottlieb Daimler (1834-1900) and Karl Benz (1884-1929). Both were engineers and both had some radical ideas about the use of the internal combustion engine. They were also astute businessmen. Benz was more successful first. By 1899, he had sold his 2,000th automobile, which made him the world's largest car manu-facturer. But Daimler came out with a new car in 1901, called the "Mercedes". It was named after the daughter of his most successful foreign sales agent. Too bad the poor girl hadn't bothered to copyright her name. The two companies, Daimler and Benz, joined forces in 1926. Off to the left – just barely visible in the distance – is the famous television tower of Stuttgart. It's almost 700 feet high, compared with the Post Office Tower in London, which is 600 feet. It is completely hollow inside, merely a huge concrete tube which is quite wide near the bottom but only a couple of inches wide at the top.

About a half-hour beyond Stuttgart, the Autobahn starts climbing. Out of nowhere, low-lying hills and mountains appear. It's a delightful break in the somewhat routine plateau. These are the hills of the Swabian Jura. "Swabia" is the ancient name for this whole area. A "jura" is a geological formation of moderately deep hills. The Swabian Jura runs roughly north and south. The Autobahn crosses over it, moving due east. Several castles appear in the distance to the right. They are perched on top of hills which rise up from the valley floor. The hills themselves are isolated from the main mountain range. They form natural fortresses, made to order for the castles built on top. The castles were built in the Middle Ages by the two greatest German families: the Hohenstaufens and the Hohenzollerns. The Hohenstaufens became known as the Holy Roman Emperors in early medieval times (1000's - 1100's). The Hohenzollerns were prominent a bit later, beginning around 1450 and continuing until 1918. The famous "Kaiser" of World War I, Kaiser Wilhelm II, was a Hohenzollern. The castles visible to the right of the Autobahn were built by the Hohenzollerns.

Life in the hills of the Swabian Jura was rugged in these times, especially for the peasants. Winters were harsh, water was scarce, and the terrain not really suited for agriculture. But the people were hardy, and used ingenuity in dealing with what they had. During long winter evenings, they would sit around the fire, thinking up ways of making life easier for themselves. They hit upon many brilliant inventions, including new weaving techniques, household utensils, and even some clever toys. In the 19th century, these ideas were developed and can now be seen at work in a string of factories to the north, where cotton is processed and where silverware, precision equipment, toys, and musical instruments (including accordions and harmonicas) are manufactured.

About 50 miles further along, the Autobahn approaches Ulm. Ulm was a great commercial center in the Middle Ages, and with its wealth it built a huge and ornate cathedral. Its spire is the tallest in the world, over 500 feet. Albert Einstein was born in Ulm in 1879. At Ulm we cross the border into the state of Bavaria. A couple of miles beyond Ulm, the highway crosses the Danube River (German: *Donau*), which flows north and then east toward Vienna, a few hundred miles away.

Next in the succession of cities is Augsburg (pop. 200,000). It is one of the oldest cities in Germany, and like Cologne was built originally by the Romans. It was important during Roman times and in the Middle Ages because it was situated on the road from Northern Europe to Italy. All kinds of goods flowed through the city. Early capitalism got its start here; powerful merchant families made fortunes in banking and finance.

During the Reformation, the Catholics and Protestants had it out here in a famous dispute which took place at the Diet (or assembly) of Augsburg in 1530. The Holy Roman Emperor, Charles V, was worried about the success of the Turkish armies in Austria. They were threatening to take Vienna, his capital. What he didn't need was a religious conflict in his empire. He wanted to bring Luther and his followers into line so that he could get on with the business of defeating the Turks.

For this reason he summoned the Diet of Augsburg. But the Lutherans were not a docile breed. Instead, they issued their famous document, the "Confession of Augsburg," which has remained the chief statement of their belief ever since. Religious wars broke out, and were not resolved until 1555, when the Peace of Augsburg agreement gave freedom of worship to the Lutherans. Meanwhile, Charles V managed to roll back the Turkish armies by himself.

Augsburg has a rich cultural heritage. The famous portraitist Holbein the Elder (d. 1525) and other painters and musicians served to make Augsburg the "town of the German Renaissance". It was here also that the first Diesel engine was produced in 1897.

About 25 miles beyond Augsburg, the Autobahn passes by the town of Dachau, about 5 miles to the left. In the 19th century, the town, with its castle, was a favorite retreat of poets and writers from nearby Munich. But in 1933, the Nazis built their first concentration camp here, and the town has acquired a very different set of associations ever since. About 200,000 prisoners were kept here between 1933 to 1945, and few of them survived the ordeal. Parts of the camp have been reconstructed, and there are various memorial chapels and a museum.

Soon we approach the outskirts of Munich, a city of well over a million people. It is the capital of Bavaria, and one of the principal cultural and commercial centers in all of Europe. It's also the "Beer Capital" of the world. The name "Munich" (German: München) comes from an old German word for "monk". It started as a village around a Benedictine Abbey in the 9th century. The emblem of the city is a little monk, and is painted on the sides of streetcars. Munich's fortunes prospered during the Middle Ages, when Duke Henry the Lion forced all commercial traffic into Munich, collecting revenue and increasing trade. It became a flourishing commercial center and has been one ever since. In the 19th century, dozens of museums, city squares, and the new City Hall were put up. The kings of Bavaria patronized artists and musicians. One of them, "Ludwig the Mad" (Ludwig II, 1864-1886), built the famous fairy-tale castle of Neuschwanstein, down near the Swiss border. This white stone castle is often featured on travel posters of Germany. It was also in Munich that Adolf Hitler got his start back in the 1920's. The Nazi party was first formed here, and its first meetings were held in various beer halls downtown. It was in Munich in 1938 that England and France decided to give the Sudetenland (and eventually all of Czechoslovakia) to the Nazis.

The one place to see Munich at its best is around the Hofbräuhaus.

The word itself means "Court Brewery Building", and it was originally built as a private brewery for the Duke of Bavaria in 1589. Various additions and extensions were added over the centuries. Between 1886 and 1891 the whole building was renovated, and drinking halls were put in. Now, it is owned by the State of Bavaria. An average of 10,000 visitors imbibe 36,000 pints of beer a day. 7000 people munch on 12,000 sausages. It's quite an operation, and deserves its worldwide fame.

About the syllable *bräu*, which is tacked onto the end of many words in German: it simply means "brew". For example: Löwenbräu = Lion's Brew, which is the largest beer firm in Munich, exporting its brew by the shipload to all parts of the world.

The Hofbräuhaus is located on a small square, called the *Platzl* or Little Square. It's right in the heart of Old Munich. Inside, the visitor can see for himself what German *Gemütlichkeit* is all about. The word is one of those untranslatable ones, but it means something like "conviviality", "high spirits", "good cheer" — exactly the sort of thing one would associate with a group of friends sitting around a table, talking and laughing into their steins. A local saying claims that "As long as the Hofbräuhaus stands on the Platzl, *Gemütlichkeit* in Munich will never die." The beer provides the occasion for a convivial get-together. It's not the purpose of the gathering. There is no "serious" drinking going on inside the Hofbräuhaus, or scarcely anywhere else in Munich.

Near the Hofbräuhaus is the New City Hall, a magnificent piece of neo-Gothic architecture, constructed at the end of the 19th century. Hundreds of statues on the façade represent the dukes and kings of old Bavaria. Nearby, a pair of matching towers reach high up into the air, capped by onion-shaped domes. This is the *Frauenkirche* or Church of Our Lady. It has been restored and the interior has been refinished in a stark modern design. Bavaria, of course, is predominantly Catholic, as is southern Germany in general.

Not only the Frauenkirche, but most of downtown Munich was completely bombed out during the war. A few monuments were spared, such as the New Town Hall, the Hofbräuhaus, and several churches, but the major shopping areas and the railroad station were reduced to piles of rubble. All the department stores along the main shopping street were built after the war. There is a brand new railroad station which has everything in it — ticket windows, theaters, outdoor beer and liver-cheese stalls, tourist information offices, and a hotel.

This is typical of the European railroad station. In the U.S., the railroad station is usually the oldest and most depressing building in town. It's a seamy place, crumbling from neglect, and usually kept going only by commuter traffic. In contrast, the airports are new and gleaming. In Europe it's different. The airports are new here too, but they're not much more important than the railroad station. For one thing, the distances in Europe are not that great. It simply doesn't make any sense to fly from Munich to Innsbruck or to Venice. By train, it takes about the same amount of time as it would to take a cab out to the airport, wait for the flight, and then take a cab into the city. The railroad station is still very much a part of urban life in Europe. It's more than just a place to get tickets, board the train, or browse among the newspapers and magazines. It's a kind of social and communications center. There's always something going on. For the visitor, there is an information center, with English-speaking clerks; a hotel register, with prices and reservation facilities; and an exchange window or two. There is a wide assortment of magazines from Paris, Rome or Frankfurt, foreign-language dictionaries, and guidebooks in every major language. Even the *Reader's Digest* is available in German, French, or Italian editions. There are usually several classes of restaurants: quick cafeterias for the harried commuter, outdoor stalls for the adventurous tourist or penurious student, and a showcase restaurant for the expense-account executive or society matron. Every European railroad station is different, of course. Some are bigger and more impressive than others. But they all have one thing in common: unlike their counterparts in the U.S., they're always centers of activity.

South and slightly west of Munich, we enter the storybook portion of Germany, where reality blends ever so slowly with fantasy and folklore. It's a spectacularly beautiful part of the country, and begins about 40 miles south of Munich. Gradually, the flat plain becomes a bit more hilly, and in the distance one can begin to make out the mountains of the Bavarian Alps. Just across the Alps lies Innsbruck. If the sun's out, it will make the clouds over the Alps a radiant gold. Soon the forests on either side of the road grow thicker. A marshy area to the right gives way to a low mountain range, known as the "Ammergau Alps". Just beyond them, about 5 miles to the right, is the town of Oberammergau, where the famous Passion Play is presented by the townspeople every 10 years. The custom dates back from 1634, after a frightful plague stopped just short of the town. The thankful people vowed to present a Passion Play every 10 years as a token of their gratitude. The actors are all amateurs, and residents of the town. They prepare for their roles long beforehand, cultivating their beards in some cases a full year in advance in order to look the part.

The river off to the left is the Loisach, and it runs straight into the resort town of Garmisch-Partenkirchen, the symbol of storybook Germany. It's a nice place to stop for a cup of coffee at one of the outdoor cafés facing the main square. During the winter the town becomes an international skiing mecca, known as the "Snow Stadium of Germany." The Olympic winter games were held here in 1936, and had a lot to do with the development of the town. In mid-winter, between 12 and 20 inches of snowfall are guaranteed by the weather conditions in the eastern Alps. The town is a favorite resort for U.S. Army personnel stationed in Germany. In the hills around Garmisch, herds of sheep and cattle graze on alpine pastures. Around dusk time, they are brought back to the town, and as they cross the main street a policeman has to hold up traffic for about a half-hour.

Alpine houses nuddle around the main square and line the narrow streets that branch out from it. There are a great many more like them up and down the Bavarian Alps. Their roofs are long, and they slope sharply to let the snow slide off. The walls are decorated with scenes from the life of the town, or with pictures of the village or family's patron saint. The window boxes are filled with flowers in bloom. One often sees an old-timer dressed in the Bavarian costume sauntering along, with his *Lederhosen,* long stockings, bright red suspenders, white shirt, and green felt hat with a red feather in it. More than likely, he will be puffing on a long-stemmed pipe.

We leave Garmisch, heading southeast and ascending gradually. Garmisch has an altitude of 2300 ft., and Mittenwald, the next town, is 3000 ft. The road becomes a bit steeper after Mittenwald. Mittenwald itself is a pure delight. It's a small town of only 8000 people, and despite the traffic going through it, it has managed to keep an unspoiled, alpine-village look. Goethe once called it a "living picture-book", and that's what it still is. The houses along the main street are covered with lavish and ornate paintings. Some date as far back as the 1700's. Entering the town by the main road, the road suddenly turns left. Here stands the statue of Matthias Klotz (1663-1743), who brought the skill of violin-making from Italy to Germany in 1684. That skill is still practiced here. The statue is at the foot of the local church that was built just after he died. The church tower is covered with paintings from top to bottom. The reason for the large, overhanging roofs is to protect paintings on the outer walls from the weather.

After Mittenwald, the road really begins to climb. Here are the Bavarian Alps, which become, just over the border, the Austrian Alps. There simply isn't a word to describe the scenery, but we can help the visitor understand it a bit better. First, the mountains themselves. About 10,000 years ago, huge glaciers in what is now Switzerland began to expand, pushing earth, rocks, and whole mountains before them. They were like giant shovels. One of these glaciers gouged its way north and east. It came to a stop just before the spot where Munich stands today. All this accumulated debris was left in huge piles, and it is these piles which are the Bavarian Alps. It has been estimated that the glacier which carved out the Inn river valley (at the bottom of which lies Innsbruck) was over 5000 feet thick. The huge peak on the right is the Zugspitze, the highest point in Germany (9700 ft.). Various cable cars and interior tunnels reach the top.

Soon we reach the Austrian border. A few formalities, and we're off again, still climbing. On the right are the ruins of an old castle, the Porta Claudia (Claudia's Gate), built in the 17th century to defend this important trade route between Italy and Northern Europe. Then through the town of Scharnitz, and still climbing. This long and winding valley is known as the Scharnitz Ravine. The little river is the "Upper Isar". The same stream 100 miles to the north becomes the Isar River which flows through the center of Munich. At the end of the long climb is the town of Seefeld, in the Seefeld Pass. The elevation here is a hefty 3800 ft. It's a popular mountain resort, with a forest and a small lake. On the mountain up to the left, construction is under way for ski lifts and other facilities for winter sports. The jagged and rocky crests off to the right are those of the mountain peak known as the Hohe Munde (High Mouth). The air up here is as clear as it is in Colorado.

Now the descent begins. It's a treacherous stretch of the road. Pretty soon the Inn River valley opens up below. It takes less than an hour to get down there. The descent is along a slope known as the Zirlerberg. Watch for the skull-and-bones warning signs. Here and there are lanes that shoot off to the right, curving up the mountainside, then disappearing after about 30 yards. These are braking roads for cars or buses whose brakes have failed. They were built in the 1930's in the days of less reliable automobiles. At one point along the Zirlerberg, there used to be a hairpin turn. It's since been smoothed out. Rumor has it that so many cars plummeted off the side of the cliff at this point, that hikers would come up every weekend, scout out a vantage point above the turn, take out their box lunches, and wait for the show to begin. The same rumor claims that at the bottom of another cliff there is a huge pile of debris that has collected there since the days of horse-drawn wagons. The spot is virtually inaccessible, and there has been no way of recovering the lost vehicles or their ill-fated occupants.

Pretty soon the whole of the Inn valley comes suddenly into view. It lies in the very heart of the Austrian Alps. Before long, we're on the valley floor, traveling east toward Innsbruck. The huge mountain range to the left is the Karwendel, a vast limestone massif whose highest point is over 9000 ft. The little town of Zirl comes into view as the road reaches the valley. Zirl is about 7 miles west of Innsbruck. The Inn is visible to the right. About 2 or 3 miles beyond Zirl, the road circles around a huge, protruding bulge from the mountainside to the left. It is known as the Martinswand (St. Martin's Wall). According to legend, the popular Emperor Maximilian, who was ruling Austria about the time Columbus discovered America, had a mishap here which turned out very well in the end. "Emperor Max", as he was affectionately called, loved to hunt, and he argued that it was an important way of getting to know his humbler subjects out in the woods and country towns. One day he was hunting on the Martinswand. At one point, his horse lost its step and threw him off, and he began to fall down the side of the mountain. An angel appeared in the form of a peasant, and caught hold of him just before he disappeared over the edge of the precipice. The kindness he had shown his humbler subjects had not been forgotten.

There is something else of interest here. The ruins of an old stone tower stand on the hillside to the left. There's another one further on. These were anti-aircraft towers during the Second World War and were used to defend Innsbruck against Allied air attacks. Innsbruck was an important railroad junction between Germany and Italy. Munitions and other supplies were always coming through the city, and it was an inviting target. The difficulty, however, was that there was only one way to approach Innsbruck by air, and that was to fly down the Inn valley. That's what they did, and the anti-aircraft crews were waiting for them. It was a harrowing mission. Many of the pilots never returned.

A few more miles and Innsbruck looms up ahead. The twin towers belong to the cathedral of St. Jakob (St. James). Another obvious landmark is the spectacular mountain range just north of the city, the Nordkette. Nordkette in German means "Northern Range". The top is covered with snow all year round. Innsbruck is a charming town, and certainly worth getting to know.

Innsbruck, the Jewel in Maria Theresa's Crown

The first thing many people ask about Austria is how it is distinguished from Germany. Everybody speaks German here, just as they do in Heidelberg and Munich. Why are the two countries separate? The explanation goes far back in history. Germany was divided into many independent states for much of its history. Austria was one of these. It happened to be the largest, and it could defend itself very well against invaders, but it was still a general part of the cultural region of Germany. Its people spoke German and they referred to themselves as Germans. Austria goes back even further. During Roman times, the whole region was known as "Noricum". Many of the Austrian cities were originally Roman forts. Innsbruck, for example, was known as "Veldidena". Vienna was "Vindobona". In Charlemagne's day, these forts were strengthened and enlarged. The whole area became known as the "Eastern March", or in German, the "Ostmark". Another version of this word is "Österreich" (Ost = east, Reich = realm or kingdom) which is what Austria is called in German today. Austria was simply the easternmost kingdom in Charlemagne's vast empire.

The country didn't really become a going concern until around 1273, when Count Rudolf of Hapsburg became king of Austria. The house of Hapsburg ruled Austria from that point on, until the monarchy was overthrown in 1918 at the end of World War I. Through a series of conquests, clever marriages, and sheer gall, the Hapsburgs added more and more territory to their realm, until Austria was the largest single kingdom in Europe. In fact, the Hapsburgs became the rulers, not just of Austria, but of the Holy Roman Empire too. The Holy Roman Empire was a second Roman Empire put together by Charlemagne and his successors. It didn't really function as an empire for very long, but remained an accepted idea over centuries that included most of Germany, Austria, and northern Italy. For a few years it really was an empire. Even later, when the Holy Roman Empire had become a mere name, the high office of its emperor still carried with it enormous prestige, and it was no small achievement for the Hapsburgs to secure this title.

So successful were the Hapsburgs in adding to their domains, that they adopted the outrageous motto: *Austriae Est Imperare Orbi Universo,* which means in Latin: "To Austria it is [given] to rule the world." Put together the first letters of the Latin motto and you have A.E.I.O.U., the five vowels. Emblems with these letters on them are still visible on some of the older buildings in Innsbruck.

Austria suffered heavily at the hands of Napoleon. In 1800, Napoleon defeated the Austrian army at Marengo and at Hohenlinden. Later, as Emperor of France, he defeated them again at Austerlitz (1805). But he wasn't content with that. He married the daughter of the Austrian emperor, Marie-Louise, after divorcing the hapless Josephine. After Napoleon was defeated at Waterloo (1815), the Austrian Empire came back into its own. This was largely the doing of the Austrian foreign minister, Count Metternich, who was possibly the most brilliant states-man of the 19th century. Austria received its lands back again, and for a hundred years after that, until the First World War, Vienna was in every sense the cultural capital of Europe.

World War I dealt a fatal blow to the Austrian Empire. The Allies stripped Austria of all its possessions, including Hungary, Czechoslovakia (which came into existence for the first time as a nation), and part of Poland. The monarchy was replaced by a republic. For the first time in its history, Austria found itself reduced to a second or even third-rate power. The territory which became known as Austria had never been economically self-sufficient, and this presented the new country with major difficulties. Its economy had depended on the former empire for raw materials and commercial markets. Austria, and espe-cially Vienna, was simply the administrative hub of a huge and pros-perous economic region. When cut off from the rest of this region, it could barely survive. It is understandable that there was some popular support for the idea of *Anschluss* (union or annexation) with Germany in the 1920's. Many Austrians liked the idea, but after Hitler came to power in 1933 most of them had second thoughts. *Anschluss* came anyway in March 1938, as the German armies rolled into Vienna unopposed. From that point on, Austria shared the fate of Germany in World War II. In 1945, the Soviet armies entered Austria from the east, and the Americans and British entered from the west. The country was divided into 4 zones of occupation, as was Germany. Finally in 1955, the Western Allies and the Soviet Union agreed on the restoration of Austrian independence. The stipulation was that Austria remain neutral in the Cold War. Austria continues to be a sovereign state, and it is nearer economic self-sufficiency that it has ever been before. It is a republic, with a population of over 7 million. The land area is 32,000 square miles, compared with 12,000 for Belgium.

Since so much of the country is mountainous, agriculture is difficult. But the Austrians bring determination and ingenuity to the task, and manage pretty well. They raise 80% of their own food. One sixth of the people are farmers, compared to about an eighth in Germany. Though crop farming is difficult, the long, sloping hillsides are perfect for cattle grazing. Beef is an important industry in Austria. One tenth of the population works in forest or wood industries, since 30% of the country is forest land. Only the Scandinavian countries can match that percentage. Austria has always been important for mining and heavy industry. Around Innsbruck, for example, there used to be large deposits of gold, silver, and copper. (All of the gold probably went into the dazzling interiors of the Baroque churches.) And with all the mountains and mountain rivers, of course, one would expect Austria to excel in hydroelectric power. It does, but the Austrians still have a long way to go in exploiting the available dam sites in the Alps. At least they are working on it. Austria also has some oil reserves, enough to keep about half its cars chugging up the alpine slopes. The rest is imported.

Austria is governed by a federal system that more nearly resembles the U.S. government than the British or the German parliamentary system. More power is retained by the individual states, however. These states or provinces (*Länder* in German) have their own provincial "Diet" or assembly. There are 9 provinces in all. Innsbruck is the capital city of the Tyrol. There are about 400,000 people in the Province of Tyrol, and it covers about 5,000 square miles. It is the westernmost province of all, except for tiny Vorarlberg, which is off to the west, bordering on Switzerland.

The Tyrol has always been proud of its traditions and of its relative independence from the rest of Austria. Though Austria is predominantly Catholic, the Tyrolese are even more so. It is in the Tyrol that Austrian patriotism finds its home. A good deal of the spirit of the Tyrolese is expressed in a local festival called the *Tirolerabend* (*Tirol + Abend* = evening). The singing and dancing, costumes and folklore all reflect the mountain and forest traditions of this sturdy people. The cultural region of the Tyrol extends further south, over the border into Italy. In Italy it becomes the "South Tyrol", and during the past 10 years there has been a movement afoot for South Tyrolese unification with Austria. Traveling through the South Tyrol on the way to Venice, one still sees armed convoys and mountain patrols looking for terrorists and other partisans of the South Tyrolese independence movement. These partisans represent the spirit of rugged independence which first built Innsbruck and made the Tyrol what it is. Indeed, only the hardiest of people could have carved out a living for themselves in the midst of such rugged and unproductive terrain.

Today, the population of Innsbruck is almost 100,000, but it still looks like the mountain town that Maria Theresa loved so well. The name simply means "Bridge over the Inn River". Innsbruck has always been an important stop on the road from Italy to Munich. For a time, it was part of the independent state of Tyrol, but soon the Hapsburgs took possession of the Tyrol and made Innsbruck one of their favorite resorts. There are two Hapsburgs whose names are important to the town. The first is the Emperor Maximilian (1493-1519), the kindly "Emperor Max" who had the hunting accident on the rocky slopes of the Martinswand. He loved to hunt in the hills and forests around the town, and built many of the buildings and churches in Innsbruck. His marriage policy was typical of the Hapsburgs in general. He married Maria, Princess of Burgundy (in what is now eastern France), and through her inherited the whole region. Two famous lines of Latin doggerel tell of this way of acquiring territories:

> Bella gerant alii, tu, felix Austria, nube
> Nam quae Mars aliis, dat tibi regna Venus.

It means roughly:

> Where others may go to war, you, happy Austria, can marry instead.
> What some people owe to Mars, you may obtain from Venus.

Maximilian's first wife died, and he married again in 1494. Later he built the "Golden Roof", one of the lovelier edifices in Old Innsbruck. He was fond of the town, and wanted to be buried here. He had the beautiful Hofkirche (Court Church) built. It is very plain and un-impressive on the outside, because it was maintained by Franciscan monks, whose architectural style stressed simplicity and asceticism. But inside, the picture is altogether different. The Emperor Max had an extravagant tomb constructed, with enormous, larger-than-life statues surrounding it. These statues are of bronze, and are supposed to repre-sent the various knights and lords who made up Max's retinue. Up on the balcony behind the tomb is a row of smaller statues. They are the patron saints of the Hapsburg family, as well as some of the Roman emperors, with whom Max, like most other Hapsburgs, identified him-self.

But even the best-laid plans may come to naught. Poor Max never got to be buried in the Hofkirche. The trouble was that the knights and lords in his retinue were larger than life even while alive. They collected taxes from the people of Innsbruck and then went on wild spending sprees. This left the people penniless and gave Emperor Max a bad name. Finally the townspeople got together and refused to allow Max and his retinue into the city. Heartbroken, he turned back to Vienna,

his capital, but died on the way there. He's actually buried in a modest church in Wiener-Neustadt, south of Vienna.

The other great name associated with Innsbruck is that of Maria Theresa, who reigned from 1740-1780. The main street of Innsbruck is named after her, the Maria-Theresienstrasse. Her reign was plagued by difficulties of all kinds, and by several personal tragedies. To begin with, several European states disputed the right of a woman to rule the empire, and used this as an excuse to invade her territories. (This led to the long War of the Austrian Succession, 1740-1748). Then the foxy Frederick the Great of Prussia began encroaching on her territories to the north. Next came a personal tragedy. Her husband was Duke Francis of Lorraine (now part of France). In 1765 the family was in Innsbruck, celebrating the marriage of Duke Leopold to a princess of Spain. There were processions, festivities, merriment everywhere. Suddenly word was brought that Maria Theresa's husband had died. Laughter turned to mourning. A monumental arch commemorates these events. It stands at one end of the Maria-Theresienstrasse.

There was another family tragedy, though Maria Theresa did not live long enough to witness it. Her daughter, Marie Antoinette, who was married to King Louis XVI of France, was the victim of the French Revolution, and was executed by the guillotine in 1793. Maria Theresa's son, the Emperor Joseph II, was a weak and muddle-headed ruler, and was either unable or unwilling to come to her aid.

Maria Theresa did a great deal for Innsbruck. She built the Hofburg or Royal Palace, which still stands, though part of it was bombed out during the war. She had the Cathedral Church of St. James remodeled. Under her, many of the city's Baroque churches were either built or refurbished. Innsbruck was her favorite place, the jewel in her crown.

The unit of currency in Austria is the schilling, worth about 4 cents; 23 schillings make a dollar. The schilling is composed of 100 groschen, just as the dollar has 100 cents. Travelers checks may be cashed at the railroad station or the American Express office. Innsbruck is a small town, and everything is easily found. Phone calls and telegrams are also handled at the railroad station.

The first day in Innsbruck is best spent sightseeing. The town is so small that it can all be done on foot. A good place to begin is along the Maria-Theresienstrasse, which begins at the memorial Arch. Both laughter and tears are recorded on this monument. Around to the south side of the arch (facing the Nordkette) are all the happy symbols:

Emperor Francis and Maria Theresa are shown together. To the left are statues of the couple being married. To the right are the sisters of the bride. Around to the other side, everything is gloomy: an Angel of Death holds a picture of the Emperor. A woman mourns his passing.

Down the Maria-Theresienstrasse, in the direction of the Nordkette, are several churches. They look rather plain on the outside, but inside everything is covered with elaborate Baroque ornamentation. Halfway down the street is a tall column in the middle of the road. This is the St. Ann's Column. Actually, the statue on top is not St. Ann, but the Virgin. St. Ann is down below, at the base, along with St. George (patron saint of the Tyrol) and two other saints. The column was built in 1706 to commemorate the victory of the Austrians over the Bavarians, who had invaded the Tyrol. The victory took place on July 26, 1703, the feast day of St. Ann.

Soon the Maria-Theresienstrasse appears to end. However, a narrow alley continues further north for a block. This is the heart of Old Innsbruck. It's a small square, with shopping arcades on either side. Caution: the prices in these shops are sky-high; the tiny restaurants are expensive too. The shops on the smaller sidestreets are much less expensive. They're actually more romantic, and the prices are a little more restrained. At one end of the square is the Little Golden Roof (Goldenes Dachl), built by Emperor Max. Legend has it, though, that it was built, not by Max, but by an earlier ruler, Duke Frederick (1406-1439), who was outraged at hearing jokes made about his empty treasury. According to the legend, he ordered the roof to be built out of hundreds of gold coins, to demonstrate that he was as rich as any other prince. The various designs on the balconies below are the coats-of-arms of the House of Hapsburg and of the various provinces of the Austrian Empire.

To the left of the corner is an elaborate house; it's known as the Helblinghaus. The extravagantly decorated window boxes were constructed in order to let in as much light as possible, back in the old days of narrow streets and alleys. It's a good example of 18th century Rococo (or late-Baroque) design. Straight ahead is the Goldener Adler (Golden Eagle) Inn, where important artists and writers, including Goethe, used to stay. The management is far from humble about it too. Right on the outside wall they have put up a guest list, carved in stone, of some famous personages who have enjoyed their hospitality over the years.

There is another tiny alley back in the square. This one doesn't seem to go anywhere. But it does go somewhere — to the Cathedral Church of St. James. The inside is pure Baroque splendor. The painting over the altar is a famous one, "Our Lady of Help" (*Mariahilfe* in German), done by Lukas Cranach the Elder. It has been greatly venerated over the years. Once, when the church building was damaged by an earthquake, the painting had to be taken out for protection while the building was restored. With great pomp and circumstance, the painting was brought back in by a solemn procession, headed by Maria Theresa herself. To the right of the altar is a glass-encased balcony. That's where the Emperor and Empress would sit during Mass. It is connected to the Hofburg Palace by a special passageway.

This about covers the main part of Innsbruck. Of course, there are other things to see too. There's the Tiroler Volkskunstmuseum (Tyrolean Folk Art Museum) right next to the Hofkirche. It's open on weekdays and Saturday and houses a large collection of peasant costumes, farming and craft tools, and furniture. They have reconstructed peasant homes by taking the walls, ceilings, and wood paneling of old Tyrolean dwellings and putting them on display, together with old stoves, cooking pots, looms, and other day-to-day items. The museum provides the visitor with a good idea of how the people lived in the days of Emperor Max. Admission: about 6 schillings (27¢).

Down on Museumstrasse (Museum Street), which angles off from Burggraben Street, there is another museum, this one devoted to fine art. It's the Tiroler Landesmuseum (Tyrolean Provincial Museum), which features artistic contributions by native Tyroleans, many of them masters of the Baroque style. Admission: about 6 schillings

Most visitors also take the cable-car up to the top of the Nordkette. A cog-railway goes halfway up the mountain to the town of Hungerburg, which has resort facilities, restaurants, and souvenir shops. From here the cable car continues to Hafelekar at the top. The entire trip takes a couple of hours. It is a good idea to bring a sweater or jacket along. There may be snow at the top. One also does well to bring a camera; the mountain is 7600 ft. high, and the view of the Inn Valley is magnificent. Innsbruck is a mere dot at the bottom. The round-trip fare for the cable car is about 35 schillings ($1.40). The cog-railway fare is about 15 schillings (60¢) round trip.

Just outside of town is a huge ice stadium and ski-jump complex. It's one of the biggest in Austria, and was built for the 1964 Winter Olympic Games. Often, a movie is shown there about the games. (They have an English version.) It's an ideal setting for winter sports. The ski-jump follows the curve of the hillside for about a hundred yards, then swoops upward, sending the skier shooting practically straight up. It's not recommended for beginners.

There are other things to do during a three-day stay in Innsbruck. The shops display fine wood carvings, porcelain beer steins, or other mountain souvenirs. Then there's the *Tirolerabend,* an evening with the Tyrolese. It's an old custom in Innsbruck, and the best way really to feel a part of this town and its people. Tyrolese musicians, dancers, and stunt artists demonstrate the skills and traditions acquired long ago by these sturdy mountain dwellers. The *Tirolerabend* is a happy way to bring a sojourn in Innsbruck to a close. There is still some mountain-climbing to do, en route over the Brenner Pass to Italy.

Over the Brenner Pass to Italy: Innsbruck-Venice

We leave Innsbruck by the south road, getting an excellent view of the Olympic stadium and ski-jump complex on the edge of town. Two churches are visible in the distance. One of them is a brilliant coral color. The other resembles the "Maria Theresa yellow" of the Hofburg Palace. They were built by a monastic order known as the "Premon-stratensians", who owned all the land around here in the 1100's. This section of Innsbruck is called Wilten, and it was the original site of the old Roman town of Veldidena. Ahead and to the left is a protrusion of the mountainside, heavily forested. The highway passes right under it by tunnel. The hillside is called the Berg Isel, and it is still sacred to the Tyrolese. It was here that the Tyrolese army fought a losing battle against Napoleon in 1809. The hero was Andreas Hofer, and his statue can barely be seen down to the right just before entering the tunnel.

When the weather's clear, there is a spectacular view of Innsbruck, the Inn river valley, the Nordkette, and beyond that the frosty peaks of the Karwendel massif. The best time of the day to catch this view is in the early morning. There's a slight mist in the air which gives the whole scene a kind of dream-like unreality.

The spectacle continues and reaches a climax at the gigantic "Europa-brücke," or Bridge of Europe. It towers about 600 ft. above the valley floor. The river seen at the bottom is the Sill, which joins the Inn river at Innsbruck. The Europa bridge is the largest in Austria. The Autobahn follows the Sill, though from a higher vantage point than the older road. The Brenner Pass comes into view as the highway rounds a fairly sharp bend in the road. It's the most important route across the

Alps between Austria and Italy. The Romans built a road along this route, parts of which have been excavated. The main importance of the Brenner Pass is that it has the lowest elevation of all the routes through the Alpine range. The railroad that passes through here is the only one that crosses the Alps without using a major tunnel. Elevation is only 4000 ft. Millions of German tourists drive through the Brenner Pass on their way to Italy and the Mediterranean. For this reason, there is usually a snake-like line of Mercedes and Volkswagens clogging the customs lanes at the pass.

In addition, there are usually dozens of heavy trucks lined up like dominos waiting for customs inspection. This is an indication of a serious economic problem confronting Europe as it attempts to compete with the U.S. Unlike our country, Europe is divided into a patchwork of relatively diversified economic regions and politically independent states. There are customs formalities at every hand, bureaucratic niceties to be observed, and the whole bric-a-brac of currency exchanges, border crossings, and cargo-declaration forms to be filled out in triplicate. This slows down trade, makes for general confusion, and allows much less economic coordination between the countries of Western Europe. Small wonder that they lag behind the U.S., with its economic homogeneity, common language, and absence of internal boundaries. Somehow, sometime, Europe is going to have to deal with this problem. But how? What can they do? Force everyone to speak Esperanto? It's hard to say. Some finance ministers are contemplating the idea of a kind of all-European currency system which major corporations would use in carrying out international business transactions. Local people and travelers would continue changing marks into schillings into lire, etc., but all major paper deals would be made with this special currency. But that's only part of the problem. There are still the border crossings, the customs tie-ups, the cargo inspections, and all the forms. There must be found a way of standardizing them, or doing away with them altogether. As it is now, U.S. corporations are buying up one weak European company after another. The problem here is anything but simple, but sooner or later the European countries will have to face it unless they're willing to have U.S. firms pulling all the strings of the European economy.

Formalities at the border should be brief, but there may be some waiting while the innumerable cars, buses, and trucks are all processed. This would be a good time to take out a Berlitz phrase-book and start practicing Italian or at least get *Buon giorno* (good day), *grazie* (thank you), and a few others out of the way. Not very many people speak English in this part of the world. The visitor has been spoiled in this respect by his experience in Germany and Austria. He may have to start "roughing it", linguistically speaking, for the next few weeks. Actually, it makes things a bit more exciting. A traveler really knows he's abroad when he finds himself on a tiny sidestreet in a remote corner of Venice, where few Americans are likely to have penetrated.

It's more or less downhill from this point on, though there will be some uphill stretches. First, one must remember to turn his watch ahead one hour. Italy is on a kind of daylight savings time. One gets the hour back when crossing the border into Switzerland.

The Austrian Alps eventually become the Dolomite Ranges. They form a spectacular limestone massif about 70 miles in length. There are several ways in which the Dolomites differ from the Austrian Alps. For one thing, they are very much more jagged and rough, with many patches of sheer rock, and much steeper mountain slopes. There aren't very many of the soft, reclining mountainsides, with lovely wooden chalets and grazing herds.

There is another way in which the Dolomites differ from the Austrian Alps. The rocky sides of the mountains have a curious color, which varies from mountain to mountain, according to the weather and the time of day. Often, it will be yellowish pink, at other times and other places, a grayish blue. The name "Dolomites" comes from the French geologist, Gratet de Dolomieu, who devoted quite a few years to the study of these rock formations and erosion patterns. These erosion patterns, by the way, have created a curious effect. The mountains are rough and jagged for about the upper two-thirds of their height. They suggest all kinds of mysterious shapes: gigantic statues, cathedrals, domes, and spires. Then, for the lower third or so, the mountain evens out into gently sloping pastureland and forest. But even here, the slope is pretty steep, and there aren't many herds.

At first, our route passes along the Isarco river valley, heading southeast. From time to time there may be military camps, mountain patrols, or jeep convoys. The Italian government is taking precautions against terrorism by South Tyrolese partisans. Actually, it's not quite as dangerous as it was several years ago, when the whole area was crawling with patrols and convoys, and when U.S. television news reports showed film strips of police stations and other municipal buildings in the area that had been dynamited. But just enough sentiment for South Tyrolese independence is still alive to prompt the Italian government to keep the area well fortified. The Italian soldiers, young recruits mostly, often wave and call *bella ragazza* (Hey, pretty girl!).

Pretty soon, we come upon evidence of real warfare. Big battles raged in these mountain valleys over 50 years ago, during World War I. It was part of the Austrian offensive against the Italians in 1917. The most famous one of all was the Battle of Caporetto in October-November, 1917. It took place to the east (or to the left), but involved the whole area of the Dolomites. The Austrians had not been doing well in mountain warfare against the Italians, who were more adept at fighting in this kind of terrain. So the Austrians asked the German allies for help. The Germans brought in officers trained for mountain warfare. They also brought in thousands of howitzers especially adapted for fairly close-range, accurate fire. The Italians weren't quite prepared for it, and when the Austro-German offensive began on October 24, 1917, it became a hecatomb. In six weeks of fighting the Italians suffered over 300,000 losses, of whom many were taken prisoner. It was a rout, the most humiliating defeat the Italian army has had in modern times. The whole Italian line would have collapsed entirely if the British and French had not rushed in several divisions at the last minute.

These events are vividly described in Ernest Hemingway's novel, *A Farewell to Arms,* which is set in the midst of the Battle of Caporetto. When the Hollywood director, Darryl Zanuck, was making a film of this novel about 10 years ago, he wanted to shoot most of it in the Dolomites where the action had occurred. But he ran into trouble with the Italian government. The Italians are still sensitive about the whole thing, and the government wouldn't let Zanuck use the Dolomites unless he agreed to soft-pedal the scenes showing the Italian defeat. He agreed, but he did show scenes of Italian officers rounding up hundreds of deserters and putting them in front of firing squads.

These bloody and tragic events account for some of the sights along the Dolomite range. Most of them are off to the left. The remains of a field hospital are still standing. A red cross is painted on the wall; it has faded a great deal but it is still identifiable. There are other fortifications along the wall, some of them rather high up the mountainside. Occasionally, old gun replacements dot the rocky cliffs, and caves which were used as machine-gun nests. The fighting that went on here over 50 years ago is awesome to imagine — quite apart from the problem of evacuating the wounded. The Austrians, for example, lost 100,000 men in one engagement alone. There were no helicopters — only rickety motor lorries, and they were constantly exposed to sniper fire, airplane attacks, or to artillery bombardment. Hemingway describes it in detail.

Our route follows the Rienza River at this point, as it snakes its way through the mountains. Pretty soon it passes through Brunico, a sleepy resort from which many ambitious hikers set off for the mountain valleys to the north. Then through Dobbiaco, another resort, and it turns right, heading due south through some of the most jagged mountains in the whole area. Someone has compared a trip through this region to a mouse's springing into the lion's mouth. It's as if one were being chewed up and swallowed by a set of giant molars. The mountains aren't even peaks anymore; they're enormous spikes. After passing through the town of Carbonin, a huge chunk of limestone towers up ahead. It is Mount Cristallo, with a peak 11,000 ft. high. The road cautiously inches its way around it, to the left. At this point, three peaks become visible also to the left. They're known as the Cima di Lavaredo, or the "combs" of the Lavaredo region. By this time we're on the other side of Mount Cristallo, and heading through the Passo Tre Croci (Pass of the Three Crosses), from which it is possible to catch a glimpse of the cable-car station for Mount Cristallo. Imagine skiing down *that* thing. This is only a prelude to the valley which can be seen below through openings in the larch trees. Any traveler who doesn't have acrophobia by now will soon get it. The road itself looks as if someone had squeezed a huge tube of toothpaste all over the side of the rock. But even this is nothing compared to the old road, which is also seen from time to time. That road was used by the makeshift ambulances as they chugged their way up and down the steep inclines.

Suddenly, an opening appears in this forest of teeth, and a lovely valley spreads itself out at the base of Monte Crepa. It's the glamorous resort town of Cortina d'Ampezzo, nestling on the slopes and extending into the valley. It's the capital of the Dolomites, and the largest town in the area. The Winter Olympic Games were held here in 1956, and ski schools do a brisk business.

Cortina is an ideal place to have lunch, and to get a first taste of *real* Italian cooking. Many American visitors have been surprised to learn that in Italy the spaghetti (*pasta*) dish is not the whole meal, as it is in "Italian restaurants" in the U.S., but only the appetizer. It is to the Italians what soup is to us. After *pasta* there's veal scaloppine or Italian roast chicken or *bistecca* — beefsteak. It is served with a good helping of vegetables and finished off with ice cream and espresso coffee.

It is tempting to eat a great deal, but the visitor is cautioned that there is more roller-coasting ahead. Cortina d'Ampezzo is almost a mile above sea level. Venice, our destination, is at sea level. We thus have a mile to descend while heading south toward the Adriatic Sea. This region of Italy is known as Venezia Tridentina, and people here are partly Germanic in language and ancestry. There are quite a few signs in German: *Zimmer frei* (room available), and most of the towns have two names, Italian and German. Bressanone, in Italian, is also known as Brixen in German. Before long, though, we enter another region, called Venezia Giulia, which extends east to the Austrian and Yugoslavian borders. The road is still descending, valley after valley, plateau after plateau; it seems to go on forever.

Finally the road turns right, into the Piave river valley, and continues on until it takes us out of the mountains altogether. The long ribbon-shaped lake to the left is the Lago Centro Cadore, or Lake in the Center of the Cadore range. Further south, past the massive Cima dei Preti, and the road passes through the flood-disaster area of Longarone. Longarone is a pitiful remnant of a town, bordering on the Piave river, and it was the scene of a disastrous flood a few years ago. On the left is a dam, up on the mountain. It has replaced the one that gave way one rainy night, back in 1966, releasing a wall of water that leveled the town.

Then a larger lake comes into view on the left, the Lago di Santa Croce, or Lake of the Holy Cross. The water looks cool, dark, and refreshing. Some townspeople as well as tourists will be taking a dip. Those who feel a little envious can cheer themselves with the thought of splashing around in something a little larger tomorrow or the next day: the Adriatic Sea. Further on is the town of Vittorio Veneto, where the Italians managed to reverse the tide of battle and redeem their national pride, having sent the Austrian army reeling back through the Dolomites. Handsome Renaissance palaces surround the Square.

Shortly after the road passes through the town of Conegliano. Just outside is the castle of San Salvatore, belonging to the counts of Collalto. It is remembered for its brief association with the 16th-century Venetian poetess, Gaspara Stampa. This is one of the richest wine, silk, and fruit regions of Italy.

About here, at Conegliano, we reach flat land again for the first time since Garmisch-Partenkirchen.The mountains are all behind us. There are some hills and even modest mountains ahead as we make our way over the Apennines in a few days, but it will be nothing like the rough terrain of the Dolomites. Later, of course, our route takes us through the Alps as we cross the border into Switzerland. But for the moment, it's nothing but plains and plateaus — specifically, the Po river plain. This plain is a huge wedge which runs east and west, beginning just south of the Alps. It has many rivers: the Po, the Ticino, the Minicio, the Adige, the Brenta, and the river we've been following: the Piave. These rivers drain off the water accumulating in the Alps and carry it to the Adriatic Sea. As they flow through the flat plains, they bring mineral deposits and other nutrients with them. Rice farming is an important industry in the Po river plain because of the abundance of water, which rice-farming requires by the ton. Around here, though, it's mainly wheat and vineyards, along with fruit trees and olive orchards. Up in the mountains, hydroelectric power is sufficient to keep huge textile plants going.

The major problem, of course, is that these rivers have a way of overflowing their banks in periods of unusually heavy rainfall. When that happens it affects cities and towns many miles away. Venice can find itself under five feet of water overnight. Florence, further south and to the west, also suffers flooding from time to time. The newspapers carried stories of mass flooding in these cities back in 1967. Hundreds of art treasures and monuments were threatened. Many of them were damaged, some irrecoverably. Of course, the solution is to develop a system of flood-control dams and dikes, and the Italians are working on it. But it's a big job and it takes time. Besides, human beings are notoriously lethargic; they usually don't go to work on a problem until it hits them over the head. It is only recently that full scale flood-control measures have been undertaken. Some say it's too late.

The road has by now entered the region of Veneto, the capital of which is Venice. On the way, it runs through Treviso, a good-sized city, and the last one before Venice. In the center of this town are old walls and fortifications dating from the 1400's, when Treviso was part of the Venetian state. Many memorial plaques on walls display the Lion of St. Mark, the official emblem of Venice, and are remarkably well preserved considering their age. Quiet, mossy canals surround the ruins. Occasionally there is a millwheel or two on them.

The somewhat crooked road now straightens out to become the Treviso-to-Venice highway. We use the term "highway" with some license, though. It's not exactly a turnpike, but it was the best road in Italy when it was first built by Napoleon, who controlled the whole area, including Venice, after his victory over the Allies in 1805. Like

most conquerors in history, he parceled out his new possessions like toys among his generals and sycophants. To Marshal Mortier he gave the city of Treviso; he made his infant son King of Rome. He thought of himself as an art lover, and ordered alterations in the layout of St. Mark's Square in Venice. He also ordered the building of the Treviso-to-Venice road. Its remarkable straightness and the trees placed at regular intervals make it resemble a French provincial highway. In fact, except for the Italian villas along the road, the whole area could be in France. The French prefer their highways, gardens, and palaces geometrical, orderly, logical. The Italians are a bit more relaxed. The English, more still. The road still has the width it had when it was first constructed, and that was very wide for those days. It is possible to catch a glimpse now and then of the fabulous palazzi on either side. They are surrounded by luxuriant gardens, and it's sometimes hard to get a view through the trees. The lovely statues, fountains, sculptured balconies, stone lattice-work, and ornamented façades all reveal how the better half lived in the days of the Venetian empire. Napoleon's generals helped themselves to it all. Now, most of them are owned by Italian oil executives and politicians. Soon the highway approaches Venice (Italian: Venezia), passing through the industrial suburbs and oil refineries which have sprouted on the mainland during the past four or five years.

Italy: Some Facts and Figures

We've crossed another border, and are in a new country. First, a few practical hints. Currency again. A ten-day stay is plenty of time to get to know the Italian *lira,* and more than enough opportunity to practice the skill. To begin with, a single lira is worth almost nothing, less than a fifth of a cent. Counting is done not with single lira, but with units of 10 lire (the smallest coin) or 100 lire (the most common coin); 100 lire are worth 16¢. In fact, "16" is the important number in Italy, and the one to remember. In calculating the dollars-and-cents value of a price tag in Italy, all one does is move the decimal back and forth around the number 16. Let us look at the following example: some article costs 1000 lire. (It would be written: "Lit. 1000.") Before writing it off as hopelessly expensive, move the decimal to the right one place from the left-hand margin: 1.6, and you'll see that it only costs $1.60. If it's 10,000 lire, move the decimal two places to the right: 16. That's $16.00. 100,000 lire are $160.00, and so on. Or take 500 lire. That would be 80¢ or .80. 5000 would be $8.00, 50,000 $80.00. There are between 610 and 620 lire to the dollar. It's impossible to give an exact exchange figure, because the rate fluctuates from day to day. Also, different banks and stores in different parts of Italy and at different times offer slightly different rates. But it doesn't really matter that much, because the difference between 600 lire (about the lowest exchange rate ever given) and 620 (the highest) is only 3¢.

The fact that the single lira is worth so little doesn't mean, of course, that the Italian currency or Italian economy is unstable or inflated. Italy has one of the stablest currencies in Europe. It hasn't been devalued since the early fifties, and the industry behind it is rock-solid. It just so happens that the lira has always been a "small" currency. The French franc was this way until the currency reform of 1960 converted 100 "old francs" into 1 new franc. There is some talk of doing the same thing in Italy.

Perhaps the most salient feature of Italy is its population. The density of the population is the third highest in Europe. But there is plenty of land to spread out on, about 120,000 square miles in fact — about the size of the state of Arizona. There are over 55 million people in Italy. It's amazing that what often looks to be a tiny hamlet is actually a city of 20,000 or 30,000 people. Many a town that seems average-sized turns out to have 70,000 to 100,000 people. Although Italy's population is dense, it doesn't *look* dense. There is a great deal of countryside left, and the visitor sees a good bit of it when traveling across the plains of Emilia and over the Apennines to Florence, through the broad, fertile valleys of Umbria to Rome, or down the coast on the way to Pompeii and Capri. In fact, Italy is one of the least "urban" looking countries in Europe.

Italy has always been an agricultural country, and this helps to explain the countryside. It presents dozens of small towns, hundreds of villages, but only a handful of large cities. Only four number over a million: Rome, Naples, Milan, and Turin. Many Italians prefer village life, with its strong local attachments. The village saint, local customs and festivals, and regional dialect influence a marked sector of the population. Their idea of life is often rooted in place, and people are not ashamed to return to their natal locality after making a name for themselves or getting a career started in the city.

Though Italy has always been an agricultural country and still produces some of the best olives, grapes, wine, and citrus fruits in Europe, a new chapter has opened up since World War II. Italy has become an industrial power of the first rank — and this in spite of some major handicaps. Italy lacks significant amounts of raw materials. It has little iron and other minerals, and not much coal. But it has tremendous hydroelectric resources. The dams on alpine streams provide power that keeps the wheels of industry turning, and at an increasing rate. Italy's production of autos and trucks is well over a million a year. The biggest automaking firm is FIAT. (The name is an acrostic for *Fabbrica Italiana Automobili Torino*. Fiat's largest plants and offices are in Torino or Turin in English.) There are other auto firms, of course, some of them specializing in the luxury car market. By now the names are familiar to most Americans: Lancia, Alfa-Romeo, Ferrari, Maserati, and so on. Italian entries in international racing competitions are often the most prestigious. To some persons, Italian designers are the best in Europe.

Most of the industrial and commercial muscle of the country is concentrated north of Rome, in such cities as Turin, Milan, Modena, and in the suburbs of Venice. It is interesting to note in this connection that the people of the North are quite aware of the economic miracle they have brought about through shrewd inventions, managerial skill, and plain hard work. They are ambitious, critical, resourceful. The people of the South, in contrast, tend to be more relaxed, generous, and even a bit gullible. (They also probably live longer.) As a result, southern Italy is still largely agricultural, and even its agricultural methods are something less than efficient. The standard of living in a southern city like Taranto is far lower than it is in Milan.

The people in the central part of the country, which includes the cities of Florence and Rome, are even prouder of themselves than the northerners, but for a different reason. It isn't so much their industry and commerce that they gloat over, though there is a lot of that too. Rather, it's the past achievements of the Renaissance that spark the pride of a Florentine or a Roman. There isn't anything in northern or southern Italy to match the creative genius of these two cities over the past 500 years. They stand in a class by themselves. The Florentine, for example, considers himself the true Italian, the bearer of his country's best traditions.

The people of Milan, the greatest city of the North, are somewhat Germanic in their habits. The workers are industrious, the businessmen thorough and efficient, and popular emotions rather heavy. After all, Milan has the greatest opera in Italy, and romanticism isn't a thing one associates with the elegant and astringent Florentine. On the other hand, the southern Italian does have a few traits in common with the pious and sturdy Moslem of northern Africa, in spite of obvious religious and cultural differences. He gets up early in the morning, works hard all day, and goes to bed with the chickens at night. This is his life, and he thanks God (or Allah) for it.

Venice, Dream City on the Adriatic

> Is there anyone but must repress a secret thrill on arriving in Venice for the first time – or returning thither after long absence – and stepping into a Venetian gondola? That singular conveyance, come down unchanged from ballad times, black as nothing else on earth except a coffin – what pictures it calls up of lawless, silent adventures in the plashing night; or even more, what visions of death itself, the bier and solemn rites and last soundless voyage! And has anyone remarked that the seat in such a bark, the armchair lacquered in coffin-black and dully black-upholstered, is the softest, most luxurious, most relaxing seat in the world? . . . .

> Thomas Mann, *Death in Venice*

Venice is a dream city – a mirage, an illusion, the figment of somebody's imagination. At least that's what many a first visitor feels, no matter how many glossy photos, travel posters, and travelogues he might have looked at. Venice is something that simply must be seen to be believed. The buildings are dirty, but it's the grime of centuries; a city has to live through a millenium of history to acquire that very special kind of dirt. The plaster's fading and crumbling. It has been there in some cases for 400 or 500 years. And the canals. The American visitor may be tempted to view them as one vast sewage system, but there is another way to see them. It is possible to visualize huge, sumptuous gondolas covered with gilded ornamentation, carrying the Doge and his retinue through the canals to his palace. Or a small, fugitive gondola, gliding quietly as it carries a single assassin to his destination. The canals have always been a part of the humdrum and throb of the great city throughout its history: armored galleys manned by slaves, setting off to do battle with the Turkish fleet; freight gondolas plying the canals with foodstuffs, wine, cloth, and lumber to keep the city alive. The canals are the arteries of Venice, and they've always smelled that way. That's the way they smelled to Marco Polo as he set off for "Cathay" (China); it's the smell he was homesick for while away at the court of Kubla Khan, and it's the smell he came back to after years of travel. Which is preferable? The straightforward, natural smell of brackish water, or the chemical odor of detergents and industrial waste? Frankly, we'll settle for the brackish water; it has something over the Hudson.

There is much more to Venice than is presented in the boy-meets-girl romances, with couples nuzzling and giggling their way along the canals in the love-seat of a gondola, the oarsman pretending not to notice, the air filled with mandolins plucking out the tune of *O Sole Mio,* and the lusty voice of a tenor filling in the words. All this has its place, no doubt, but the Venice one comes to love after a while is the city behind the façade, away from the grand palaces and squares – the Venice of a hundred secluded little spots, of dark and foreboding alleys, spread out like a maze, most of them leading nowhere. Or the smell of cooking at suppertime as one walks past open kitchen windows; the cracked and crumbling plaster on the walls of old villas; the brawling sounds of alley cats as they run in packs through the streets or fight each other for a piece of meat that fell from a vendor's cart; and yes, the delightful, unforgettable, irreplaceable smell of the canals. That too is part of the mystique of Venice. Thomas Mann sums it all up in a famous passage:

> Yes, this is Venice, this the fair frailty that fawns and that betrays, half fairy-tale, half snare; the city in whose stagnating air the art of painting once put forth so lusty a growth, and where musicians were moved to accords so weirdly lulling and lascivious. The adventurer feels his senses wooed by this voluptuousness of sight and sound, tastes his secret knowledge that the city sickens and hides its sickness for love of gain, and bends an ever more unbridled leer on the gondola that glides on before it.

When strolling around the streets and squares of Venice, the visitor comes to value it just the way it was, or as near to it as is possible in the 20th century. In fact, things are not exactly all that antique. There is a new railroad station – brand new, in a stark modern design. There is the Piazzale Roma, the big square that greets the visitor as he drives into Venice from the mainland. All the buses and cars coming into the city must park here; it's as far as they can go into Venice. There is no traffic except for the *vaporetti,* the water buses that ply the Grand Canal and the lagoon. More than 400 bridges link the canals. Venice is built on 117 islands. The Canal Grande runs from the Piazzale Roma to the far side of the city, where the famous art exhibition (the Biennale) takes place every two years. Beyond is the outer island of the Lido, famous for its beaches, which Thomas Mann memorialized in his *Death in Venice.* Little has changed there in the last half-century. A sunset return to the city offers one of the most spectacular land-and-seascapes known to travelers.

"Canal" in Italian is *Rio*. There is *Rio* this and *Rio* that on most of the street signs – or *Campo* (square), *Calle* (street), *Riva* or *Fondamenta* (two words for "quay"). These terms are from the special Venetian dialect, and are not necessarily standard Italian. *Palazzi* (palaces) line the Grand Canal and many of the other large canals. The streets are paved with flagstones. There is little earth or grass inside the city, but there are a few trees and many flowers, especially in the window boxes and patios of the palazzi. The palaces themselves are of all colors: coral, yellow, blue, gray, green, and white. There are striped "barber" poles where gondolas tie up. The most famous bridge of all is the Rialto. The *vaporetto* or ferry, which goes from Piazzale Roma to St. Mark's Square, passes under the Rialto. The bridge was built in the later 1500's and was arched just high enough to allow a fully armed galley to pass underneath. All sorts of shops are crammed into the interior of the bridge. The area around it is a bustling business quarter. The name *Rialto* comes from *Rivo Alto* (High Bank), where, according to legend, the very first settlers started the town.

As the visitor approaches St. Mark's Square – the center of Venice – two islands come into view on the opposite side of the Grand Canal. The smaller of the two is the island of San Giorgio (St. George), dominated by the huge Church of St. George, a magnificent early Baroque structure. The other island, much larger, is the Isola della Giudecca (Island of the Jews), where the Jewish population lived during the Middle Ages. The word "ghetto", by the way, comes from *"borghetto"* (little town). It refers to another quarter of the city where the Jews settled in the 18th and 19th centuries. It is in the northern part of the city, not too far away from the Piazzale Roma.

Americans invariably ask about the drinking water in Europe and particularly in Italy. Some people have doubts about the drinking water in Venice, or even assume that the tap water in the hotels is drawn from the canals. Italians are highly incensed when asked about their drinking water. They are just as susceptible to dysentery as anybody else. They know about the canal water too. The drinking water in Italy, and especially in Venice, is probably purer than it is in your home town, which, admittedly, isn't saying too much these days. The water is piped in from the Dolomite mountains. The drinking water drains into the canals, along with much of the city's sewage, but it is not drawn from them. Moreover, the canals of Venice are flushed out twice a day by the movement of the tides.

The best place to begin a trip through Venice is at St. Mark's Square.

This is the center of the city and possibly the most spectacular square in Europe. It is dominated by the ancient cathedral of St. Mark. St. Mark is the patron saint of the city, and his emblem, the lion, appears on many monuments and statues. The cathedral, or basilica, dominates the square. Next to it on the right is the Doge's Palace, the political and administrative center of Venice until recent times. The Doge was the head of state in the days of the Venetian Republic. The term comes from the Latin word *dux*, meaning "leader."

The arrangement of St. Mark's Square is typical of medieval European cities. The cathedral is downtown, in the center of the city, symbolizing the spiritual and cultural identity of the people. Next to it, or facing it on the main square, is the palace or town hall or state building, representing the secular authority. The two have always gone together in Europe: church and state, sacred and secular. The first provides the substance of the life of the people, the second gives that substance concrete form. There can hardly be anything like a "political" history of Europe without a history of its religious and cultural institutions, and vice versa. St. Mark's Square demonstrates this fact all by itself.

The first thing to do after arriving at St. Mark's Square is simply to stand still for a minute and take it all in. Here is the center of one of the greatest cities of the West, and yet the whole scene is a mixture of East and West. The style of the basilica is largely Byzantine. Byzantium was originally the eastern half of the Roman Empire. Its capital city was Constantinople, which the Roman Emperor Constantine modestly named after himself. After the fall of the Roman Empire, Byzantium continued as an independent Christian kingdom, until it was overrun by the Turks in 1453. Constantinople was re-named Istanbul and has retained that name to this day. Byzantium developed its own peculiar style of architecture and art, including the famous mosaic. The mosaic is a way of forming a picture by putting together many tiny stones of different colors. There are mosaics inside St. Mark's cathedral and in many other churches and palaces in Italy, including St. Peter's in Rome. Generally speaking, the Byzantine style is characterized by richness of ornamentation, often in gold and silver, by the use of mosaics to cover many of the walls and ceilings, and by the use of domes and round arches instead of pointed spires and Gothic arches.

Both the basilica and the Doge's palace almost seem to be made of candy. In fact, Venice itself looks a bit like a candy village. The "barber" poles where the gondolas are tied up look like peppermint sticks. Notice the stripes and other designs on the Doge's palace and on many of the other palaces of Venice. However one sees Venice, it is simply impossible to give a straightforward description of it. The city itself is one big metaphor. When anyone enters Venice, he enters a different world and has to start thinking in different terms and describing things in different ways.

The basilica of St. Mark is one of the oldest cathedrals in Europe. It dates from about the 1060's. According to tradition, the remains of St. Mark were brought here and are still preserved under the altar inside. Various alterations and additions were made over the centuries, many of them in the 1600's during the Baroque period. The sumptuous decoration of the church has earned it the title of Chiesa d'oro (Church of Gold). Many of the artistic treasures inside were pilfered from other cities and countries as the armies of the Venetian Empire swept through one territory after another.

The most notorious example of this sort of thing took place during the Crusades. Venice made a good deal of profit on the Crusades: it could supply food and ships to take the knights and their vassals to the Holy Land, and at a substantial price. The Fourth Crusade took off from Venice, but instead of heading south to the Holy Land, it veered east toward Constantinople, a more lucrative target. Constantinople was a Christian city, the capital of a Christian empire, but that did not deter the Venetians. They, along with the other Crusaders, descended on the city and plundered it from top to bottom. Among other things the Venetians brought back with them was a set of four bronze horses; they are still standing on a balcony out in front of the basilica. They were originally Greek, and according to legend were done by the famous Greek sculptor Praxiteles. Eventually they reached Constantinople, and were brought back to Venice by the Doge Dandolo after the sack of Constantinople in 1204. Much later, Napoleon, true to form, absconded with them to Paris, but after he met his Waterloo, the outraged city demanded and got them back again.

Once indoors, the visitor can catch a glimpse of some of the brighter as well as the darker sides of Venetian history as they are revealed by the different parts of the cathedral. In the narthex, various floodings over the years have left giant bathtub-rings all around the walls. The highest ring is also the most recent; it's about 5 feet high, and was caused by the flood of 1967. Inside the church proper, the features are especially intriguing: there is an air of antiquity everywhere. The pulpits, for example, date from the 1100's; one of them is placed inside the other.

The floor is just as old, and very uneven. The walls are inlaid with mosaics, and gold decoration covers almost everything. Inside the south transept is the treasury of the church. Here the darker side of Venetian history is displayed in the form of spoils which the Venetians brought back with them from Constantinople. The ceiling and the domes often have a curious effect on the visitor. One is struck by the brilliance of the decorations on the one hand, and by the overall darkness and the impression of mystery on the other. It's hard to believe that this is Europe. One could just as well be inside a Turkish mosque or a Cambodian temple, it seems. In fact, nothing sums up the Venetian aura of secrecy and intrigue like the basilica of St. Mark. It goes together with the city of Venice just as Westminster Abbey goes with London.

Outside the basilica and on the left is the old clock tower, which has been ringing the hours ever since the later 1400's. In addition to the time, it has the signs of the zodiac. On top are two mannequins, representing two Moors. The best time to be in the area is around 11 a.m. or at noon. The mannequins strike the gong in a little ritual they've been doing for 500 years. Next to the clock tower, and extending all the way down the square, is a magnificent arcade. It now houses various shops, banks, and cafés. In the 16th century, when it was built, it was the residence of the "procurators" who were responsible for the upkeep of the basilica. It was a sort of luxurious custodians' quarters for the church.

In the direction opposite the basilica, facing the other end of the square, is the newest part of the square. This section was built on orders from Napoleon in 1810. Originally, this end of the square was open, with only a lovely little church in the center. Napoleon didn't like the idea and had the church torn down and the arcade put up in its place. Actually, the arcade blends well with the rest of the square. Across from the main entrance of the basilica and to the left, is the *campanile* or bell tower of the basilica. It is isolated from the main building. The bell tower is the highest building around and much simpler than St. Mark's, though quite imposing in its own way. The original bell tower was built just before the basilica itself (10th century), but the whole thing collapsed in 1902 and had to be rebuilt all over again. For this reason it looks much newer than the basilica, and considerably more stable.

From the bell tower one can see the Grand Canal, where the Doge's gondola and other state galleys used to dock. On the quay are two massive columns; both of them were brought from Constantinople. One of them, the Winged Lion Column, is the symbol of Venice. The other one has a statue of St. Theodore. The Winged Lion Column is the most popular meeting place in Venice. There is always a knot of people clustered around the base, and most of them are waiting for someone. They walk briskly up to the column, as if they were keeping someone waiting. Relieved to see that they haven't, each invariably strikes a relaxed pose, rocks on his heels, or starts thumbing through a newspaper. Five or ten minutes later, he grows anxious again, alternately looking at his watch and thrusting his hands in his pockets. He starts pacing around the column. He looks back into the square, and down the quays of the canal. Another look at his watch. Now he's agitated: he's been stood up. Finally he gives up in disgust and walks away.

Running between St. Mark's Square and the Grand Canal is a wide corridor known as the Piazzetta (*little square*). It used to be known as Il Broglio (*intrigue*) because it was reserved each day from 10 a.m. until noon for the noblemen and powerful merchants of the city to meet. They would group together in tight cliques, buzzing and whispering together about their business deals or their political plots. It was a typically Venetian institution.

Perhaps the most interesting part of a stay in Venice is a trip through the Doge's Palace. A local guide takes visitors inside in small groups, showing them the various rooms and halls where the ruling councils of Venice used to meet. The building dates from the twelfth century, when the Venetian Empire was at its height. It has been remodeled many times since. The council chambers and reception rooms dazzle with luxury; everything is covered with gold leaf. Huge marble staircases lead from one floor to the next. Enormous paintings by Tintoretto, Veronese, and their pupils cover the walls and ceilings. The largest and most impressive of the rooms is the Grand Council Chamber, measuring 170 ft. by 75 ft. It is still considered to be one of the most perfectly proportioned rooms in the world. A visitor can test his self-confidence by imagining himself as a new ambassador from some small and rather remote country, trying to wring a deal out of the Venetians in this room.

Then the group is led across the famous Bridge of Sighs, constructed about 1600. It crosses a canal, leading from the Doge's Palace to the dungeons. All kinds of stories have circulated about this bridge, many of them started by Lord Byron. He was captivated by Venice, and intrigued by the mood of romance and mystery surrounding the city. He wanted to record his impressions, and in order to enter into the right mood for describing the dungeon, he slept for a night in one of the cells. His descriptions are vivid indeed. He tells of a poor wretch sentenced to life imprisonment in one of the law courts of the Doge's Palace. The prisoner is led, in chains, over the bridge to the dungeon. Knowing he will never see daylight again, he takes one last look out ·the window of the bridge. He sees the splendor of the Grand Canal, and· the island and Church of St. George in the distance. But it only lasts a minute. The guards gruffly push him on, into the darkness and gloom ahead. Realizing for the first time how awful his fate really is, he lets out a long, loud sigh which carries out the window of the bridge and can be heard on the streets below. Byron thus called it the Bridge of Sighs, and it has retained the name ever since. (In Italian: Ponte dei Sospiri.)

The various cells and passageways are still intact, and visitors are led through them by the guide. The cells are of different sizes. Some were for solitary confinement, and some for groups of 10 or 15 prisoners. For the most part, however, common criminals were not kept here, but in one of the less renowned prisons of the city. This dungeon was mainly for political prisoners, traitors, and people of high rank who had fallen out of favor with the ruling councils.

Lunch can be had at a nearby hotel or in one of the dozens of restaurants just off St. Mark's Square. The afternoon would be well invested in a visit to the beach. The beach is out on the Lido, a long, tree-shaded island separated from Venice by a wide lagoon. A steamer goes from St. Mark's Square to the Lido. The Lido is one of the most chic resorts in Italy. Its wide beach extends for miles along the outer shore. The sun is hot, and it burns, so caution is advised.

In the evening, a whole different set of activities opens up. Gondola rides are always enchanting, with gondoliers in blue and white striped jerseys, and mandolin players plucking out dreamy Italian ballads. St. Mark's Square at night is something to behold. It's a very different scene after dark. The arcades are all lit up, and bands play in the various outdoor cafés along the arcades. The square is so large that their music does not compete for attention. Walking around the square, one hears a band playing something, with people dancing, laughing, and eating. As one continues walking, the music fades, and some other band becomes louder, with another scene of conviviality and commotion.

Another favorite pastime in Venice is getting intentionally lost. It's best to do it in the daytime, of course, and with a few fellow-navigators. First, get a map of the city. Then stuff it in your back pocket and take off from St. Mark's, heading in any direction. Venice is a small city, and it's an island — or more correctly, a series of islands. Its greatest width, from east to west, is about 3 miles. So one never really gets lost — at worst, just temporarily misplaced. The point is to get into the "real" Venice — into those secluded little places mentioned earlier. It's a whole different world away from the big squares and stores. Sometimes the canals are so narrow one can almost jump over them. Tiny little bridges lead from one quarter of the city to another. Small, ornate churches appear out of nowhere. Little squares open up around a corner; they seem like miniature versions of St. Mark's. Most of all, though, it's the quietness that is striking. Walking along the quay of a canal, one hears a gondola approaching nearby. It may be a freight barge or a pleasure boat full of laughter and conversation. It passes, the noise dies down, and one is left alone again. The streets are narrow, and one walks past open windows with people jabbering away inside in their Venetian dialect. After about an hour of this, one may simply take out a map and ask the first person that comes along to locate a position on it. This can be done without speaking a word of Italian; one simply points to the map, looks quizzical, and makes a sweeping gesture as if to indicate "here". Whoever it is will hunch over the map and point to the spot. There's an even better way: one asks, "San Marco? San Marco?" The person will point the way. Actually, it's fairly easy to find one's way around the city. All the streets, the quays, and the inter-sections are clearly indicated with signs, most of which are painted on the sides of houses. Everything has a name, even the back stoop of a palace.

A late-afternoon or evening vaporetto ride is the way to witness Europe's most bizarre spectacle: the Venetian "rush hour". It's an aquatic version of the Tokyo-Yokohama express. But even under these conditions, the faded glory of the Palazzi still glitters as the vaporetto glides past each one. It follows the Grand Canal past the 200 or so marble palaces, most of them at least 300 years old. The canal is almost 2 miles long, and circles up past the Rialto Bridge to the Piazzale Roma, where all the cars and buses are parked.

There are several things to do on a last morning in Venice: a second look around St. Mark's Square, or some shopping for glassware. Or some browsing in the Academy of Fine Arts (open from 9 a.m. to 1 p.m. in the summer). It has an excellent collection of paintings, most of them by the Venetian masters. There are works by Giovanni Bellini, Gentile Bellini, Carpaccio, Mantegna, Veronese, Giorgione (especially his

"Tempest", 1505), Tintoretto, Titian, and Hans Memling. To get there, the visitor gets off the vaporetto at the *Accademia* quay. Finally there is one last look at the Dream City of the Adriatic and then it's off to Florence.

Over the Apennines to Florence

The trip from Venice to Florence takes a half day, and passes through the cities of Padua and Ferrara, circles the city of Bologna, and continues down the new Autostrada del Sole (Highway of the Sun) to Florence. It takes the visitor through some of the richest agricultural areas of Italy; they're also some of the loveliest. He also gets his first taste of the Apennine mountain range, the backbone running through Italy from north to south.

The road out of Venice is straight and fast, and it brings one to Padua (Italian: Padova) in no time at all. This is still the general region of Veneto, and Padua has long been its religious and cultural center. Two things about Padua are of special interest. First, the life and legend of St. Anthony, who is still one of the most popular saints in the Catholic world. Second, the great University of Padua. In the Middle Ages and in Renaissance times, the university was one of the most important centers of learning in all of Europe. It goes back to 1222, when the Holy Roman Emperor Frederick II founded it. Later, during the Renaissance, the scientist Galileo was a professor here. It was also here that modern medicine began to develop on an experimental basis. In fact, the medical students had plenty of patients to practice on. During the Renaissance, Italy was divided into a host of city-states and small countries which were constantly warring among themselves; one duke or prince was always fighting another. They brought the wounded in by the wagonload. Small wonder that all sorts of medical discoveries were made: new drugs, surgical techniques, better sanitary conditions, and so on. Most of this activity took place at Padua. A lecture hall which was used for anatomy classes is still preserved in the town.

The University of Padua wasn't limited to the study of science and medicine. Several of Italy's literary giants also studied there: Dante, Petrarch, and Tasso. The great Renaissance painter Mantegna was from Padua. At its height, the university had over 6000 students. It was a sprawling affair, a kind of medieval Berkeley. They also had plenty of "Young Turks" to keep the place jumping. Diaries and local reports tell of riots, kidnappings of professors, duels, drunken sprees, and other academic diversions. The flavor of town and university life in Padua is amply conveyed by Shakespeare's play *The Taming of the Shrew* which is set in this city.

Padua is also the town and tomb of St. Anthony. St. Anthony was Portuguese in origin, and was born in Lisbon in 1195. He entered the Franciscan order and became known as a powerful and stirring preacher. After spending some time in Africa, he came to Italy, where he died in 1231 just outside Padua. Various miracles were attributed to him, including the ability to preach so forcefully that even fishes in a stream could understand him. Just as St. Christopher is the patron saint of travelers, so St. Anthony of Padua is the saint who helps the faithful find lost articles. The most imposing building in Padua is the Basilica of St. Anthony, or the "Basilica of the Saint". It is in the center of town, and was built in 70 years, beginning just after the saint's death. It strongly resembles St. Mark's Basilica in Venice because of its many Byzantine features. There are six domes, much like the domes of St. Mark's, and the whole building is elaborately ornamented. It's the second most famous Byzantine church in Italy. One of its most spectacular parts is the treasury chapel, which is just behind the high altar. Various relics of St. Anthony are preserved in dazzling gold vessels. Around them is an extravaganza of Baroque sculpture. The saint is buried in a chapel which is located just off the north aisle. Most of the people inside the church are clustered here, holding lighted candles. Outside the church, in the courtyard in front, is the famous bronze statue by Donatello, the "Gattamelata" (1447). It shows the great Venetian naval commander, Erasmo di Narni, who was nicknamed "Gattamelata" (Tabby Cat), and is the statue most often cited in art history books as an example of early Renaissance sculpture.

The highway continues south, and about 20 miles later crosses a broad, drowsy-looking river – the Adige. Another 15 miles later, it crosses an even wider river, the Po. The area between the Adige and the Po is known as the province of Polesina. This is a very fertile region, and one of the most flourishing agricultural centers of Italy. There are rice fields on both sides of the road, with occasional patches of sugar-beets. Vast amounts of water are required for rice cultivation, and these two rivers bring the required quantities in from the Alps, which are about a hundred miles to the northwest. Soon the highway passes through the capital of this province, Rovigo. A castle is perched sleepily on the hill which overlooks the town.

Further south, the road crosses the Po, the river after which the whole area from here to the Alps is named. Shortly after this it enters the city of Ferrara. Today Ferrara is mostly agricultural, but during the Renaissance it was a thriving artistic and cultural mecca. Its political history during these times is almost as seamy as that of Venice. In fact a simple (if somewhat cynical) way to gauge the importance of any of these cities for the Renaissance is to count up all the intrigues, plots, assassinations, and double-dealings which took place in the city as one party battled another for power. If the city's history is full of blood and gore, then it is sure to have had an illustrious place in the Renaissance, contributing more than its share to the fine arts. If its history is relatively tranquil, then it's probably only worth a footnote in a history text. The period of the Renaissance was one of constant scheming, ambition, and blood-letting, side by side with enormous creativity in every field of art, science, and literature. Most of the dukes and princes who ruled the cities of Italy and who patronized the arts had made huge fortunes in trade, often by the sort of deals and exploits associated with the "robber barons" in the U.S. during the 19th century. Having secured their fortunes, they turned to culture as an outlet for their patronage or vanity, or in many cases as a distraction from the proddings of their conscience. Of course this doesn't make the art they patronized any less brilliant or lasting, but it does shed some light on the conditions under which much of it was produced. Nor was this typical of all the great patrons of the Renaissance. But it was typical of a good many, including many of the rulers of Ferrara. Nicolo III, for example, caught his wife in the arms of a lover; he killed them both on the spot. Ercole I attempted to poison his nephew, who had claimed the throne of Ferrara for himself. The nephew was later beheaded by Ercole's wife. And on it goes.

The famous castle of Ferrara stands by the side of the highway, near the center of the city. During the Renaissance, Ferrara was ruled by a single family, the House of Este. The castle dates from these times (14th century). It is one of the best-preserved castles in Italy, and it has that fairy-tale look one often expects a castle to have. It boasts turrets, moats, and drawbridges, and the viewer half expects to see the White Knight come crashing through the front gate any moment. Inside are magnificent gardens and salons, as well as prison cells where many a ghost could tell a gruesome tale.

But Ferrara has its bright side. Two of the greatest literary figures of the Renaissance made their reputation here. One was Ariosto (1474-1533), author of the poem, *Orlando Furioso;* the other was Tasso (1544-1595), author of the even more famous *Jerusalem Delivered,* a poem about the capture of Jerusalem by the Crusaders. Both works became sensations overnight; everybody read them and quoted from them. Later, many of the Romantic poets, including Shelley, made pilgrimages to Ferrara to admire the birthplace of Tasso, and Napoleon counted him as one of his heroes.

Some auto buffs may be tempted to ask whether the Italian sports car, the Ferrari, is made in Ferrara. It's a shrewd guess, but not quite the right one. The Ferrari is made in Modena, a city some 30 miles west of Ferrara.

Once outside Ferrara, our route takes us on the Via Adriatica, or Adriatic Highway. It runs north and south, from Padua down to Bologna, and is one of the newest highways in Italy. By now we have left the region of Veneto and are in Emilia. Emilia is a broad, flat plain which extends southward to the Apennine mountains. The Via Adriatica cuts across it on its way to the Apennines. The name "Emilia" is derived from an old Roman road which used to run through here on the way to the sea. Now, a new highway follows the old route, and has the same name, the Via Emilia. The landscape is fairly uniform, consisting mostly of wide fields, largely for wheat, but occasionally punctuated by tall vines. We are nearing the vine-growing region at the foothills of the Apennines.

The highway skirts Bologna, which is off to the left. Like most Italian cities, it goes back to Roman times, when it was called Bononia. It is an important city in a number of respects. First and foremost, for its food. Bologna is the culinary capital of Italy. Many of Italy's most famous dishes were invented here; the city used to be called "Bologna the Fat". It is in the center of some of the richest agricultural country in Italy, with wheat for macaroni and other types of pasta, vineyards for wine, pork for sausages, and many fruit and vegetable farms. Bologna is also a prosperous industrial and commercial center, and the capital city of Emilia. Its population numbers almost half a million.

Bologna has the oldest university in Europe. It goes back to late Roman times, about 400 A.D. or so. Over the years it grew as it attracted scholars from all over Europe. In the Middle Ages, it boasted 10,000 students, an enormous enrollment for those times. It was perhaps the most famous university in Europe, rivaling Paris, the other great medieval university. It has often been said that women occupied the lowest rung of the social ladder in the Middle Ages — that their place was in the kitchen, that most of them couldn't read or write or ever hope for an education. At Bologna it was different. Not only were women students allowed, but many of the professors were women. The women would put on the same black gowns as the men and solemnly give instruction on such subjects as canon law, theology, or logic. Reports tell of a woman professor so shapely and appealing that she had difficulty communicating the subject matter to her students. She finally had to lecture from behind a screen.

Bologna is still a great university. It is especially well known for its medical school and for the scientists who have done important research there. For example, the physicist Marconi (1874-1937) pioneered in the development of radio. Bologna almost rivals Padua for the medical studies that went on in the Middle Ages. Corpses, fresh from the latest battle, were wheeled in and dissected on the spot. In times of peace (which were few and far between), the local prison was besieged by students who desperately needed a cadaver in time to complete their dissertations. In our own day, Bologna has acquired a reputation as the largest Italian city to have a Communist administration. This is mainly due to the fact that most of the voting population is made up of workers in the huge industrial and food plants in the city. To the surprise of many, however, the Communists have played down ideology since they assumed power, and have been running the city in middle-class fashion. They offer tax incentives to lure investment capital into the city, negotiate with the biggest Italian corporations for plant sites, and sponsor huge trade fairs every year in May. Few people seem to mind, least of all the businessmen, and so they keep on getting re-elected.

As the highway skirts the city of Bologna, the foothills of the Apennines come into view in the distance. In fact, the whole city is surrounded by them, and soon the road begins to climb. The country-side around here is magnificent. Lush green valleys nestle among the craggy hills and ridges. Off to the right, down in the valley, are little farming villages; from the highway they look much like confetti: all that can be seen is the sunlight reflecting off white stucco walls. There are wheat fields, dark green vineyards, and fruit trees of all kinds. This is some of the best wine country in Italy. The weather is usually clear in the summertime, with only a few puffs of cloud in the sky.

The Apennines get steeper after a while, and the Autostrada passes through a series of tunnels. This is the heart of the Apennine mountain range and almost the exact center of the Italian peninsula. The Apennine range covers most of Italy, starting in the north around Genoa, then sweeping all the way south to the toe of the Italian "boot"

It is impossible to go from one side of Italy to the other without passing over the Apennines. In some places, the mountains are volcanic. Mt. Vesuvius is still active. Most of the Apennines are not very rich in ore and other minerals. There is one exception, however. Southwest of Florence, a good deal of mercury is produced, making Italy the largest supplier of this metal in the world.

By now we have left the region of Emilia and are in Tuscany; Florence, our destination, is its capital. The name "Tuscany" (Italian: "Toscana") comes from the word, "Etruscan". The Etruscans were among the earliest settlers in the Italian peninsula. They were related to some of the peoples in ancient Turkey, or "Asia Minor" as it was called in Biblical times. The Etruscans had a thriving civilization in Italy long before the Romans extended their rule over the peninsula. But the future lay with the Romans, who defeated the Etruscans in a series of wars and drove them up north, to the region we are now passing through. They settled here, and gave their name to the region. Though the Romans were stronger militarily than the Etruscans, their civilization was not nearly so advanced at this time. Indeed, the Romans learned a great deal from the Etruscans, just as they borrowed heavily from the Greeks much later. From the Etruscans they learned many of their engineering and building crafts, as well as pottery and cloth-making, weaving and dyeing. The art, if it can be called an art, of gladiatorial combat was also an Etruscan invention. Many of the Roman gods and goddesses were borrowed from the Etruscans, who had picked them up from some of the Greek settlements in southern Italy.

The countryside of Tuscany is renowned throughout Italy, and it deserves to be. The hills are round and graceful; the cragginess observed earlier (and which has its own charm) has given way to soft green slopes. The air here is crystal clear; one can see for miles. The different types of vegetation go together surprisingly well. It almost looks as if some landscape artist had thought it all out in advance: here and there is a patch of forest, a vineyard, a stretch of plain, a small stream, and clumps of cypresses and pines. It's not exactly the spectacular sort of beauty one witnesses in the Bavarian Alps or the Dolomites. It's a calm, serene beauty of the kind one associates with Florence and the Renaissance.

Soon a long, low valley opens up to the left. This is the Arno River Valley. Everything grows here: vines heavy with grapes, olive trees, wheat, corn, tobacco – even the weeds are luxuriant. To the south, the famous Chianti wines are produced. Some have called this spot the garden of Italy. In the center of this garden lies Florence (Italian

Firenze). The late afternoon is the ideal time to arrive, as the Florentine sunset bathes the whole valley in radiant gold. There isn't a scene quite like it anywhere else in Italy.

The first thing one sees when entering Florence is the red tile dome of the cathedral, which dominates the whole city. The branch road from the Autostrada passes through the outskirts of the city, approaching Florence from the west. Villas dot the hillside to the south. Soon the traveler is in the thick of things, with cars honking and clattering over the cobblestones, scooting around trucks stacked high with wine bottles. Most of the traffic is heading for the suburbs. This is the Italian equivalent of our rush hour, and it's the time of day to see the city at its liveliest. A harassed cab driver shakes his fist at a white-uniformed policeman. A housewife haggles with a fish vendor on the street. Five or six university students are packed into a tiny Fiat 500, shouting and whistling at a young woman walking home with a bag full of groceries.

Unlike the U.S., the rush hour doesn't begin until dusk in Italy. In fact, the whole working day is pushed back about two or three hours in relation to our own. People don't get to work much before 9 or 10 a.m. (They've been up the night before sipping wine and playing cards or talking politics.) They work until about 1 p.m., when the sun scorches even the coolest heads, then take a long Italian "siesta". Most of the stores and banks close up between 1 and 3 p.m. In mid-afternoon, the city comes back to life and stays that way until 6 or 7 p.m. Then everybody goes home – all at once, and that's when the honking begins. This is the pattern followed in most Italian cities. It is easy enough to get used to, particularly after one has set out on a shopping safari after lunch, only to find the whole city a ghost town. The best time for shopping is in the late afternoon or evening. It's cooler then anyway.

An ideal way for the newly-arrived visitor to get acquainted with the city of Florence is to take advantage of the cool evening air to do some shopping. Leatherware has long been a specialty of Florence, and there are good bargains in jewelry and woolens as well. Or one may prefer to get one's bearings first, and there is a spectacular way to do so. From the Piazzale Michelangiolo one gets a magnificent view of Florence and the whole Arno River Valley. This short excursion takes only about 45 minutes. The Piazzale Michelangiolo is named, of course, for the great sculptor and architect Michelangelo. A copy of his *David* stands in the center of the square, looking out over the city and the hills beyond.

On the left are the Giardini Boboli (Boboli Gardens), dominated by the massive Pitti Palace, built by a wealthy Florentine merchant at the height of the Renaissance. The palace was designed by Brunelleschi, the architect who built the famous dome, which is clearly visible from the Piazzale Michelangiolo. The sumptuous gardens around the palace are speckled with fountains, statues, and rows of cypress trees. The palace is now a state museum, and well worth a visit. It has a magnificent collection of paintings by Raphael, Andrea del Sarto (about whom Robert Browning wrote his famous poem), Tintoretto, and Rubens. (Hours: 9:30 a.m. to 4:30 p.m.).

After getting an idea of how the city is laid out, it is often pleasant to take an evening's coffee at one of the outdoor cafés in the Piazza della Repubblica. It's a big shopping mall two blocks south of the cathedral. Department stores and outdoor cafes line the square. There is usually something going on at night: a small band and singing troupe turning out "Santa Lucia" or "Ciao, Ciao, bambino". The Florentines don't mind if the foreigner joins in — whatever his language might be.

Florence, The Renaissance in Miniature

> Take a look around. You're in Florence, the birthplace of the Renaissance. It's more than just a city on your itinerary. It's the whole Renaissance in miniature. Does that mean much to you? Well, it may and it may not. But if you could get just a glimpse of what the Renaissance means for the modern world and for us today, you might want to know at least a little more about it.

At least that's the introduction given by the more effusive guides in Florence; and it does have its point. But it's best to discover these truths for oneself. Some of the greatest architectural achievements in history and some of the greatest painting and sculpture are to be found within a tiny square mile area in central Florence. It's worth at least a morning's trip around the city in the company of a local Florentine.

By the way, being a local guide in Italy isn't an easy job — not when the city is one like Florence or Rome or Venice. The guides must take courses in the history of art and Italian history. They have to know practically every street, building, and stone of the city, and to demonstrate their knowledge in a tough state examination. Otherwise they don't get a license. The Italian government is very fussy about these requirements, and in Florence especially, the competition for these jobs is so keen that the exams are made as stiff as possible to weed out all but the best.

Florence is laid out very sensibly, so it's not a difficult city to get to know. The River Arno flows from east to west. At the center of the city, an old and venerable-looking bridge crosses the river. It is the *Ponte Vecchio* (Old Bridge), built in the Middle Ages. Its interior is lined with leather and jewelry shops, and from the inside it looks more like a street than it does a bridge. These shops have been there, most of them, since the 1500's, and have displayed about the same type of wares almost as long.

A few blocks north of the Ponte Vecchio is the cathedral. The name of the cathedral is *Santa Maria dei Fiori* (St. Mary of the Flowers). The dome is clearly visible from almost any point in the city. The Italian word for cathedral is *Duomo,* and there are signs throughout the city which point the way to the *Duomo.* It is a giant of a building and has dominated the city ever since the Middle Ages. In fact it's the second largest cathedral in Italy after St. Peter's in Rome. It was paid for by the city of Florence, and most of the funds were provided by the guild of cloth-makers. The cloth-makers were the largest and most influential guild in Florence during the Middle Ages and the Renaissance, and it's still an important trade in the city.

The façade of the cathedral is an elaborate geometrical design put together out of hundreds of blocks of marble. Some of these tiny blocks are dark green, some white, some pink. Fortunately there are large deposits of marble in Italy, most of them in the town of Carrara, not far from Florence. Without this marble the Italian Renaissance would have been a very different thing. All these cathedrals and churches, with their façades, and the many palaces with their luxurious interiors — not to mention the hundreds of statues and fountains — were all dependent on an abundant supply of marble.

Out in front of the façade and separated from it by a few yards is the famous Baptistry. The *campanile* or bell tower is a little to the right. The whole scene offers a capsule definition of the Renaissance. It's spectacular enough as it is, but it seems even more spectacular when one realizes how *old* it all is. These exquisite buildings stood here when the rest of Europe was still in the Middle Ages. Think back to the cathedral in Munich, with its two onion-shaped domes. It was awfully bare and austere: nothing but dark gray stone. It looked more like a fortress than a church. While the citizens of Munich were congratulating themselves on their progressive new church, the Florentines had already come to take these buildings for granted and were looking around for something even bolder. Part of the difference is due to the fact that marble was rather plentiful in Italy but scarce in northern Europe. But the difference is more than just a matter of building materials: it's the

whole design, the plan, the *idea* behind the cathedral which distinguish
it from the cathedrals that were being built in northern Europe at the
time. This cathedral demonstrates how early the Renaissance started in
Italy. It was a hundred or two hundred years ahead of the Renaissance
in northern Europe. In fact, historians begin to speak about the Renaissance in Italy as early as the 1300's. By the 1400's, when the doors of
the Baptistry were installed, the Italian Renaissance was already at its
height.

Three names are worth remembering in connection with this great
cathedral. First, the name of the man responsible for that enormous
dome: Filippo Brunelleschi (1377-1446). The dome was the greatest
architectural marvel in Europe when it was built, and is still one of the
greatest. It required nothing less than a revolution in the principles of
engineering to design it. Brunelleschi actually constructed two domes,
one inside the other. The lower one provides support for the higher
one. The whole structure took 14 years to complete.

The *campanile* or bell tower outside recalls the second great name in
Florentine architecture, that of Giotto (1266-1337) who designed it. He
lived just long enough to see the lowest tier completed; the rest of it
was constructed under the supervision of his pupils. The dates are once
again astonishing: 1266-1337. It hardly sounds like the Renaissance.
When most people think of the Renaissance they think of dates like
1475-1564, when Michelangelo lived, or 1466-1536, the lifetime of the
great Dutch humanist Erasmus. By 1450 or 1500, when the Renaissance
was spreading to northern Europe, it had already been transforming
Italy for a hundred years.

In front of the cathedral is the Baptistry. The name to remember in
connection with this is Lorenzo Ghiberti (1378-1445). He designed the
gold doors on the side of the Baptistry which faces the cathedral.
These are perhaps the most famous doors in Europe – if not in the
world. Ghiberti spent almost 20 years working on them. When Michelangelo saw the doors he exclaimed that they were worthy to be the
gates of paradise, and they have retained this name ever since. The
doors have 10 panels depicting scenes from the Old Testament. During
the floods of 1967, some panels came loose. They have since been
cleaned and restored. The guide will point out Ghiberti's self-portrait,
which is tucked in among the other figures in the panels. Today,
the Baptistry is entered by another door (the "North Door") and there
is an interesting tale about this one too. As was often the case in the
Renaissance, the city of Florence offered a competition for the decora-

tion of the doors of the Baptistry. Several of the greatest sculptors and goldsmiths participated, including Ghiberti, Brunelleschi, and others. Ghiberti won, and Brunelleschi, outraged, vowed to give up sculpture and turn to architecture. He did, and one of the results was the magnificent dome on top of the cathedral. Inside the Baptistry is an enormous 13th-century mosaic depicting Christ in Majesty, surrounded by a panoply of saints.

Inside the cathedral, the visitor is invariably amazed to see how bare and simple it is compared to the sumptuous exterior. Michelangelo's third Pietà stands in front and off to the left. He started it when he was 80 years old, but left it unfinished. This Pietà should not be confused with his first one completed when he was only 25. The latter was displayed at the 1964-65 World's Fair in New York, and is now back at St. Peter's in Rome.

A block north of the cathedral is the Medici Chapel, which is connected to a larger building, the Church of San Lorenzo. One way to reach the chapel is from the cellar, which is a full 10° cooler than the sidewalk outside. The visitor must walk over several tombs in the floor while passing through this dark and gloomy crypt. Then he proceeds upstairs to the chapel itself. It's one of those things that has to be seen to be believed – pure opulence; everything is made of marble. The chapel was built to house the tombs of the Medicis, who ruled Florence during its Golden Age and patronized many of the artists, including Michelangelo. They are the very epitome of the type of wealthy merchant family which played so important a role in the Renaissance: shrewd, treacherous, cruel – but with a refined and cultivated taste for the arts. The walls around the tombs are covered with elaborate mosaics. They are made of hundreds of tiny stones of different colors, some of them semi-precious. The ceiling is gorgeous with mosaics dating from around 1800; they haven't been retouched or even dusted since that time. Yet they look as if they were done yesterday.

From the Medici Chapel a corridor leads down to the New Sacristy, which is decorated with a set of famous statues by Michelangelo. They represent Day and Night, Dawn and Sunset. It has often been remarked that the female figures look massive and muscular. There are several theories to explain this. One is that when Michelangelo studied anatomy he limited himself to the male form. Thus he gave the nude women male bodies; only the faces look female.

A few blocks from the Medici Chapel is the Piazza della Signoria, the cultural and commercial center of Florence and a mecca for art lovers.

This is the ideal place to feel the pulse of the city. Here, old and new come together in an exciting and unforgettable way. Art treasures and cafés stand side by side; it's one big outdoor museum. The word *Signoria,* by the way, means "lordship," *not* "lady"; it refers to the Lords' Council which used to rule Florence and which met in the Old Palace on the square.

Outside, along the wall of the Old Palace, is a row of statues. One of them is a copy of Michelangelo's original *David.* The original used to stand here, but during the wars which plagued the city in Renaissance times, one of David's arms was knocked off. The arm was put back on, but the statue was moved inside the Academy for safekeeping, where it stands today. Next to the copy of *David*, the visitor will find a copy of Michelangelo's *Hercules.* Near the Fountain of Neptune is a pavement plaque indicating the place where the ill-fated Savonarola was burned at the stake in 1498. One of the most amazing buildings in the square is the one which looks like an arcade. Inside is a gallery of statues. Some of these are from ancient times, the others are from the Renaissance. This hall is known as the Loggia dei Lanzi (Loge, or Hall, of the Lancers). The lancers were guards who protected the palace nearby, and their headquarters used to be in this hall.

The palace itself is unmistakable. It's the storybook castle behind the statues of David and Neptune, and is called simply the Old Palace (Palazzo Vecchio). It has been well taken care of and conveys a feeling for the old Florence as nothing else can. It was designed by the same architect (Arnolfo di Cambio) who started the cathedral. The style is pure Gothic (around 1300), though the interior dates from the early Renaissance. (Hours: 9 a.m. to 6 p.m. Admission: about 200 lire or 32¢.) The courtyard and apartments inside are an extravaganza of tapestries, statues, paintings, and gold embellishment. As is so often the case with castles which were built in the Middle Ages but redecorated in the Renaissance, this one is severe and foreboding on the outside (all the better to discourage invaders), but sumptuous and ornate on the inside.

Right off the Piazza della Signoria is the Uffizi Gallery, the most famous museum in Florence. Some say it's the best museum in Italy. If so, that would make it the best in the world, — at least as far as Renaissance art is concerned. The building was put up originally to be the Town Hall of Florence. Hence the name Uffizi, meaning "offices" in Italian. Inside is a rich collection of painting and sculpture dating from the late Middle Ages (Cimabue, Giotto), including the Early

Renaissance (Masaccio, Uccello, Fra Angelico, Filippo Lippi) and the High Renaissance (Botticelli, da Vinci, Raphael, Memling – of Bruges fame – and the only surviving painting by Michelangelo, apart from the frescoes in the Sistine Chapel). There are many others, of course. In fact, one can practically follow the whole Renaissance without stepping outside these walls. The museum is that complete. Small wonder that art historians and students come from all over the world to visit its treasures.

Michelangelo's *David* can be viewed in the gallery of the Academy in Florence, which is open to the public. The statue is a colossal piece of work. It can be seen down a long corridor from the entrance of the building. Though it seems large to begin with, it gets even larger and more massive as one approaches it. By walking around it, viewing it from different angles, the visitor can come to understand the "agony and the ecstasy" which went into its making. More than any other work of art in Florence, the *David* sums up the entire meaning of the Renaissance. If for some reason there were only one thing we could see in Florence, this would be it. And one doesn't have to be an art historian or even an art lover to be overwhelmed by it. What does it mean? It means this: the *David* is the very essence of Renaissance man. He stands tall, strong, proud, and even a little arrogant. He is the image of Promethean man – man on his own. He doesn't bow to anyone or ask anyone – not even Heaven – for favors. He has discovered what it means to be a man, to be free to shape his own destiny, and he takes supreme pride in that discovery. Michelangelo's *David* is the very Credo, the "faith", if it can be called that, of the Renaissance. It is the whole Renaissance in miniature, it is humanism embodied in a single statue.

Between the front door of the Academy and the *David* is a long corridor. On either side of the corridor are other statues by Michelangelo, done much later and all of them left unfinished by the artist. On the back of one of these unfinished statues, Michelangelo has carved a tiny self-portrait. The statues are of prisoners or slaves. Many critics consider them more impressive the way they are, suggesting that Michelangelo might have had a reason for not completing them. It's hard to resist this interpretation. The figures seem to be struggling to free themselves from the stone in which they are encased. Though still held back by the stone, they somehow triumph over it. Once again we find the very essence of the Renaissance revealed in a few blocks of stone. These men are humanists, just as the *David* is the exemplar of humanism in general. They are breaking the bonds which hold them back, asserting their individuality for the first time. They rely on nothing in heaven or on earth other than their own strength and self-affirmation. This Credo may have its fatal flaw — who among us would dare to claim such strength for himself today? — but it is glorious nonetheless.

Finally, there is one other monument well worth seeing in Florence — the Chiesa di Santa Croce (Church of the Holy Cross). It's about 5 blocks east of the Piazza della Signoria. The church is almost gaudily ornate on the outside, and in fact it looks rather like the main cathedral, but a bit smaller. The façade is made of the same multi-colored pieces of marble: dark green, white, and pink. Inside, there is considerable excavation in progress. Some remains of an ancient church have been discovered below the floor, and their identity has so far remained a mystery. It is uniquely appropriate, then, that the great Michelangelo is buried here, along with Machiavelli, the composer Rossini, the scientist Galileo, and the sculptor who cast the "Gates of Paradise": Ghiberti. Up toward the front, the walls of the chancel are covered with Giotto's frescoes. These date from the 13th century. In fact, Santa Croce is one of the oldest churches in Florence. The whole inside of the church used to be covered with such frescoes; that is why it was called "The Bible of the Poor". It was only in this way that the Bible stories could be communicated to the common people who couldn't read. But during the later Renaissance the artist Vasari took control of most of the art work in Florence. He had definite ideas about "improving" some of the churches in the city and painted over most of the frescoes in order to put up these huge, awkward tombs, though it is an "improvement" most art critics bitterly resent. They sometimes call the man "Vasari the rascal", scowling as they do so. Vasari also designed the Uffizi Gallery; that may partly redeem him.

There is much more for the visitor to do in Florence than browse inside museums and churches. Shopping is excellent around the Piazza della Repubblica, a general meeting place for Florentines in the daytime, and a rendezvous for others in the evening. Adjoining are two avenues running north and south, the Via Roma and Via Calzaioli. The stores on them are among the best in Florence. After finishing downtown, the visitor may be tempted to take a horse-drawn carriage back to the hotel. They rent for very little: about $3 an hour; they seat 4 people comfortably.

In the afternoon, the visitor can soak up some sun to deepen the tan he started at the beach in Venice — or take a visit to the Pitti Palace Museum. The museum is 6 blocks south of the River Arno. Another place worth visiting is Michelangelo's house, near the center of the city.

Or one may take a short walk along the banks of the River Arno to the Ponte Vecchio. During World War II, the Germans blew up all the bridges over the river except the Ponte Vecchio. They valued it as a work of art, but they did dynamite the approaches to the bridge on both sides of the river. This did some irreparable damage to a part of the Uffizi Gallery. The bridge downstream is also famous. It's the *Ponte Santa Trinità* (Holy Trinity Bridge). Though it was blown up, its importance is so great that the Florentines set about retrieving all the pieces from the river. Bit by bit they put the bridge together again. All the pieces were put in place except the head of one of the statues. When one crosses over the bridge today, it is possible to make out where all the pieces were joined together with mortar. A few years ago, the missing head of the statue finally turned up a short distance downstream. Practically the whole city came out to see this last piece fitted into the puzzle.

The sensitive visitor always feels that Florence is trying to tell him something, to whisper the mystery of greatness in his ear. Florence gives him a taste of the most important experiment Western man ever made: to stand up on his own two feet, proclaim his independence, and see what would happen. But it didn't happen all at once; it happened over a long period of time. At first it was all grand and glorious: optimism everywhere, unbounded self-confidence. A new world was discovered, and in several respects: a New World across the Atlantic Ocean, and a "New World" within man himself. Suddenly, man was doing things he could hardly have imagined before. Who in the Middle Ages could have conceived the *David* or the *Mona Lisa*? But every coin has two sides. For every Michelangelo there is a Machiavelli. The Renaissance wasn't all creativity and self-discovery. It was also violence, warfare, ambition, cruelty. These too must be included in the picture. And as they are, the image of the Renaissance changes drastically. Optimism began to turn sour, even in Michelangelo's own lifetime. Doubts crept in where self-confidence had previously reigned.

Breakfast in Florence. Lunch in Assisi. Dinner in Rome.

Back on the road, this time for the trip to Rome. Of all the one-day trips in our itinerary, this is one of the most delightful. It's not because the rural scenery is spectacular, but because Assisi, where we suggest having lunch, is a perfect gem of a place to see in the summertime. It's a journey through the heart of medieval Italy. We head further south, along the backbone of the Apennines, skirt Lake Trasimeno — about the biggest lake in the itinerary — pass through Perugia, and then stop at Assisi for lunch. After a relaxed visit through the town, we rejoin the Autostrada del Sole and arrive in Rome by late afternoon. It's an easy, unhurried day. The highway is straight and fast, and the shifting scenes outside the window liven things up considerably.

The best way to leave Florence is by way of the Piazzale Michelangiolo, from which there is a parting glimpse of the cypresses and pines, the villas and gardens, and the little churches and chapels tucked in among the folds of the hillside. The road connects with the Autostrada del Sole outside of town. Off to the right runs the Arno River, heading back to Florence. It originates high up in the Apennines at a point some 20 miles off to the left. This is Chianti wine country: that's what all the vineyards are about. The very flavor of the region is captured in the wine which is named for it.

Pretty soon the Autostrada crosses the Arno River, which wanders off to the left and disappears into the hills. Soon after, we exit from the Autostrada and head east, into Arezzo. It's one of the loveliest towns in Tuscany — after Florence, of course. The whole town is built on a hill, and it has the appearance of a giant staircase leading up to a fortress on top. Arezzo dates from Etruscan times. It was a thriving commercial center even then, and continued to be under the Romans. Arezzo is the birthplace of some luminaries: for example Petrarch, who rivals Dante as the outstanding literary genius of the early Italian Renaissance. The artist Vasari, who painted over the frescoes in the church of Sante Croce in Florence, was born in Arezzo.

About 20 miles south of Arezzo is the town of Cortona. Like many towns in the foothills of the Apennines, it is spread out over the slopes of a hill and can be seen for miles. Like many other Italian towns, it is dominated by a castle which looks down on narrow streets, small tile-roofed houses, and olive orchards. It too was an old Etruscan town, and hasn't changed much since the Renaissance. St. Francis walked these hills 800 years ago. He was well known in Cortona and established a hermitage outside the town.

A few miles beyond Cortona, a large patch of blue materializes gradually out of the mists in the distance. It is Lake Trasimeno, the largest body of water in Italy outside the Alps. (The signs in Italian read *Lago Trasimeno.*) Before actually coming to the lake, the highway crosses a broad, marshy plain which extends roughly from the lake back to Cortona. It was here that one of the most savage battles of the Punic Wars was fought. Hannibal the Carthaginian had entered Italy from the north by crossing over the Alps. Like most of Hannibal's moves, it was a daring operation. In 217 B.C., Hannibal approached Lake Trasimeno, taking roughly the route the highway follows today. The Roman forces were led by the Consul Flaminius, who approached the area from the east (i.e. the left), circling around the lake. It was in June and the heat was ghastly. Flaminius consulted the omens, which were full of gloomy predictions. Hannibal was shrewd. He withdrew before the Romans, luring them into a fairly narrow area between the lake and the hills to the left. Then he struck. The Romans were all but annihilated. Their chariots and horses had been mired down in the bog and could not move. Flaminius and about 20,000 of his men were slaughtered. Thousands were driven into the shallow water, where they stumbled over themselves and drowned. No one knows how many bones are piled up at the bottom. It was said that the marshy areas around the lake were red with blood for weeks afterward. Nearby are two villages which still have the names Ossaia (Bones) and Sanguineto (Bloody). The Roman historian Livy describes the battle in grim detail in his *History of the Roman Republic.*

The lake is beautiful during the summer. Umbrella pines are spread along the shore. They're aptly named. Cypress and olive trees are also legendary in this part of the country. The olive oil produced here is supposed to be the best in Italy. The lake itself is quite shallow: the average depth is less than 30 feet. Fishing in Lake Trasimeno is excellent, especially for trout. In the summer when the weather's nice, the skies are crystal clear and the air is Alpine fresh. The road climbs up some small hills, and the lake recedes from view for a few minutes. Then the road descends, and the lake appears on the right, just a few yards away. Any of these places along the lakefront are excellent for a rest stop. Many visitors like to wade a few feet out in the water. Occasionally they trip over a bone or an old rusty helmet. Archeologists haven't picked up all the battle debris by any means.

Soon the road turns east, and Lake Trasimeno fades in the distance behind us. We have left the region of Tuscany and entered Umbria, the land of St. Francis. It's a country of rocky hills, broad flat valleys, and lush green patches of pine and poplar trees. All the towns around here were originally Etruscan settlements. They're among the oldest in Italy.

Next we enter Perugia, the capital of Umbria. St. Francis was a familiar figure here, and it seems that the city really needed his preaching. In Assisi, one of Giotto's paintings of the life of St. Francis is about the city of Perugia. Apparently the city had been besieged by devils. All kinds of wars, conspiracies, and betrayals wracked the town. The painting shows St. Francis preaching in the city and praying for peace. In the background, the devils and demons are shown fleeing the city in dread of the Saint's power, flapping their tails and wings. Once Perugia was cured of its demons, it settled down to become a peaceful place, and its people acquired a reputation for gentleness and religious devotion.

These traits are seen in the work of the Perugian painters of the Renaissance. Though they shared much of the humanism of the period, they retained a medieval piety which strongly affected their work. Bonfigli is an example. A famous painting of his shows the Virgin standing guard over the city during a plague. The whole population of the town is sheltered under the mantle she spreads over them. A painting like this offers a vivid impression of the sort of day-to-day fears and concerns which occupied most of the people during these times! Their fears were basic: plagues, fires, and famines that could destroy half the population overnight. Florence, for example, was hit by the Black Death in 1348. It carried off three-fifths of the population. Events such as these make Bonfigli's picture seem a little more down to earth than it might at first appear. Perugia was also the town of the painter Pietro Vanucci, known as Perugino. One of the pupils in his painting classes seemed unusually bright and gifted. This young man was Raphael.

Just beyond Perugia the road starts winding its way down the hillside, and before long a huge valley comes into view below. It's a magnificent sight, one which the visitor is sure to remember every time he recalls Umbria. The valley is sprinkled with small hills which rise up like bumps from the valley floor. On top are villages. This is the pattern followed by almost all of the towns in this region, including Assisi. They utilized the natural protection furnished by the hills, and were built right on top of them. Unfortunately, it makes for a good deal of hard walking to go from one side of town to the other. But the Umbrians have always been good walkers. St. Francis himself seems to have set the example.

Soon the rocky summit of Mt. Subasio appears up ahead. On top and spreading down the slopes is Assisi, the town and tomb of St. Francis. The road is straight and even at this point. Assisi lies directly ahead.

The visitor almost feels that he's journeying down the aisle toward the altar. No approach could be as spectacular or as appropriate as this.

St. Francis lived from 1182 to 1226. He was the son of a wealthy cloth merchant in Assisi. His mother was French. He received an excellent education and was prepared to follow in his father's footsteps or even make a name for himself on the battlefield. But something happened which changed all that. Perugia and Assisi were in the midst of one of their interminable wars. Francis, at the age of 19, went off with his countrymen to battle, but was captured by the Perugians. As he lay in his cell one day, wracked with fever, a vision came to him He was converted, and vowed to devote the rest of his life to a moral reform of the church and to purge it of all secular ambition. He thought that the best way to do so was to begin at the bottom, with the ordinary people in the towns and countryside, and to bring about a revival there that would gradually spread to the higher echelons of the church and society. He seems a very contemporary figure in the light of current events. He walked through all the towns of Umbria, preaching the love of God and compassion for one's fellow man. He was especially known for his love of nature and his kindness to animals. He felt a personal relation to everything around him, referring to "Brother Sun" and "Sister Moon". He addressed animals by name and composed a Hymn to the Sun and other songs. People spoke of him as "God's troubadour". Soon he became a very popular figure among the common people, and attracted a small circle of followers. They vowed to live in poverty and to emphasize preaching and visiting the sick. One of his disciples was a young and very beautiful woman, Clara, who organized a similar company of women. After Francis' death, his followers became known as Franciscans, an order of monks who made their living entirely by begging. Today they are one of the largest monastic orders in the Catholic Church. Clara's followers became the Order of Poor Clares. Francis was made a saint two years after his death, in 1228. Later, Clara was canonized as well.

The visitor enters Assisi through one of its medieval gates, and must walk up the steep, narrow streets and past the tiny shops and white stucco houses to the top of the hill. The balconies above the street are decked with flower boxes. The town looks practically the same as it did in St. Francis' time. Everything except the telephone poles is the same: the cobblestones, the stone wall around the city, the huge fortress at the top of the hill, and the old churches. Even more than that: the crystal clear sky, the soft breeze, the valley, and the many brightly colored flowers. These, the contemporary visitor still shares with St. Francis.

The walk is bound to create an appetite, and a delightful place to have lunch is in one of the restaurants at the top of the hill. The whole valley can be seen from the top of the hill — miles and miles of it. The town fans out along the hillside. Red tile roofs follow each other down the slopes like a set of stairs. The churches, shops, and many of the houses are all made of a soft cream-colored stone. They're clustered together on the hillside, baking under a brilliant white sunlight. It's a perfect picture of Italian village life in the Middle Ages. It's not to be found in any textbook or travel guide. One has to be here, out under the sun, one's skin tickled by the breeze blowing in from the valley. It's breathtaking to see how sharply the geraniums in window-boxes and the dark green pines in the garden below contrast with the overall lightness of the other colors around. And over everything a blinding white sunlight, burnishing all it touches.

The central attraction in Assisi is the Basilica of St. Francis. It is constructed of brilliant white limestone. It is actually two buildings, one on top of the other. It was designed by Brother Elias, one of St. Francis' closest disciples, and completed in 1253. One enters the lower church first. The sun is so bright outside that on stepping inside one is blinded for a few moments by the darkness. Off to the left of the main entrance are several relics of St. Francis, including one of his robes. When a group of visitors assemble, an English-speaking guide takes them downstairs to the crypt in which St. Francis is buried. They proceed through the rest of the lower church and then follow the stairs to the upper church. On the wall to the right of the staircase are frescoes done by Cimabue, who taught painting to Giotto. The largest and most famous of them is the *Madonna with Four Angels and St Francis.*

But the most famous frescoes of all are in the upper church. They are Giotto's series on the life of St. Francis. There are 28 frescoes in all. The last four were done by one of Giotto's pupils. The guide points out each one, explaining the events they portray in the life of St. Francis. One of them is about his visit to Perugia, and depicts him driving the devils away by his preaching.

The frescoes are important because for the first time in European painting there is a marked emphasis on individual expression in the faces and gestures of the characters. The pictures are not just of saints but of men, individual men. Each of them differs slightly from the others; some are handsome, some ugly, some short, some tall. Of course, these frescoes are still a long way from the *David* or the *Mona Lisa*. But they're on the way. Giotto's paintings are basically medieval in spirit and inspiration. But in style and expression, they belong to the Renaissance.

Outside, and the visitor is blinded again, this time by Brother Sun himself. Down the narrow streets, past the shops, and he's back to the bus ready for the remaining miles on into Rome. The road continues along the old city wall as it makes its way out of Assisi. Mt. Subasio runs alongside the road for a few miles on the left, and soon the town of Spello appears on the slopes. The ancient gateways and city walls are older than anything else in the town. They were built by the Romans. It was a rich agricultural center in those days. Wealthy Roman merchants had their villas up on the hillside above the town; the plebeians were huddled together inside the city wall. After a few miles the road comes to Foligno, which is a good bit more modern looking. There are limestone quarries and other signs of industrial activity. The air is tainted momentarily by a noxious odor from the chemical works in the distance. Even a town this small had its own school of painters in the 15th century.

The countryside remains much the same for the next hour or so. Small towns spill over rocky hillsides, each one boasting its own local traditions, many of them involving St. Francis. And in all of them there are traces of old Roman fortifications, mixed with newer ones dating from medieval or Renaissance times. It is lovely terrain, though very placid. The road is small, and there is never much traffic. It heads due south toward the Autostrada del Sole, which continues into Rome.

Spoleto soon appears on the right. Spoleto is yet another old Roman town, with an amphitheater dating from the days of the Caesars. It was a special favorite of St. Francis, who liked its plain, rather austere look. Directly in front, on top of the hill, is a castle built by the Popes. The road passes directly under it through a tunnel. After passing through the tunnel, an aqueduct emerges from behind the hill. It was built by the Romans and then enlarged in the 14th century. For a while it was used as a fort to defend the town.

Further south, the road passes through Terni, a city of steel mills, foundries, and a population of almost 100,000 people. Much of the military hardware for the Italian army is manufactured here. The city has often been called the "Arsenal of Italy". The Roman historian Tacitus, who first described the Germanic peoples encountered by the Roman legions in the north, was born in Terni in 54 A.D. After Terni, our route continues on a smaller road, which leads to Narni.

A few miles beyond Terni/Narni we rejoin the Autostrada del Sole. From here, it is a fast trip into Rome. The countryside changes: the hills become a bit steeper, the valleys deepen, and there are a few short tunnels. Signs point out the River Tiber (Italian: Tevere), which the Autostrada crosses several times. It more or less follows the river into Rome. We've left the region of Umbria now and are in Latium, from which the word "Latin" is derived. The capital city of Latium is Rome. Latium was the cradle of Roman civilization. It was here that those values were born which made Rome a unifying force in Italy and eventually throughout the whole Mediterranean world.

Eventually the hills even out and the road signs begin to announce the different entries to Rome. The Autostrada enters the city from the north, then heads west on several of the major arteries, including the huge "Raccordo Annulare" or Ring Road. Pretty soon the whole city comes into view. The scene resembles the entrance into Florence. Rome, after all, is a city of almost 2½ million people. On the outskirts are the apartment buildings of factory workers and office clerks. Then the artery we follow becomes a tree-lined boulevard, and the buildings begin to look older and more distinguished. Toy-sized Fiats give way to Jaguars, Alfa-Romeos, and Mercedes. Here and there a marble fountain peeks out from behind a pine grove. Soon we near the center of Rome. It's as if the whole throb of the city were converging on one point. It's a sensation the visitor experiences every time he enters this city. It makes Assisi and the hills of Umbria seem light-years in the past. It's all one can do to remember them. There's too much to do in trying to make sense of the barrage of sensations going on around you – like that pack of Vespa scooters swarming around the bus, some with three people on them. Or that black-and-green taxi parked in the middle of the street, the driver haggling over the fare with a departing passenger. Or the truck full of soldiers in battle gear yelling and waving at the girls in the street. Everywhere – noise, commotion, intensity. This is Rome.

Where to Find It in Rome

For all its glamor, Rome is one of Europe's most impractical cities. It's best to be resigned to this fact and to be more patient than usual. A city the size of Rome really should have a subway system. One short line was completed a few years ago. But they soon discovered that it would be impossible to dig any more without destroying the accumulated layers of history that lie underneath the city. So they left all further digging to the archeologists. The city transit system could be a bit more efficient, as could the Italian postal and telephone systems. The city is overcrowded to begin with, and the post-war economic boom has left many utilities a little behind the times. There is much crowding, much waiting, and some less than efficient service.

Most Italian buses and trolleys are entered from the rear. Look for *entrata* by the door. The conductor collects 50 lire and hands out a ticket. Debarkation is from the front of the bus. All stops have signs indicating the route of the bus or trolley. It's best to read them with a map in hand.

The main points of reference are the following: Piazza Venezia is the center of Rome. To the south are the Victor Emmanuel Monument and the Forum. To the east is the Via Nazionale. It leads uphill toward Stazione Termini, the main railroad station. The Via del Corso leads north to the shopping district around the Piazza di Spagna, where American Express is located. The Corso Vittorio Emmanuele heads west across the Tiber to Vatican City. The main east-west bus in Rome is No. 64, a double-decker. It goes from the main railroad station to St. Peter's and back. There is no single effective north-south bus route, but most shopping can be done on foot around the Via del Corso.

Stazione Termini (railroad station) is worth mentioning again. Aside from its importance as the largest railroad station in Europe, it's also a convenient place for money-changing, postage stamps, long-distance calls, and general information.

The *Piazza di Spagna* (Spanish Square) is a lovely place from which the famous Spanish Steps lead upward to the Villa Borghese Gardens. Aside from the American Express office, there is a variety of fine shops and handsome cafés in the immediate area around the Piazza.

Changing money in Rome involves the same procedure as elsewhere in Italy. Just about any bank can do the job, but it's best to get there early. Banks close for a siesta between noon and 3 P. M.

Italian telephones don't use coins. Instead, there is a special brass token with a slot in it. (It's called a *gettone*.) Tokens can be purchased at any place that has a pay phone. (Cafés are the best bet.) In most places it costs 50 lire (8¢). The token goes in the slot on top of the phone. But one doesn't push the bottom releasing the *gettone* until someone has answered. Until the *gettone* is released, only the other party can be heard. If there is no answer, one simply hangs up and retrieves the token. It can be changed back into currency at the counter.

Stamps are available at the post office, but it's easier to look around for cafés that have a blue sign with a capital "T" out in front. Inside, stamps can be bought at any hour of the day or night.

Suggested Activities in Rome

There is a great deal to do during a week in Rome, and each visitor brings his own expectations with him. We therefore confine ourselves to the highlights.

1. *Shopping and/or browsing.* From Piazza Venezia, one walks north on Via del Corso. Every side street is crowded with elegant stores; the show-windows here are among the handsomest in Europe. They are filled with everything from shoes and handbags to sunglasses. (Persola sunglasses are perhaps the best in the world. They're impossible to buy in the U.S. Price = 10,000-20,000 lire, or $16-32.)

2. *Via Veneto.* This is the place to see and be seen. There's a string of chic (and expensive) sidewalk cafés where international celebrities cluster like hornets. Yves Montand has a favorite table at Doney's.

3. *The Forum.* An afternoon should be set aside for a walk among the ruins. (Entry: about 300 lire.) There are still chunks of Roman marble, which one can sit on, and imagine very clearly what it must have been like. This is hallowed ground.

4. Rome's art treasurers are scattered among many musems. The Roman National Museum contains the best collections of ancient works. It's in the Baths of Diocletian, across the huge square from Termini, the main railroad station. The richest holdings in Renaissance art can be found at the Borghese Gallery Museum inside the Villa Borghese. The morning is the best time to visit either one. Entry is about 300 lire.

5. No one should leave Rome without visiting several other churches besides St. Peter's. The Gesù, just off Piazza Venezia, is the most typical Baroque church. It is the Mother Church of the Jesuit Order. A few blocks south of Termini Station is the massive Saint Mary Major. Further south on Via Cavour (heading toward the Colosseum) is the Church of San Pietro in Vincoli (St. Peter in Chains). Michelangelo's *Moses* stands inside by the tomb of Pope Julius II. Finally, at the Spanish Steps is the church of Trinità dei Monti. It's simple and unpretentious despite its spectacular location.

6. Trastevere is the "left bank" of Rome, and a good place to lose oneself for an afternoon amidst the maze of tiny streets and the open-air concert of sounds. One shouldn't miss the tiny Isola Tiburtina island in the middle of the Tiber. It's a great place to spread out and

relax. Young couples come here to picnic.

7. For those who want to do what the Romans do, a leisurely afternoon around the Spanish Steps is in order. (To get there: Via del Babuino to the Piazza del Popolo, then up the Spanish Steps). The view of Rome from here is spectacular. Also worthwhile are the several sweet shops at the bottom of the steps, which serve excellent *gelati* (ice cream: Italians invented it).

8. Just across the Tiber from Trastevere is the district around the Pantheon. To get there: bus 64 from St. Peter's for three blocks after crossing the Tiber. It's a short stroll up to the Piazza Navona. Many visitors like to sit down on the edge of one of Bernini's massive fountains and watch the children play tag. This square has been a playground since Roman times and was often flooded for use as a swimming pool.

9. If one happens to be in the vicinity of St. Peter's, a visit to the Vatican Museum can be arranged easily. (Entry 500 lire). It is here that the famous *Sistine Chapel* is located. Inside is the spectacular ceiling by Michelangelo, including The *Last Judgment.* The election of Popes is held inside this chapel; Catholic bishops assemble here from all over the world for the occasion.

10. *Fountains.* Rome has over 400 of them, and no two are exactly alike. They're everywhere. This is the real Rome. There is something of beauty on every street corner.

The Week in Rome

This is our second stay in a major European capital. The pattern of activities will naturally parallel those in London to a large extent. It ought to reflect the same balance of sightseeing and rest plus a few other activities unique to Rome – an afternoon under the sun at the beach, shopping along the Via Veneto, an evening's trip to the Tivoli Gardens, and a day's trip to Pompeii and Capri.

Rome is not one city, but three. There is classical Rome, found in the old Forum, the Colosseum, and in dozens of ancient ruins scattered around the city. Then there is Renaissance Rome, the city of worldly Popes who patronized the arts and showered the city with palaces, museums, and churches – including St. Peter's. Third, there is modern Rome, perhaps the most exciting of all. It can be seen downtown along the Via Veneto, Rome's "Fifth Avenue". All the embassies, swank airline offices, department stores, specialty shops, and some of the best restaurants in town are found here.

Rome is three cities in one, and all are important. None of them can be understood without the other two. It's best to begin with ancient and Renaissance Rome in the first day of city sightseeing. As in Florence, there are guides to take groups of visitors around the city. The place to start is the Basilica of St. Peter, the most majestic building in Rome and the center of the Catholic world. It is in the middle of Vatican City, an independent city-state established in 1929 by the Lateran Treaty. It covers just two-tenths of a square mile, and is ruled directly by the Pope. In spite of its small size, it is one of the most important spots in all of Italy. Some 50 countries send ambassadors to the Vatican. It has its own newspaper, the *Osservatore Romano* (Roman Observer) – an influential one too – and its own postal system, currency, radio station, railroad, and police. It exercises sovereignty over other church buildings in Rome as well as over the Pope's summer villa, Castel Gandolfo, just south of the city. Economically, however, it is completely integrated with Italy. Postcards and colored slides can be purchased in lire from the hawkers who gather around the buses in St. Peter's Square.

Looking up from the square, the window on the top and to the right, just behind the Colonnade, is the one from which the Pope gives his blessing every Sunday at noon, except when he is away at Castel Gandolfo during the summer. The Colonnade itself is the magnificent work of Bernini, a name to remember in Rome. The design of the Colonnade is symbolic: its huge twin arms reach out to gather the world into the Church's embrace. The façade of the church was the last part to be completed, and by the time it was put up the style of the Renaissance had given way to the Baroque. It remains the greatest Baroque building in the world. It is also the largest church in the world.

As one approaches St. Peter's Square from the broad boulevard in front, on can clearly make out the vast dome on top of the Basilica. But as one comes nearer the church, the dome recedes. As one walks through the square to the front steps, the dome disappears entirely. It's a fascinating effect, though not exactly what Michelangelo had in mind when he designed it. He wanted the dome to be seen at all times, but his successors altered the blueprint. Like the one in Florence, it's actually two domes, one inside the other. There is a fantastic view from the lower rim of the dome, which can be reached by elevator. From there one can look down on the whole interior of the church. For the adventurous, there is a stairway which runs between the inner and outer dome, up to the tip of the dome. From here there is a spectacular view of the whole of Rome, and even the seacoast in the distance. (The elevator is at the far left of the church as one enters. Admission: 300 lire, or 48¢ for the elevator and the entrance into the dome; if one walks up to the dome, the admission is only 200 lire, or 32¢.)

Just outside the Basilica are the Swiss Guards in their striped uniforms and pointed helmets. They have guarded the Vatican since the days of Michelangelo, who designed their uniforms. Inside, one is overwhelmed by Baroque splendor. There isn't a square foot that isn't taken up with a fresco, mosaic, statue, or dazzling gold filigree. It's quite a contrast to the plain interior of the cathedral in Florence. The guide points out the major features, including Michelangelo's Pietà, completed when he was 25. Up fairly near the main altar, at the last pillar on the left, is a much-venerated bronze statue of St. Peter. A few pilgrims are usually clustered around it. St. Peter is shown seated, and his right foot has been worn smooth by the kisses of the faithful since the 1200's when it was cast. It was done by the same artist who designed the cathedral in Florence and who put up the storybook castle at the Piazza della Signoria: Arnolfo di Cambio.

At the large chapel about half-way down the right aisle, Masses are said continuously. In the front of the nave is Bernini's sumptuous bronze canopy over the altar. The supporting pillars writhe in a dizzying vortex of shapes. Below the altar is a crypt in which excavations were conducted recently. The whole basilica is set on a spot where, according to tradition, St. Peter was martyred in Nero's huge circus. St. Peter's remains are thought to lie deep in the ground under the main altar.

Almost directly in front of St. Peter's, and about 7 or 8 blocks away, is a massive round fortress. That is the Castel Sant' Angelo, which was originally an enormous tomb built by the Emperor Hadrian for himself in 136 A. D. Sculptures and other decorations have been added in the meantime. In the Middle Ages it was a convenient fort, and was often used by the popes when Rome was invaded by the Goths, the French, and then the Holy Roman Emperor Charles V. An underground passageway was built connecting it to the Vatican, so that the Pope could get there quickly and safely when the city was being invaded.

The castle is on the Tiber River, and just across the river is the Pantheon, the best preserved building of ancient Rome. It's a spectacle to behold. Several wealthy Romans built it as a temple to the seven planetary gods: Venus, Mars, Jupiter, etc. Later it was made into a church. The hugh bronze doors are original, and have been there almost 2000 years. But the most spectacular part of all is the dome. At the very top is a round opening. It was designed to let in the sunlight in such a way that it would shine on one god or goddess after another as the day wore on. It still does, except that the pagan deities have been replaced by altars. The painter Raphael and several kings of Italy are buried inside. The whole interior used to be covered with pure marble, but Pope Julius II stripped it off in order to decorate St. Peter's. There was also much bronze work inside. This was taken off and used to make the enormous altar canopy in St. Peter's. This sort of "pious plundering" was quite a common thing in those days. One's first and natural reaction to this is probably one of anger. When visiting Pope Julius' tomb (where Michelangelo's *Moses* and other works are located), one may wonder why Pope Julius did not quarry marble for himself, instead of pillaging everyone else's. Unfortunately it's easier said than done. Italy is rich in marble, but it's a problem to get it out of the ground and transport it all the way down to Rome, especially when it has to be done with ships and oxcarts. There seemed little reason to do this when an abundant supply of marble was right at hand among the "worthless" ruins. This at least was the reasoning behind the borrowings. The idea of preserving and venerating the monuments of the past is something relatively new. It is largely a product of 19th century Romanticism. Keats' *Ode to a Grecian Urn* is a good example. The notion of idealizing the past was unheard of in Julius' day. He was interested only in the present and in getting a new church built. He thought he was doing these old ruins a favor by putting them to use for a change, instead of letting them crumble in neglect as they had for centuries. So he stripped the Pantheon, and while he was at it he raided the Colosseum too.

Not much of the original Colosseum is left either, at least as far as luxurious trappings go. But it's still easy to imagine what it must have been like in the days of the Emperors. The outside was coated with pure white marble and there was a statue in each of the arches. The top was ringed with banners. The visitor can go up and around the various tiers, but must be careful on the stone stairs; they're very uneven. By the way, the Colosseum was not used for the persecution of Christians. It was used mainly for animal fights or for mock sea battles. The lower part would be flooded with water for these occasions. Christian martyrs lost their lives at the nearby Circus Maximus. Most of the building there is gone, but the foundations are still visible. Behind the Colosseum, on the Esquiline hill, is where Nero had his famous Golden House. It's now an attractive garden, though a few ruins are left. Bas-reliefs of Nero's face appear at the top of the gateposts. Next to the Colosseum is the Arch of Constantine, the first Christian emperor, who built it in 312 A. D.

The Roman Forum is nearby, and guides are available to point out the most important sites, including the spot where Julius Caesar was assassinated. One of the best places to get an overall view of the Forum is from the Piazza Campidoglio, which is above and behind it on the Capitoline hill. This square is a gem by itself, and was designed by Michelangelo. At night there is a "Sound and Light" show in the Forum. Various historical events are reënacted, and the buildings are flood-lit in ingenious ways to make the dramatizations as convincing as possible.

Next to the Forum is the Piazza Venezia, the geographical center of Rome and its most prestigious location. The name comes from Renaissance times, when the Venetian Republic had its embassy there. At the Piazza Venezia, ancient, Renaissance, and modern Rome all converge. All the traffic in the city converges here too, and it's the place to see the Italian "traffic ballet" in action. Ancient Rome is represented by the Forum, a stone's throw away, and by the Colosseum, just a few blocks down the Via dei Fori Imperiali. This impressive boulevard, starting at the Piazza Venezia and passing the Forum on the way to the Colosseum, was built by Mussolini. Halfway to the Colosseum, next to the Forum, are several stone panels which he also ordered. They show the various stages in the expansion of the Roman Empire. *Il Duce* thought of himself as a kind of reincarnation of the Roman Emperors, and of his political program as a restoration of the Roman Empire.

Renaissance Rome is represented by the Palazzo Venezia, the Venetian embassy building, and it stands in the center of the square. Aside from the Vatican, it's probably the most expensive piece of real estate in the city, and so Mussolini used it as his official residence. In the center of the building is a small balcony from which *Il Duce* delivered his famous Shakespearian orations to the throngs of delirious followers. A block away is the Gesù church, a huge Baroque building and the Mother Church of the Jesuits. St. Ignatius Loyola, founder of the order, is buried here.

Modern Rome is the most conspicuous of all at the Piazza Venezia. The square is dominated by the colossal Victor Emmanuel Monument, which commemorates the reunification of Italy in 1871. Romans laugh at the thing and call it the "wedding cake" because all that white marble looks like frosting. There is even talk of tearing the monument down some day to make room for office buildings and efficiency apartments.

A visit to Rome isn't quite complete without a look through one of the catacombs. The Catacombs of St. Callisto, outside the city proper, are among the largest. There are tombs of some of the earliest popes, and many of the remains date nearly from New Testament times. Several primitive mosaics are there, some with Latin, some with Greek lettering. It's dark and rather damp in these long passageways and a sweater or light jacket is advised. To get there and back, the bus or car goes along the Appian Way, the oldest and most famous of the Roman roads. It's lined with dark green pines and old villas, and captures perfectly the mood and flavor of ancient Rome. It is here that the composer Respighi drew inspiration for his symphonic poem, "The Pines of Rome".

An ideal way to spend an evening is at the Tivoli Gardens. The gardens belong to an old estate and palace about 20 miles northeast of Rome, and give the visitor a vivid sense of the life style enjoyed by the great merchant princes of the Renaissance. The prince in this connection was not a merchant but a wealthy and powerful churchman, the Cardinal Ippolito d'Este. He took an old monastery on a hillside and transformed it into a sumptuous palace. The whole hillside was terraced with gardens and fountains. The fountains themselves are the most spectacular feature of all. There are hundreds of them: some are huge waterfalls, cascading down 30 feet; others are tiny jet streams. Several fountains are set inside dark mossy grottoes. The effect is overwhelming.

There are two beaches near Rome, both about 20 miles west of the city on the coast. The most popular one is the Lido, and that's where most American tourists go. In the summer, the place becomes an Italian Jones Beach, with every variety, shape, and size of tourist. A far better place to try is the beach of Fregene, some 10 miles up the coast, and much more secluded. The tourists haven't discovered it yet. Fregene is popular with Italian film directors and other celebrities. The sand is so fine it's almost powder. Along the beach are dozens of villas belonging to the Roman jet set. It is said that Sophia Loren was discovered here one day back in the 50's as she sauntered past Carlo Ponti's beach cabin. It's still a popular place to spend an afternoon, splashing around or napping in the sun. Paddle boats are usually available. The sun is very strong, and one does well to avoid getting too much of it at first.

A morning's trip to the Pope's summer residence at Castel Gandolfo,

some 25 miles south of Rome, is also a worthwhile excusion. Special arrangements can be made for a general audience with Pope Paul, but even for non-Catholics the trip is a pure delight. It covers some of the loveliest countryside in central Italy. The scenery isn't as spectacular as the Dolomites or as rocky as Umbria. Instead, it features soft green hills and shady valleys. The center of the area is the Alban Hills, and the Pope's summer residence is on one of them. The hills are volcanic in origin and several of the largest craters have become lakes. As the highway approaches the area from Rome it passes through a broad plain at first, dotted with live orchards and vineyards. The wines from this region, "Castelli wines," are light and golden; huge barrels of it are seen on old-fashioned carts and wagons. The earth here is volcanic, and looks it — jet black, lush and fertile. Vegetables of all kinds cover the valley floor.

Then the road starts climbing. Vineyards give way to shadowy chestnut groves. Suddenly, as the road rounds a bend, the whole valley comes into view below, and far in the distance, like a silver thread, is the sea. This is summer resort country. Famous Romans built country estates here, including Cicero, who claimed that he did his best work away from the crowd and clatter of Rome and in the peace and quiet of his estate at Tusculum. Many others agreed, including powerful dukes and princes in the Middle Ages, who decked these hills with castles and gardens. The region became known as the Castelli Romani (Roman Castles), and it still is. There are 13 of them in all, and most of the towns are names after them.

One of them is called Castel Gandolfo. The Roman Emperor Dominitian built a villa here. Later, a papal estate was built, and the Popes have used it as a summer retreat ever since. The castle is superbly situated and offers a serene view of Lake Albano and the richly carpeted hills around it. It's a quiet spot, affording the Pope respite from the cares and turbulence of Rome.

The original villa is not large enough to accommodate visitors, so the papal audience is held in a special hall built in 1963. The Pope is carried into the assembly by the Papal chamberlains, and the crowd hails him with chants and cries of *Viva il Papa!* (Long live the Pope). The Pope then welcomes the visitors and addresses them briefly on the major problems facing the Church today. He speaks alternately in four different languages. As he leaves, he imparts his blessing and offers a warm smile or gesture in every direction. The whole scene combines the majesty of the Pope's office and responsibilities with a sense of the human affection which unites the Pontiff to the faithful.

There are other things to see and do in Rome during a week's stay, both by day and by night. There is the Piazza del Popolo, with an enormous Egyptian obelisk in the center, and the opulent Medici Gardens nearby. There are the famous Spanish Steps, in the heart of the "Foreigners' Quarter", where writers and artists from all countries have congregated since the seventeenth century. Goethe, Shelley, and others lived here, and at the foot of the steps a plaque indicates the house where Keats died in 1821. Today, many actors, models, and fashion designers have apartments nearby.

Trastevere, the oldest section of Rome, is also very interesting. It's almost exactly across the Tiber River from the Piazza Venezia. In ancient times, Roman slaves lived in this section. Nowadays, in the summer, the place becomes one big carnival. Streets and squares are jammed with artists' stalls, outdoor markets, and bazaars. Everything is decked with banners and awnings. One of the oldest churches in Rome is in the area, Santa Maria in Trastevere. Some of the best cooking in Rome is to be had at any of the restaurants tucked away in tiny squares and alleys. The sign *Trattoria* points the way.

Across the river from Trastevere are two of the loveliest temples in Italy. They stand near each other on the banks of the Tiber. They are the Temple of Vesta (the round one) and the Temple of Manly Fortune (square-shaped), both dating from the late Roman Republic. The temples aren't exactly grandiose and overwhelming like the Colosseum, but petite and graceful. Aside from the Pantheon, they are the only pagan temples in Rome that have remained completely intact.

In many parts of the city, Rome comes alive only at night. Romans can boast of the Piper Club, the largest discotheque in Europe, with English rock groups, banks of strobe lights, and 104 loudspeakers all blaring at once. It's located on Via Tagliamento, just off Viale Regina Margherita. Hours: 10 P.M. to 3 A.M. There's a cover charge of 2,000 lire and drinks go for about 1,500 lire. Mick Jagger and others have played there during the summer.

There is one Roman institution everybody sees at night: the Trevi Fountain. It's located about six blocks north of the Piazza Venezia. The fountain is a huge affair, with rocks, rapids, and statues of gods in repose. It's the most restful sight anywhere in town after dark. Streams of water cascade over the rocks and down to a flood-lit pool. The water cools the air, and is supposed to bring thoughts of romance to even the gravest cynic. A coin tossed in the fountain is said to guarantee a speedy return to Rome.

These, then, are some of the possibilities offered by a week in Rome. We've only hinted at some of the things awaiting the visitor in the hubbub and excitement of Europe's oldest capital. It's impossible to catalogue it all, much less put it down in print. There's the Rome of history, the Rome of business and politics, the Rome of the Popes, "mod" Rome (in a suitably Italian version); the Rome of carnivals and cuisine in Trastevere; of fashion shops on the Via Veneto; of the Forum and the Colosseum, melancholy with the weight of history; of St. Peter's, mecca for the faithful; of the Spanish Steps, haven for artists; of the Trevi Fountain, cue for the romantic. It's a city to be savored in small doses, one place at a time.

Pompeii-Capri-Naples Field Trip

There is a completely different side of Italy to be seen in the south, and there are many important landmarks along the way. There is the ancient Roman city of Pompeii at the foot of Mt. Vesuvius, Sorrento — the orange juice capital of Italy, Capri — the magical isle in the Bay of Naples, and the bustling port city of Naples. One must be up early in the morning to cover all of this in one day. The Via Casilina leads out of Rome to the southeast. There isn't much traffic early in the day — mainly trailer-trucks carrying sewing machines or motor scooters to Naples — and one can make excellent time.

The route southward passes the old abbey of Monte Cassino, which comes into view on the left. The abbey is perched comfortably on top of a low, flat mountain. This is one of the most sacred places in the Catholic world. Western monasticism got its start here in 529 A. D. when St. Benedict established a monastery and drew up a rule of life that became the basis for most monastic orders. St. Benedict's rules stressed a life balancing intellectual activity and manual work. Monte Cassino is still the Mother House of the Benedictines. In the Middle Ages, under the Abbot Didier, Monte Cassino became one of the wealthiest and most powerful of all abbeys. It had a huge library and was a flourishing center of learning. Artistic activity was intense; the technique of mosaic-making, which had been perfected by Byzantine artists, was brought to Monte Cassino, from which it spread to the rest of Europe.

For non-Catholics, Monte Cassino is best known for the battle which raged along this valley in World War II. The Nazis made a last-ditch stand here in early 1944, hoping to prevent the Allies from taking Rome. Monte Cassino was heavily fortified, and bristled with long-range artillery. The Allies could not advance to Rome without taking it. Time and time again they hurled their best troops at the mountain stronghold and were thrown back every time. Finally, a corps of Polish soldiers stormed the bastion; they too had to retreat, with heavy losses. They tried again. The fortress fell to them in May, 1944. The Allies were free to proceed to Rome, and the Nazis retired to the east. In all this fighting, the old abbey was bombed repeatedly by the Allies. It has since been rebuilt along the old lines, and many of its art treasures have been recovered. Military cemeteries dot the area, and there is a monument to the thousands of soldiers who fell in the Battle of Cassino.

By this time, the rough, stern-looking mountains to the left have evened out, and the highway enters a broad plain which carries us toward Naples. We've left the province of Latium and have entered Campania, which circles the Bay of Naples. It's a region of rich volcanic soil and flourishing agriculture: cereals, vineyards, olive orchards, and citrus fruits grow in Campania around the Bay of Naples. This is "volcano country", and one can almost sniff the sulphur in the air. The big brute of a mountain looming up ahead and slightly to the left is the famous Mt. Vesuvius. It's the last active volcano on the mainland of Europe. Vesuvius is sinister and unpredictable. It will launch into a tantrum of eruptions, spilling lava all over the countryside and down to the sea, then settle back into a long and misleading period of dormancy. One long and quiet spell was suddenly interrupted in 79 A. D., when the whole area around it, down to the coast, was buried under ashes and lava. The town of Pompeii was completely smothered. Several other eruptions confirmed Vesuvius' re-awakening. In the Middle Ages, however, the mountain went back to sleep again, and as always the towns around it were lulled into a fool's paradise. Vineyards and vegetable gardens were planted on the slopes, practically up to the summit. It was all for naught. In 1631, Vesuvius took revenge. The whole area between the mountain and the sea was devastated. Peace continued until 1944, when a final blast blew off the top of the mountain. It has been quiet ever since, but geologists are predicting another eruption sometime in the next five or six years.

Just beyond Vesuvius is the ancient city of Pompeii. No doubt the visitor is inured to ancient ruins by now, having seen them every day in Rome. But in a sense the ruins in Rome are spoiled by the newer buildings, streets, and all the commotion of a modern city. In Pompeii, it's different. There are no modern boulevards, no smog, no urban skyline - just the town of Pompeii, preserved in its original condition. We have the eruption of 79 A. D. to thank for that. Many, in fact, most, Roman remains aren't what they used to be because they have been plundered, scavenged, and "improved" over the years by robbers or architectural do-gooders. Not Pompeii. The heavy fall of cinders and ashes completely buried the city and like a protective blanket kept all hands off the town. When excavation began around 1750, everything was found exactly the way it was on that terrible day back in 79 A.D.

Even before the ruins were rediscovered, historians knew a great deal about Pompeii from ancient records. They knew, for example, that it was a favorite resort for wealthy Romans and a rich and thriving city under the Roman Emperors. The Emperor himself would come down from time to time for some fun in the sun and a sip or two of the local wine. The town had a population of over 20,000, a sizable one for those times.

A vivid impression of Pompeiian life just before (and during) the holocaust of 79 A. D. is conveyed by the famous novel *The Last Days of Pompeii,* by Sir Edward Bulwer-Lytton. Hollywood made it into a film some years ago. The best account, however, and the most distinguished, is given by an eyewitness. It was the Roman writer Pliny the Younger, who watched the spectacle from a safe distance. He tells of earthquakes in the morning, and then a rain of cinders which soon reached three feet. Vesuvius seemed to be giving a hint, and many of the townspeople took it. Pliny describes the traffic-jam of oxcarts, carriages, and slave-carried litters, all heading for the city gates. Terror and panic were everywhere: hysterical women looking for their husbands or children, the children crying and trying to rub the cinders from their eyes. Pliny's description of the earthquake is classic. It wasn't just a rumble, it was literally an earth-shattering event. The ground would move a few feet to the right. All the oxcarts and traffic would then change their course, since the city gate was now in a slightly different direction. Then the earth would move a few feet the other way. All the traffic would change course again. It was a nightmare with an air of bizarre comedy.

Many people lost their heads in panic, and took refuge inside their houses just to get out of the rain of cinders. But soon something else came: the lava. Most of it descended on the nearby town of Herculaneum; Pompeii was buried under tons of cinders. At first there was a long low rumble, fused with a hissing sound. The juggernaut worked its way down the mountainside, snapping trees and releasing huge boulders, which crashed into the houses on the edge of town. The din came nearer. Only then did the people indoors realize what was happening. It was too late. A tidal wave of steaming ash engulfed the houses in a few minutes. Then it all stopped. The traffic ceased, the crying and shouting were stilled. Pompeii was through; it belonged to history.

Most of the town has been excavated. Guides are available by the main gate to conduct the visitor through the ruins. Most of the roofs are off the houses (they weren't built to withstand tons of congealed ash) but some have been restored. Everything else is pretty much intact, including the streets, which are laid out geometrically, and are paved with stones. There is an ingenious bit of city planning. At every intersection, there are huge stepping stones for pedestrians to walk over. The distance between the stepping stones is just wide enough for the wheels of an oxcart to pass through. There are spots where wheeled traffic has worn ruts in the stone. Here and there are potholes. Street signs are carved in stone on the corners of the buildings. They are actually numbers – Roman numerals of course. There are all kinds of houses: small shops, larger offices, workrooms, and finally the great estates.

One is particularly worth seeing. It has the AVE (Welcome) spelled out in small stones in the doorway. Inside is the Atrium or parlor, with a small bronze statue in the center. The Atrium was open to the sky. The small pool in the center of the room, where the statue stands, was the *impluvium,* designed to catch the rain water. Various rooms branch off in all directions, some for servants and slaves, and the larger ones for the family.

The most luxurious buildings in town are the baths. Pompeii, after all, was a resort town, and bathing was the Romans' favorite indoor sport. The visitor can barely make out traces of the mosaics on the walls and ceiling. There are men's and women's changing rooms, pools, and stone pipes which brought in the water. In the changing rooms are small cubbyholes where the people put their tunics, togas, and other apparel. It was all very orderly.

All sorts of relics and remains are exhibited in special museums. It's a good place to get a vivid picture of day-to-day life in ancient times. Cooking pots, plates, wash basins, shoes – all the artifacts of daily life are still there. Many plates were found with food still on them. The most grisly sight is that of several corpses. They are the remains of townspeople who were asphyxiated by smoke and fumes. The figures are hunched over, clasping their sides as they gasp for air. A dog's corpse is also displayed. One of the corpses is that of a small boy. It was found in the women's changing room at the baths. This has led to speculation that the boy was an attendant in the baths, faithfully performing his duties to the very end.

The visitor leaves Pompeii lost in thought. A trip through it is a

somber experience. The whole town is wrapped in a kind of serene silence. Only the chirping of birds and the sound of bumblebees break the stillness.

Thoughts liven up, however, as one reaches the coast. The blue expanse of the Bay of Naples appears over the tall and rugged cliffs. The coastal road heads toward Sorrento. This is a magnificent stretch of seacoast. The sight of the "wine-dark sea", as the ancient Greek sailors called it, mixed with the copper-colored cliffs, dark green cypresses and pines, and pastel-shaded houses (pink, yellow, coral), is a spectacle to keep all noses to the window. Then Sorrento comes into view. It's a small town, dangling precariously on the cliffs, and has been a favorite of many poets and writers over the years. Nietzsche, after he fled from Bayreuth, wrote his book *Human, all too Human* in Sorrento. The Renaissance writer Tasso, who later gained renown in Ferrara for his epic poem *Jerusalem Delivered,* hailed from Sorrento. The main square is named for him.

Launches for Capri are to be found on the docks just below the city. There is a hairpin turn at the bottom that calls for a virtuoso performance from any driver. He must maneuver his car or bus backwards and forwards five or six times before making it. It's the famous "Sorrento turn". Some bus drivers have been driven to drink by it. The best always do it in fewer than seven tries.

Several motor launches are docked at the wharf, their keels slapping the brine like a tap dancer in slow motion. With a short peremptory hoot on the horn, they set off for Capri. Just off Sorrento is the spot where, according to Homer, Odysseus stopped up the ears of his crew and had himself strapped to the mast in order to resist the call of the sirens on the shore. On the other side of the Bay of Naples is the spot where the Greeks thought Hades began. The Greeks were great seafarers, establishing many settlements along the southern coast of Italy. But by the time they reached Italy, they were far from home. This seemed to be the end of the world and the beginning of the under-world. Later, the Romans, who were closer to home, used many of the hot springs in the area for spas and thermal baths. They took "Hades" and turned it into a string of extravagant resorts.

A few minutes after leaving Sorrento, the visitor can just barely make out the Isle of Capri ahead. Before long the launch approaches the rocky coastline. The island is about 4 miles long and 1½ miles wide at its greatest width. It's really two mountains joined by a small valley. If the weather's nice and there's time, the Blue Grotto is worth seeing. It's a cave in the side of the mountain. Little rowboats take the visitor inside. The sunlight comes in through the water underneath and it makes everything inside a brilliant blue. The waters around Capri are legendary. They're deep and crystal-clear. The sky is a light silvery blue. And there's no forgetting the Capri sun: it makes the colors of the houses almost incandescent. They're the same colors as the ones at Sorrento — light pastels. The harbor is full of little fishing boats and yachts. On the beach, fishing nets are spread out to dry in the sun. The vegetation around the town and up the mountainside is sub-tropical.

The funicular railway goes up the mountain to the town of Capri. It works like a cog-railway, except that it is operated by a long cable. Occasionally one still hears a little ditty, *Funiculi, Funicula,* which people used to sing when the first funicular railway was built on Mt. Vesuvius. The walk through the narrow streets of the old town leads to the Tiberio Palace Hotel, one of the finest on the island. This is the time for lunch and relaxation. From the hotel there is a magnificent view of the harbor below and of the other mountain, with the village of Anacapri nestling on top. All around the island is the deep blue Tyrrhenian Sea. Though the sun is out, and almost blinding, the air is a moderate 75° or 80°. A breeze is always blowing, carrying the aroma of jasmine and rosemary bushes.

After a good long look around Capri, it's time to be heading for Naples. The funicular railway goes back down the mountain to the wharf, where one boards the ferry that steams across the bay to Naples. The voyage itself is a lazy affair. Soft drinks and snacks are available downstairs. It's possible to get a nice tan in these two hours.

Eventually the city of Naples comes into view. It's the second largest port in Italy, after Genoa, and the headquarters of the NATO fleet. U.S. warships are lined up in the harbor. Soon the ferry pulls up to the dock, which is swarming with buses, cars, postcard hawkers, and olive-skinned Neapolitans.

Naples (Italian: *Napoli*) is a huge city of 1,300,000 people. It goes back to ancient times, when it was one of the wealthy Greek trading settlements along the coast. The Greeks called it *Neapolis* (New Town), from which the name "Naples" is derived. The city has been passed back and forth among several countries. The French and Spanish had it in the late Middle Ages and in early modern times. Napoleon gave it to his brother Joseph, who became King of Naples.

The people of Naples are known for their song and laughter. Such popular songs as *Santa Lucia, O Sole Mio,* and others were born here. Most Italian restaurants in the U.S. serve Neapolitan cooking. Pizza is a

Neapolitan invention. What is most impressive about Naples are the crowded, noisy streets and the people leaning over the balconies above or hanging strings of lemons to ripen in the window. Of all the people in Italy, the Neapolitans are the favorites of many foreign visitors. Everything they do is spontaneous. They are vivacious and emotional, much less inhibited in their gaiety and sadness than the elegant Florentine or wary Venetian or businesslike Roman.

Naples has a certain artistic disorderliness. Unlike modern Rome, the streets are choked with horse-drawn carts, loaded with fresh vegetables, wines, and citrus fruits. Buzzing around them are the ever-present Fiats. Anything and everything is draped over the balconies above the street. The first floor of all the buildings is a succession of different colored awnings. Small shops and wooden booths are bunched up along the sidewalk and spill into the street. Naples may not boast the historical or cultural achievements of Florence or Venice or Rome, but it's a gem of its own.

Rome to Milan on the Highway of the Sun

Our route from Rome to Milan once again is on the Autostrada del Sole. We were on this same road for a while from Venice to Florence (we picked it up just outside Bologna) and from Florence to Rome (we left it in order to circle around Lake Trasimeno and see Assisi). The way out of Rome is on the "Raccordo Annulare", which affords the visitor a final look at the city. Parks and fountains give way to efficiency apartments and industrial suburbs. In a way, it's a suitable preparation for Milan, which reveals another whole side of Italy. Not so much the Italy of the Renaissance, of the past, but the Italy of the present and future; the Italy of modern industry and finance. Milan is the industrial center of Italy and one has to see it to understand the economic miracle of post-war Italy.

In the meantime, however, there's a full day's driving ahead. The Autostrada makes the trip straight and fast. The Autostrada is itself an engineering marvel, the biggest and one of the newest of the Italian superhighways. In fact, it makes an American feel right at home. Except for the Italian road signs along the way — signs like *Stazione* (Toll station), *Uscita* (Exit), *Alt* (Stop), and so forth — one could just as well be driving from New York to Boston. There are a few other differences too. For one thing, there is beautiful countryside outside the window, not just a string of industrial suburbs. And there's less smog in the air. Also, one is passed by Ferraris and Alfa-Romeos, not Mustangs and Corvettes. Some other things are the same, though. There are Howard Johnson-looking service centers along the way. The biggest chain is called "Pavesi". Several Pavesi restaurants are built over the highway, just as some are in the U.S. Italians seem to think it's glamorous to have lunch while getting dizzy from the traffic racing by underneath. These service centers have candy stores, snack shops, drug stores, and magazine racks. Another big chain of service centers is Motta. Motta is one of the largest candy manufacturers in Italy.

The most common gas station chain is Agip. It is run by the Italian government, and the stations are modern and clean. It has been a very successful operation in Italy and in other parts of Europe, and Italy has planted its Agip stations all around Africa and the Middle East. Italians take pride in Agip: it is a symbol of their growing economic influence. Though Agip is the largest and most successful gasoline chain in Italy, it's not a monopoly. Other brands, including American ones, are also sold.

Since the onrush of tourism in Italy, the Italian government has committed itself to developing a modern and efficient network of highways. The system is practically complete, and it has transformed tourist traffic overnight. The Italian superhighway system was begun in the late 1950's, and had to overcome all the difficulties posed by the rugged Italian terrain, the preservation of antiquities, and the irregular scattering of the major sites of importance.

Italy is first in the world when it comes to tourism — some 30 million tourists come to Italy every year. Many of Italy's tourists are Germans, but the majority are still American. The second country for tourism is Spain, with about 25 million visitors every year. France is third, with 22 million people. France was once first on the list, but its popularity has slipped a bit in the past decade.

Our route to Milan retraces in reverse sequence the part of the Autostrada which brought us into Rome from Assisi. There are the same steep hills and deep ravines and valleys; the same tunnels too. Signs point the way to "Terni/Narni" off to the right. We don't follow them but continue straight north. The highway has left the region of Latium and re-entered Umbria. Signs point left to the town of Orvieto, which sits grimly on top of a mound of volcanic rock. Small wonder the Etruscans made a fort out of it, and the Popes, much later, a medieval stronghold.

About 40 miles up the road the signs point left to Chianciano Terme, a small town with an international reputation for its mineral water. In Rome many signs direct one to such health springs. Chianciano Terme boasts an abundance of sulphur and calcium springs. In fact there are hot springs throughout the entire area. Europeans, especially Italians, worship them as cure-alls, and head for a spa at the drop of a headache or the slightest rumbling of indigestion. Europeans are great hypochondriacs, particularly in the Latin countries. It's all a part of their national culture − a game everyone plays and takes pretty seriously, or at least as seriously as they take anything else. Although they're as healthy as anybody, they enjoy *feeling* unhealthy and fussing about themselves as if on the verge of collapse. They count and classify all of their internal organs, spinning an elaborate mythology about each one. The capstone of the whole system is the liver. Americans tend to be concerned about the heart or the lungs, but in Europe the liver takes center stage. If one's liver is happy and content, nothing serious can happen. One is invincible. If the liver is upset or unhappy, an attack of something must be on the way.

A European always knows how his liver is feeling; he recognizes its subtlest whims, and he knows how to satisfy each of them. He has a wide assortment of potions, pills, exercises, special diets, and hot-spring baths to keep the liver in optimum condition. "How are you?" asks one Italian of another. "My liver isn't feeling well today," replies his friend, downcast. It's the Frenchman who takes the cake, however. He has a classification of the moods of the liver that makes the Italian seem positively insensitive by comparison. When a Frenchman is really upset about something and wants everyone to know it, he throws up his hands and exclaims: *C'est une crise de foie!* (It's a crisis of the liver!).

The Italian praises *acqua minerale* (mineral water), not so much for its tart effervescence, but because it's enthusiastically received by the liver. The liver likes it; therefore he likes it. Hypochondria aside, the visitor owes it to himself to have some Italian mineral water. It's quite cheap in Italy, much less expensive than coke. Imported Italian mineral water is available in the U.S. The best brands are Pellegrino and Appia. But nothing the U.S. produces can come close to the brisk flavor of Italian mineral water. It doesn't have any taste of its own. What it does is to cleanse the mouth and stimulate the taste buds for the food to follow. It's about the most refreshing thing one can have on a hot day, especially at the beginning of a meal. The label on the bottle is an education in Italian psychology. There is invariably a long and involved statement by a distinguished physician, singing the praises of this or that brand. The statement usually dates from the 1930's or 40's. The point that Dr. so-and-so works up to is his solemn testimony that this brand of *acqua minerale* is especially beneficial to the *fegato* (liver). That's what sells the bottle.

By now the Autostrada is well into Umbria. Lake Trasimeno is off to the right, about 10 miles. Before long the road crosses into Tuscany. The signs point the way to Florence, off to the right. The Autostrada circles around it to the left, heading due north. Soon it starts over the backbone of the Apennines, through one pass after another and then descends to the broad plain around Bologna. This is the heart of the "Romana", a part of the region of Emilia just south of Bologna, reaching up to the Apennines. It's full of fertile river basins, sprouting wheat, maize, and row after row of vineyards.

The scene is enough to give anyone an appetite, and any one of the motor inns just outside of Bologna is a good place to stop for lunch. We're' more than halfway to Milan by now. From here it's all flat plains and straight driving. After lunch, we head west and north. The Autostrada continues past Modena to the left, where the famous Ferrari and Maserati sports cars are manufactured. An occasional smokestack or industrial plant signals our entry into the commercial and industrial heartland of Italy. More and more of them sprout up as the Autostrada approaches the outskirts of Milan.

Just before reaching Milan, the highway runs along the southern edge of the huge Po River basin, ideal for all kinds of farming. There are vineyards and wheat fields, and here and there a herd of cattle is grazing lazily in the sun. Then an oil well pops up out of nowhere, then another. There isn't much oil in Italy, but where there is, the Italians make the most of it. The oil derricks and tanks off to the right announce the town of Cortemaggiore, too small to appear on most maps, but very important for such state petroleum firms as Agip.

The signs point to Parma, off to the left. This is the setting of Stendhal's famous novel *The Charterhouse of Parma.* Then Piacenza, in the thick of gas and oil rigs. This was the starting point of the old Roman road which ran across the region of Emilia to the Adriatic Sea. The highway soon crosses the Po River, a wide, slow-moving waterway that rather resembles the Mississippi. Upstream, to the left, it continues until it disappears into alpine streams at the French border.

Once across the Po River, we enter the region of Lombardy, the last region on our route in Italy. The region takes its name from a barbarian tribe known as the "Lombards," who invaded this area at the fall of the Roman Empire and settled down to stay. It's a busy and prosperous region. Huge rice fields make use of the abundant water supply, and herds of cattle yield a great many dairy products. Among the best and most popular is *Gorgonzola* cheese. It's so mellow and milky it's almost sweet. (The sweet version is called *Gorgonzola dolce:* Gorgonzola soft.) The mulberry bushes around the edge of the wheat fields are used to raise silkworms. Silk is a big industry in this part of the country.

Before too long, we're in Milan. The city is one huge power plant. Fortunately, however, one doesn't see too much of the industrial works from the Autostrada, which heads for the center of town. The central square is dominated by a massive cathedral. This one especially is worth seeing. It's sometimes called the "sand-castle" cathedral because of its almost unreal appearance. It bristles with 135 needle-shaped spires and over 200 statues, all pointing up from the roof. People have compared it to a porcupine. Though the building goes back to the Middle Ages, it wasn't completed until Napoleon took a personal interest in it around 1805. He added a few ideas of his own, then ordered the structure finished right away. It was, 4 years later. It has often been said that the best time to see the cathedral is in the late afternoon, when the rays of the setting sun peer through the forest of spires and statues and cast a golden glow over the white marble.

In front of the cathedral is a large esplanade. There are always pigeons milling about, just as in St. Mark's Square in Venice. On the left facing the cathedral is the famous Galleria, a long indoor arcade lined with shops and cafés. This is the time of the afternoon when the Milanese, exhausted after a full day's work (there's no "siesta" in Germanic Milan), crawl out of their offices, drag themselves to the nearest café, slump into a chair, and bury their faces in the evening newspaper. Women shoppers meet their friends, and tourists relax after sightseeing.

Milan was a commercial center even in Roman times. During the period of the barbarian invasions, the Roman Emperors had their headquarters here in order to be near the skirmishing. One of them, the Emperor Constantine, issued the famous Edict of Milan here in 312 A.D., making Christianity the official religion of the Roman Empire. St. Ambrose, the patron saint of the city, was Bishop of Milan. He converted St. Augustine to Christianity. Then came the barbarian invasions. One tribe, the Longobardi (Long Beards), settled around Milan and set up a kingdom. Later, Milan became part of Charlemagne's vast empire. Throughout the Middle Ages, it was a thriving commercial center. All sorts of goods going back and forth between Italy and northern Europe passed through Milan. Today Milan is a big silk market. The Alfa-Romeo sports car is manufactured here. It's also a mecca for international banking, with over 300 banks in the city.

But Milan isn't all business and industry. It has always been renowned for its cultural life. The Sforza family, who ruled Milan during Renaissance times, were great patrons of the arts. They were to Milan what the Medicis were to Florence. One of them brought Leonardo da Vinci to Milan. Later, he was captured by invading French armies in 1500. His famous fresco, *The Last Supper*, is painted on a wall of the Church of Santa Maria delle Grazie (St. Mary of Grace) in Milan. Da Vinci finally died in France and was buried in Amboise. The most famous opera house in the world is here too, the La Scala Opera, where such vixens as Maria Callas have kept audiences calling for encores.

The Swiss Alps

The Bavarian Alps and the Dolomites are bumps on a log compared to the peaks of the Swiss Alps. Even in summer, there's snow up on the mountains. Our route takes us to the Italian-Swiss border town of Chiasso, over the St. Gotthard Pass, and down to the lakefront resort of Lucerne.

The road out of Milan to the north is a fast highway. At first the countryside is still rather flat, but far ahead one can just begin to make out, in the mist and clouds, the foothills of the Alps. The highway skims through the town of Como which sits at one end of Lake Como. It's a lovely spot, and the lake looks fresh and cool. Como was originally a Roman camp, and part of the old Roman wall is still standing. Pliny the Younger, the Roman writer who described the eruption of Vesuvius, was from Como.

A few miles down the road from Como is the border town of Chiasso. Customs formalities are brief, and the visitor is seldom detained for long. The road begins to climb almost immediately after entering Switzerland. Watches should be turned back one hour. The visitor is recovering the hour he lost when crossing the Brenner Pass into Italy. Many Swiss flags are displayed along the way. The flag is solid red with a white cross in the center. (The exact opposite of the Red Cross emblem). It's an imposing sight fluttering against the deep blue sky. The air is crystal clear, and Alpine breezes have already cooled things off.

The hills make a beautiful panorama, but these are still only the foothills. We don't *really* start climbing until after Lugano.

Switzerland is divided into 22 cantons. Each canton is relatively independent, much more so than most European provinces or the American states. The first canton on our route is Ticino, the only Italian-speaking canton in Switzerland. Lugano, the next stop, is its largest city. The Swiss cantons are divided into four different language areas. The largest is the German-speaking portion. It consists of 16 cantons, including the canton of Lucerne, where we are headed. It also includes the commercial and banking cities of Basel and Zurich. The next largest is the French-speaking portion, consisting of five cantons. Its important cities are Geneva and Lausanne. There is also the Italian-speaking portion, Ticino, which makes the third. The capital city of Ticino is the town of Bellinzona, which lies just ahead. There is a fourth language spoken in Switzerland: Romansch, a language coming directly from Latin. It is spoken in the easternmost canton of Graubunden, even though the dominant language of that canton is German. These four languages are all officially recognized by the Swiss government.

Soon a sparkling Alpine lake appears up ahead. This is Lake Lugano, and it's shaped like a shoestring, as are most Swiss lakes. It can't be seen all at once, only in segments. Nestling peacefully along the lake front is the town of Lugano. It's a perfect place to take a rest stop and to get the feel of Swiss town life.

The air is cool, fresh, and a bit nippy, though the sun is warm. In the town itself everything's as neat as a pin. It looks something like a big watch, with everything ticking away in perfect order. Along the lake-front are parks and gardens, abrim with fountains and flowers. It's enough to make a visitor settle down permanently. The prices here are quite high. The people live well, about as well as in America, and the visitor pays for it. But it's not at all unreasonable, especially for items like clothing and wood carvings. Chocolate is also a specialty in Switzerland. Extraordinary care and effort are lavished in making it.

The highway proceeds through the town of Lugano, zigzagging up the slopes on the St. Gotthard Road. These are still in the foothills, and traffic moves along briskly. About 20 miles north of Lugano is the town of Bellinzona. The castles up on the hills around the town were part of the medieval fortifications, and they date from the time when this area was controlled by the German-speaking cantons to the north. The three castles are named after three of these cantons: Uri, Schwyz, and Unterwalden.

Now we start our long and harrowing climb up to the St. Gotthard Pass. At first there are moderately steep and craggy hills on either side of the road. A stream runs alongside the road to the left. Occasionally, one comes across hikers walking in single file, with their lederhosen, long stockings, rucksacks on their back, alpine hats with a feather in them, and knotty walking sticks. The tiny stream on the left is the Ticino River, after which the canton is named.

Just beyond the town of Airolo lies the entrance to the famous St. Gotthard Railroad Tunnel. The tunnel is 9½ miles long, one of the longest in Europe. It was finished back in 1882, and is used today by some of the heaviest electric locomotives in the world — 240 tons or more. The trains need that much power to pull them up the steep grades. In the winter, the road is snowed in, and automobiles and trucks are loaded onto flatcars and taken through the tunnel to get to the other side. We see the other end of the tunnel later, at the town of Göschenen.

After Airolo the road starts climbing in earnest, winding up the mountainside. The vegetation gradually thins out as the elevation increases. Trees give way to shrubs. Then only grass remains, plus a hardy evergreen or two. The visitor is thankful for the new highway when he catches a glimpse of the old one. It's off to the right, below. It takes twice as long to get up the mountain as the new one does. From time to time the bus turns a corner, and the whole valley opens up below, all at once. Further up, the road climbs higher and higher. More and more of the valley comes into view. It's possible to see almost all the way back to Bellinzona. Soon the road nears the top. There's one spot just before the top of the pass where banks of snow are piled up on the left hand side of the road. It's a nice place to stop for a few minutes — perhaps even for a snowball fight.

Less than a mile later, the road reaches the top of the St. Gotthard Pass. The elevation is well over a mile high at this point, 6,915 feet to be exact. The temperature is in the 50's. It's absolutely quiet on top, except for the soft tinkling of cowbells coming from the mountainside below. Nearby are two small lakes. The enormous rockpile that dominates the scene is Mt. Prosa. The pass is named for the old St. Gotthard Chapel, built in the Middle Ages in honor of a German bishop. Then, abruptly, the road begins its descent. From time to time, one sees squads of Swiss soldiers out on maneuvers. At one point the emblem of a bull with a ring in its nose is painted on a rocky cliff to the left. The colors are yellow and black. It is the coat of arms of the canton of Uri. The road has just left the Italian-speaking canton of Ticino and is now in German-speaking Uri. The road signs will be in German from now on until we cross the border into France.

The stream to the right is the Gams River, after which the valley is named. The road is steeper and slower now; in fact it's the original road. The newer highway coming up the mountain has been finished only to the top of the pass. From here on down, the original one must be used. Fortunately, this road isn't nearly as winding as the old one on the other side. There is evidence of construction work on the new highway from time to time. Everything looks bare and rocky, but a soft blanket of grass seems to tame the rugged slopes. A lovely stream can be seen splashing its way along the valley floor. It flows over rocks and waterfalls, making for an endless succession of shapes and patterns.

Next we reach Andermatt, the "cross-roads of the Alps." Several valleys branch off it. In winter, this is spectacular ski country. After Andermatt, the road squeezes through the Schollenen Gorge. The best way to see it is on the old road. The new highway bypasses it completely by using tunnels. On either side of the road, steep granite walls head straight up. They're perfectly smooth. These walls kept traffic from moving through the gorge until the 1200's, when the first road was hacked through the mountainside. In fact, the route we're following dates from that time. Soon it passes the Devil's Bridge, dating from 1830. Legend has it that the original bridge was built by the devil, who used to stalk this whole area. Nearby is a shimmering waterfall. Then a large cross appears in the side of the rock to the right. The inscription is in Russian. It honors the Russian soldiers under General Suvorov who forced their way through these rocks back in 1799 in order to try to help the Allies defeat the French. Unfortunately, they didn't make it on time.

After some more twisting and turning the road reaches Göschenen. Off to the right a valley opens up and one can see railroad tracks running into the town. By following the tracks backwards, the visitor can see them emerge from the St. Gotthard Railroad Tunnel. The road becomes a bit more even now, and follows the Reuss River, which continues north until it finally flows into Lake Lucerne. The next town is Wassen, a resort area in summer and winter. Often there are Swedish or Dutch students on outings around here in the summertime. They pitch tents on the field just outside of town.

About a mile outside of Wassen is a reservoir. At the end of the reservoir, just after the road rounds a bend to the right, is a dam with a spectacular waterfall. It is visible only for a split second. The sunlight plays on the water as it plunges over the rocks, giving off an eerie light show with a myriad of colors. This is the *Pfaffensprung* (Priest's Jump). An old legend tells of a monk whose indiscretion with a young village lass caused a scandal in the town nearby. The monk couldn't face the outraged citizens and leaped over the waterfall to his doom.

The road follows the Reuss River down the mountainside, through one valley after another until it comes to Altdorf (Old Village in German). This is the capital of the canton of Uri, and like so many other spots around here, it goes all the way back to the original founding of the Swiss Confederation. In the Middle Ages, Switzerland was nothing but a loose collection of cantons which officially belonged to the Holy Roman Empire. The cantons enjoyed relative independence, so most of the Swiss didn't mind the arrangement. But when Rudolf of Hapsburg became the Holy Roman Emperor and began the long Hapsburg dynasty, he took his sovereignty over the Swiss cantons a great deal more seriously. He and his successors appointed "bailiffs" to collect taxes and administer justice. They became so unpopular that a series of revolts broke out, subsiding only when Swiss independence was recognized by the Hapsburgs in the Treaty of Perpetual Peace (1474). In the meantime, the three famous "forest cantons" (*Waldstätten* in German) of Uri, Schwyz, and Unterwald had joined together. A pact directed against the Hapsburgs was signed on August 1, 1291, and the date is still the Swiss national holiday.

The legend of William Tell provides a picture of these times. Tell was a hardy Swiss archer who refused to pay reverence to the Austrian coat of arms: a hat on a stick. Outraged, the bailiff Gessler had Tell's son tied to a tree and placed an apple on the boy's head. He commanded Tell to shoot an arrow into the apple from 50 paces. If the arrow missed the apple, Gessler would kill the boy – unless Tell's arrow did the job first. Tell aimed his crossbow, drew the cord, and the arrow shot straight to the mark. The boy was saved. Later Tell killed Gessler on a lonely road in Küssnacht, a small town which lies ahead.

Altdorf is a small and colorful place. The road comes to the center of town, then turns left. At this point if one looks out the window to the right, a statue of William Tell can be seen standing in the square. It is said to be an exact picture of the way he looked.

Off to the left is Lake Uri, actually an arm of Lake Lucerne. Our route follows it as far as Brunnen. On the way, the road passes through six tunnels. After the fifth tunnel, a lovely vista opens up on the left. The grassy slope on the other side of the lake is the historic field of Rütli. This is the place where the original alliance between the three "forest cantons" was signed in 1291. The field is now a national shrine.

From Brunnen we head through Schwyz, where the original document drawn up on the field of Rütli is preserved. The town of Schwyz is the capital of the canton of Schwyz. It is from this name that the words "Swiss" and "Switzerland" come. (In German, *Schwyz* is pronounced "Shvuts", sounding the "u" as in "put".) The Swiss national flag derives from the coat of arms of Schwyz. The coat of arms is a red banner with a white cross in one corner. The Swiss flag puts the cross in the center. The Swiss flag is prominently displayed in every major Swiss city.

In medieval and early modern times, many European kings hired Swiss mercenaries to fight their wars. Most of them came from Schwyz. After making a fortune in battle, they came back home and built mansions which still stand. On the road leading out of Schwyz is the *Bundesbriefarchiv* (Archives of the Federal Charters), where the original documents founding the Swiss Confederation are kept.

Soon a small lake appears on the right. It is Lake Lauerzer. Later, a larger one appears, also on the right. That's Lake Zug, after which the canton of Zug is named. Then the town of *Küssnacht,* where William Tell slew the wicked Gessler. Lake Lucerne soon appears on the left. As soon as it does, a little chapel comes into view, between the road and the lake. It honors poor Queen Astrid of Belgium, who was driving along this road back in 1935, planning to spend a pleasant vacation in Lucerne. Suddenly the royal car veered off the road to the right, and plowed into a tree. She was killed. A cross (to the right) indicates the site of the accident.

The lake disappears for a few miles, but then comes back into view. Ahead and slightly to the left is Lucerne. The road heads straight into town, along the quays of the Reuss River. The old covered bridge, which crosses the river, is called the *Kapellbrücke* (Chapel Bridge).

Lucerne: Switzerland at a Glance

Switzerland at a glance: that's exactly what Lucerne is. The traveler has seen a bit of Switzerland already, and has a more than passing acquaintance with the Alps. But much of it seems to come together in this little lakefront town of 70,000 people. There's the Switzerland of the common folk — full of alpine houses with sloping roofs and windowboxes dense with flowers, rolling pastureland at the base of the mountains, goatherds with their six-foot horns, and dozens of clinking cowbells off in the distance.

Switzerland can also boast of its ultra-modern industries — especially the manufacture of precision watches. Watches can be purchased here for about half the U.S. price. The major stores are on the Schwanenplatz (Swans Square), the big square in the center of town. Bucherer's (Bucherer and Rolex watches) and Gübelin's (Omega) are the largest. The Swiss are very fussy about the quality of their watches. The Swiss government has a complicated set of quality-control procedures, and regularly tests and rates the products of the major watch-making firms. The highest category is that of "chronometer". A watch which has "Officially Certified Chronometer" on it has been through the testing mill and is about the best one money can buy. It's not supposed to gain or lose more than a few seconds a day.

The Swiss unit of currency is the franc. It's usually written "Fr.S.", and is worth about the same as the German mark: 28¢ or about 4 to the dollar. The Swiss franc is divided into 100 centimes. There are 3 centime coins, 10, 20, and 50. The 50 centime coin has "½ franc" on it. Swiss bills are rather odd-looking. For one thing, they're huge, and impossible to lose. The 5 and 10 franc notes are more or less conventional, but the 20, 50, and 100 franc notes make the wallet bulge. Italian lire and travelers' checks can be exchanged for Swiss francs either at the hotel, any of the banks downtown, or at the train station. All these places offer about the same rate of exchange. The large stores do too. In fact, the stores sometimes give a better rate than the banks in order to attract business. Long-distance phone calls or telegrams can be taken care of at the main Post Office downtown, which is located across the street from the railroad station. Most people in Lucerne speak English, so there is little difficulty in finding one's way around.

Switzerland is Europe's most international country. In fact, apart from national traditions, legends, and heroes like Wiliam Tell, Switzerland might strike the visitor as little more than a sort of economic junction point for the rest of Europe. Switzerland is the nerve center of international finance, business, and politics. Not surprisingly, the most important international organizations have their headquarters here. It's the place to be if one happens to be negotiating a treaty with some country, or setting up a big international conglomerate, or looking for a place to stash away a few million for safekeeping. The League of Nations was located in Switzerland, and the International Red Cross was founded here in 1863. It is impossible to list all of the international agreements concluded in Geneva.

Ever since 1815, the country has been politically neutral in international affairs, and this has enabled it to ride out so many of the storms that have swept across Europe. But it wasn't always that way. Swiss history is full of the same invasions, wars, and wranglings that have beset most European countries. The Romans first invaded the country; they occupied it back in the days of Julius Caesar. Their name for the area was "Helvetia". The name stuck. In fact, the official name of the country is the *Confederatio Helvetica,* Latin for "Helvetian Confederation". The expression appears on Swiss coins, and the "CH" which is seen on Swiss-owned automobiles comes from this same expression. *Helvetia* also appears on Swiss postage stamps. The Swiss always use Latin for official purposes. With three major languages operating in the country, the government couldn't very well put just one of them on currency and stamps.

Switzerland has a land area of almost 16,000 square miles, somewhat larger than Belgium. Its population, however, is smaller than Belgium's. It has about 6 million people. Swiss citizenship is almost as highly prized as Roman citizenship was in New Testament times. A great many Europeans would love to possess Swiss citizenship and enjoy the high standard of living. But to do so, they must first be admitted to membership in a local community, and that isn't easy. This reveals how strong local and regional feelings are in Switzerland. But it's more than just a feeling, it's part of the political structure which Switzerland has had ever since the beginning: the canton system. The Swiss cantons are something like the American states, except that they are much more independent of the central government. In fact the central government is dependent on them. The mountains divide the country into a checkerboard of different regions and local communities. Each canton is jealous of its sovereignty. It passes its own laws, supports its own schools, and has its own unique political customs. For example, some of the mountain cantons still hold open-air meetings where public issues are debated and then voted on by everyone present.

Each canton has its own capital and officially recognizes one of the three major languages of Switzerland. It gives semi-official status to either the Protestant or Catholic Church. The majority of the Swiss are Protestant (53%), but many are Catholic. Most of the French-speaking cantons are Protestant, while the German-speaking cantons are mainly Catholic. The Italian-speaking canton of Ticino is Catholic. The canton of Lucerne is German-speaking and Catholic. In fact, the city of Lucerne was a mainstay in the Catholic Counter-Reformation. The Jesuits opened an important college in the city, and built the *Jesuitenkirche* (Jesuit Church), which stands next to the river. It's a magnificent Baroque structure.

The capital city of the country is Berne, some 50 miles west of Lucerne. The name "Berne" comes from *Bärn,* an old German word for bear. Up until recently, women were not allowed to vote in national elections. Some have attributed Swiss political stability to that fact alone. But the ladies do make their opinions felt. They are responsible for laws against gambling and drunkenness. Switzerland has about the lowest proportion of alcoholics of any country in Europe.

The Swiss are a sturdy people, rugged and independent. They have to be if they are to survive the rugged environment. They're fair-minded, hard-working, sober, and prudent. In many ways they're rather like the British. They don't get overly excited about anything, and yet they can hardly be called lazy. Their industriousness has made Switzerland one of the most prosperous nations in the world, and this in spite of obvious handicaps. Switzerland doesn't have many natural resources, except hydroelectric power. Because of the mountains, agriculture is difficult and sparse. Barely a fifth of the population are farmers, and even that figure is declining. But the Swiss make up for it in manufacturing, especially in precision instruments and textiles. Watches, clocks, diesel engines, locomotives, optical instruments, and steel and aluminum plants are the largest industries. Swiss clothing is well made and relatively inexpensive. Sweaters and scarves are good buys in the stores downtown. But above all, the Swiss are precise; they're best at small, painstaking jobs, like diamond-cutting, watchmaking, or wood-carving.

Switzerland has also been an important financial center of Europe since early in the Middle Ages. Switzerland was the crossroads of the great trading routes of Europe. This meant that the Swiss could collect taxes and control the flow of goods in and out of the country. Great financiers arose, accumulating vast amounts of capital. With it, they sponsored local industries, and that has been the pattern ever since. Today Swiss bankers practically control the economy of Europe. They are the "gnomes of Zurich" that the British government continually reproaches. The Swiss franc is backed by gold, 100%. It's a diamond-hard currency. Behind it is an economy which is extremely stable. And behind that are people who get up early in the morning, work hard all day, and go to bed early at night.

Activities in Lucerne can be varied and exciting. No visitor will want to miss a cable car ride up to the top of Mt. Pilatus. The trip takes about 3½ hours. Since it can be quite cold on top, it is a good idea to bring a sweater or jacket along. About a half-hour outside of Lucerne is the hamlet of Alpnachstad, at the base of the mountain. Nearby is the station for the cog railway, from which the tracks wind up the mountainside. The trip up to the top is a lesson in geography. The vegetation changes from thick fir trees to low shrubs to Alpine pastures to bare rock — all in 45 minutes. One doesn't see much at first, but when the trees start thinning out, the whole valley comes into view. For every two feet forward, the car moves up one foot in elevation. It is the steepest cog railway in the world. High up in the mountains are herds of cows grazing in the sun. Their bells can be heard for miles. Then it becomes very steep, and the tracks run over bare rock. Occasionally the car passes through tunnels cut into the rock. As it approaches the top, the car no longer moves forward, but almost straight up.

The area round the summit is called Pilatus-Kulm, with an elevation of almost 7,000 feet. There is a huge round building at the top. It's a station, and it also has observation platforms with binoculars, information offices, and a very good restaurant. The other building is a hotel. Aside from these two, there's nothing up here — except a view of the whole of Lake Lucerne and a good part of the rest of Switzerland.

There are several things to do on top of the mountain. Signs point to various "walks" around and through the big rock at the peak. They are labeled by the amount of time they take. (The "8 minute" walk actually takes about 15 minutes.) Each walk passes through tunnels with openings cut out of the stone. Way down below are lakes and towns, spread out like a map.

There are two parts to the trip down. First, there is a large cable car, holding about 25 people. That's the harrowing part, so it's nice to have other people around. Not that it isn't safe. There has never been a mishap up here. There was one a few years ago in the French Alps, but that was caused by an airplane that flew too low and cut the cable.

At this point it's easy to understand why the Alps in general and Mt. Pilatus in particular have been the object of so much dread and supersition. This was especially true in the days before cable cars, when one had to see the mountain from a distance. It was said, for example, that the ghost of Pontius Pilate haunted the mountain, and that the Devil himself would visit here from time to time. Hence the name

"Pilatus", Latin for Pilate. An old proverb explains how to tell the weather by looking up at the mountain.

> When Pilate hides his head (in clouds), sunshine below will spread.
> When Pilate's head is bare, of rain you'd best beware.

Halfway down the mountainside, the passengers get off and transfer to smaller cable cars, which hold four people apiece. The mountain begins to level off. Occasionally a team of hikers can be seen below, with their inevitable rucksacks and walking sticks. Then the cable car reaches the bottom, at the town of Kriens. It's just a 15-minute ride from Kriens back into Lucerne.

Among the most impressive sights in Lucerne is the Kapellbrücke. (Chapel Bridge). This old covered bridge, with the stone water tower in the middle, dates from the Middle Ages and was used to defend the town against invaders. Inside are 110 painted panels showing the history of Lucerne. Nearby, little swan families paddle single file along the river.

There's another old bridge just up the river from the Kapellbrücke. This is the Spreuerbrücke, or Mill Bridge, and is almost as old as the first one. The panels inside are about the plagues that wracked the city in the 17th century. They are called the "Dance of Death". In the middle of the bridge a tiny chapel juts out over the water. It is just large enough for a priest and altar-boy to stand inside.

Also worth investigating is the great "Panorama". It's a large round building, and the whole inside wall is covered by an enormous painting showing the French army marching through Switzerland in 1871. The painter was Castres, and it took him almost 12,000 squre feet to make his point. The Panorama is located on Löwenstrasse (Lion Street), which begins at the lake, just one long block from the Schwanenplatz. Admission is about a franc (28¢).

A block past the Panorama on Löwenstrasse is the Löwendenkmal (Lion Monument). This is certainly among the most impressive sights in Lucerne. The best time to see it is in the evening, when it's illuminated. A huge figure of a lion is carved from the side of the rock. The lion has been stabbed with a spear and lies dying. The monument honors the Swiss Guards who protected King Louis XVI and Queen Marie Antoinette of France during the Revolution. The Guards were killed defending the royal family when a mob stormed the Tuileries Palace in Paris in 1792. What is most moving about the lion is the expression on its face. It is a picture of nobility mixed with tragedy. The warrior has fought to the very end, giving his life in the service of duty. Now he lies dying. He suffers, but without resentment or self-pity. Instead he

turns to face his final challenge: death. He does so bravely and on equal terms. Yet there is just a hint of pathos on his face.

The Verkehrshaus (Museum of Transport and Communications) has an old steamboat from the days of "Fulton's folly", and one of the first cog-railway locomotives. There are a lot of other specimens of rail, road, and air transportation, along with old telephones and telegraphs. To get there, walk a few hundred yards along the lakefront from the Schwanenplatz. It's two francs (50¢) to get in.

Also found near Lucerne is a museum in honor of Richard Wagner. It's housed in the building where Wagner composed some of his most important operas, and where the young philospher Nietzsche visited him on weekends. Many original scores and other mementoes are still preserved. A kind of reverent hush surrounds the place. The house is built on a promontory out on the lake near the village of Tribschen, a bit outside of Lucerne. The museum can be reached by launch over the lake (fare: 4 francs). The trip is a nice excursion in its own right.

An evening at the Stadtkeller provides an ending to a visit in Lucerne as nothing else can. The Stadtkeller is an old inn where the best of Swiss cooking is served, particularly the Swiss specialty: cheese fondue. Fondue is a cheese sauce served in an open casserole. The casserole is kept warm by a gas flame. The whole thing is put down on the table, piping hot. There are baskets full of little chunks of bread, which are speared with a long fork, and then dipped into the cheese. It's a delicious treat. Entertainment is also provided, usually in the form of Swiss folk music and dancing.

In the morning, one last look at Mount Pilatus and then off for Paris.

Across the Provinces of France to Paris

The trip from Lucerne to Paris is the last big one on our itinerary. We go through the rest of Switzerland to the north, proceed through the city of Basel, cross the French border at Saint Louis, continue northwest across one province after another, and then stop for lunch at Langres. A few more hours to Paris. It's a day full of variety. The trip starts out in the foothills of the Alps, pauses for lunch way out in the French countryside, and ends with dinner in the most glamorous city of Europe.

The town and lake of Lucerne recede in the distance. Ahead are small towns and low-lying hills. The lake off to the right, about 15 miles outside Lucerne, is Lake Sempach. Just beyond it is the town of Sursee, a sleepy hamlet full of Gothic towers and timbered houses. Our route passes quickly through one corner of the canton of Aargau, which is German-speaking and Protestant. It's named after the River Aare. But by the time we reach the river, we're in another canton, Solothurn, which is also German-speaking but Catholic. The largest town we see in Solothurn is Olten on the River Aare, and the road crosses the river right in the center of town.

Then the road enters the last canton, Basel, which is German-speaking and Protestant. Basel is one of those cantons that is divided into two parts. There's the District of Basel, whose capital, Liestal, lies on our route. Basel, a city of 200,000 people, is the second largest city in Switzerland, after Zurich. It's an international trading and banking center of the first rank. Here our route once again passes the Rhine — this time several hundred miles upstream. The Rhine is Switzerland's most important waterway, and Basel the country's only port. Most goods being exported from Switzerland are loaded onto ships in Basel and leave the country via the Rhine.

Basle goes back to Roman times. In the Middle Ages it was ruled by a prince-bishop. Several famous religious controversies took place here. The most important was the Council of Basel, which met from 1431 to 1448. This council was not altogether unlike what's going on today in some quarters of the Catholic world. The Pope and many of the bishops simply couldn't agree on some issues. The result was that the bishops set up their own Pope, Felix V. This began the Great Schism, when two Popes claimed to be the Vicar of Christ, each one excommunicating the other. Finally, Felix V renounced his claim to the papacy and peace was restored. But religious controversy flared up again during the Reformation, when Basel joined the Protestant side. It has remained Protestant ever since.

A few miles beyond Basel is the border town of Saint Louis. Part of the town is in Switzerland, part of it in France. The border is a spot along the main street where two flagpoles stand peacefully side by side. On one, the flag is Swiss, on the other it's French. We're completely out of the mountains now. From here on into Paris the trip is over fairly smooth plains and gently rolling hills. The road is straight and even, and is typical of most French secondary highways. Unlike Germany or Italy, the French don't have many Autobahns or Austostradas. Some American travelers regard the French highway system as primitive. That's unfair and it misses the point. The French are in fact excellent road builders. The reason France doesn't have a brand-new highway system is that it started building highways before the rest of Europe. Its highway system was constructed in the 19th century, when the Germans and Italians were rattling over dirt roads. The French roads were laid out like the Treviso-to-Venice highway: straight and tree-lined. But the French paid a price for jumping the gun on the rest of Europe. All their energies and capital were put into the 19th century highway system. Now, they need the capital for other things. Besides, France has the best secondary road system in the world. It would be somewhat of a waste to put millions into big highways. But they are making a start. There's a fast "Autoroute" going into Paris; it's part of the Autoroute from Paris to Marseilles.

There isn't too much going on right away. In fact, it hardly seems like France at first. Many of the towns have German names: Tagsdorf, Wittersdorf, Altkirche, Ballersdorf, etc. This is the southern tip of the old province of Alsace. Alsace and Lorraine are two provinces which have been passed back and forth between the French and Germans every since the days of Charlemagne. They were part of Charlemagne's empire. But after his death, his domains were divided into three parts and given to his three grandsons. Charles the Bald took the French-speaking lands to the west; Ludwig the German took the German-speaking lands to the east. Lothair took the part in the middle, which was made up of both French and German-speaking people. This fateful agreement was made at the Treaty of Verdun in 843 A.D. The French-speaking kingdom to the west made sense; it was the origin of modern France. The German-speaking kingdom to the east also made sense; it eventually became Germany. But the polyglot kingdom in the middle brought nothing but trouble. The French and the Germans fought over it from that time on. It eventually became the provinces of Alsace and Lorraine. (The word "Lorraine" comes from Lotharingia, and this in turn comes from the name of Charlemagne's grandson who first ruled it: Lothair.) The Germans took the two provinces in 1871 and held them until the end of the First World War, when a referendum was held and the people voted to become a part of France again. But many of them still speak German and have German names.

Twenty miles farther along, the town names become French: Valdieu, Chaveannes-sur-L'Etang, Foussemagne, and so on. At Valdieu the road crosses the canal that links the Rhône and the Rhine Rivers. France has an extensive canal system. The importance of waterways for commercial transport is decreasing, as trucks and superhighways take over. But it was once otherwise. Europe as a whole is laced by a vast network of canals. They were dug out in the 17th and 18th centuries to

carry goods from one region to another. They formed the main transport arteries of the Continent. Now, with their diminishing importance,
the canals are not so well kept up, though they are ideal for rowboats and
romantic weekends.

The first real city on our route is Belfort, with a population of about
50,000. It's an industrial town of spinning and weaving mills. It was
here that the French General Denfert-Rochereau withstood a siege by the
German army back in 1870. He became a hero overnight. In Paris, the
battle is commemorated by a huge statue of a lion in red sandstone. It's
the "Lion of Belfort". The statue stands in the middle of a large square,
the Place Denfert-Rochereau.

After Belfort our route continues through the countryside. Small
villages pop up suddenly and then disappear. They're just a set of signs
with a few houses and a parish church wedged in between: "Port-sur-
Saone," "Combeaufontaine," "Fayl-Billot," etc. Fifteen miles after
Fayl-Billot, the road crosses the River Marne, one of the Armageddons
of World War I. Then the road comes to Langres, an ideal place for a
luncheon stop. It sits proudly on top of a hill, commanding the whole
valley, around it. In the Middle Ages it was a powerful stronghold, and
some of the old fortifications are still standing. The French philosopher
Diderot came from Langres.

The highway continues west from Langres. Another mountain stronghold looms up ahead. It's Chaumont-en-Bassigny, full of tiny streets and
turreted houses. The U.S. Army had its headquarters in this town
during World War I. A great deal of fighting took place north of here at
the Battle of the Marne. Most of the trenches have been filled in, the
debris has been picked up, and the countryside has settled back into its
peaceful slumber. Seventeen miles outside Chaumont the highway skips
through the village of Colombey-les-Deux-Eglises (Colombey of the Two
Churches), the family estate of the late General Charles de Gaulle.

Next through Bar-sur-Aube, where big trade fairs were held in the
Middle Ages. Now, they sell wheat and Vichy water. The highway
crosses the River Seine in the center of Troyes, an industrial town of
65,000 people. It's the largest city between Basel and Paris. Gothic
churches and ancient houses blend into the smokestacks. A bit later the
road skirts around the town of Sens. Off to the left stands the
Cathedral of Saint-Etienne in Sens. It's the oldest Gothic cathedral in
France, begun in the 1100's.

Soon after Sens, the road joins a larger highway and traffic moves
along briskly. A little further on and we reach the huge forest of
Fontainebleau. In the middle of it stands the Palace of Fontainebleau.

It goes back to the Middle Ages, but was rebuilt by the lusty, fun-loving King Francis I back in the early 1500's. Francis I loved only two things: hunting and the ladies — though not necessarily in that order. He has left his stamp all over the area. Later, several of his successors added on to the palace. King Louis XIV once entertained his mistresses here in grand style. Napoleon and Josephine used it. Today it is a museum. Nearby, on the edge of the woods, is the town of Barbizon. This area became a popular retreat for writers and artists in the 19th century. Here began the "Barbizon School" of painting, which is characterized by a return to realism from the earlier romanticism of the 19th century.

The rest of the way into Paris is on a fast Autoroute. Soon the signs point to Versailles on the left and Orly Airport on the right. The Eiffel Tower appears in the distance, somewhat to the left of the highway. The Autoroute enters the city from the south, through the Porte d'Orleans, one of the major traffic gateways of the city. From here it's just a few minutes to the center of Paris.

The best way to begin a week in Paris is to walk through the city in the evening. A good place to start is Boulevard St. Michel, lined with fashion boutiques and outdoor cafés. From there it's a short distance across the Seine, for a look at Notre Dame, which is flood-lit at night, then on to Place de la Concorde, where the U. S. embassy is located, and on down to the Champs-Elysées, the most famous boulevard in the world. At the end of the Champs-Elysées is the Arc de Triomphe, which is also flood-lit. Parisians are proud of their monuments. They want them to be seen day and night.

The Palais de Chaillot provides the climax of the evening. It's not that the palace itself is all that important. What's important are the fountains in front. They are not as graceful nor as artistic as the Tivoli fountains in Rome. They're something else: a huge spectacle of light and water. The fountains are not jet-streams or trickling spouts, but enormous geysers, shooting tons of water up in the air. There are big spotlights down below, shining through the spray and foam. Just across the river is the Eiffel Tower, all aglow with different colored lights.

This is Paris summed up in a single scene. The visitor can feel it all at once. Everything here is intense, extravagant, monumental.

France: Some Facts and Figures

France is the one country of Europe Americans are probably most familiar with. French is the most studied foreign language in the U.S., and this puts American students in a position to get to know Paris fairly well by themselves.

The most striking feature about France is its bigness. In land area it's the largest country in Western Europe. It covers 212,000 sq. miles, making it about the size of Texas. Half of the land is taken up with agriculture. In fact, until recently agriculture was practically the sole basis of the French economy. For many people it still is. A quarter of the population is still engaged in it. Unlike England, Germany, and Austria, France is self-sufficient in wheat and other staple foods and no one has to be told about French wine. It's exported to every corner of the globe. One peculiarity about French agriculture is worth noting. Unlike the U. S., most French farm lands are owned by the families that work on them. The average homestead covers less than 25 acres. Huge agricultural combines are practically unknown. 80% of French farms have no hired help; the sturdy French farmers do all the chores themselves. This makes French farming less efficient, no doubt, but it suits the character of the French people.

Though France is the largest country of Western Europe in land area, its population is only 50 million — smaller than that of Great Britain or West Germany. Like Italy, its people are spread fairly evenly all through the country. There aren't too many large cities in France. Aside from Marseilles, Paris is the only city in France with more than a million people. Most of the people live in medium-sized cities like Tours and Rouen, or in smaller towns and villages.

It's not hard to understand why agriculture is such an important part of French life. The country is fairly flat and even. Much of the soil is lush and fertile, and extremely well suited for farming. A good 40% of the land can be cultivated — and it is, every bit of it. But there are other aspects of the French economy. There is iron ore and coal in the east, near the German border, and French textiles are the most famous in Europe. The country exports everything from silk to hopsacking.

The aircraft industry is also very important. It was French fighter planes that did the job for the Israelis during the six-day war in 1967. France's automobile industry exports almost 800,000 cars a year. They're all over the U.S., elbowing over the VW's and MG's. They include the Peugeot, the Renault, the Simca, and of course, the Citroën.

Almost everything about France is unique. Unlike many European countries, such as Germany, Austria, and Italy, France has had relatively stable boundaries throughout its history. France didn't have to be "re-united" in the 19th century. It had not been fragmented into tiny states to begin with. France doesn't have any obvious geographical barriers to break it up into separate regions. It's mostly flat and even; it belongs together. This gave the French people a feeling of national identity from the very beginning. For this reason, France didn't experience the sort of nationalist upheavals which Germany or Italy endured when achieving national unity in the 19th and 20th centuries. The French solved that problem long ago. This left the French free to get on with other things.

France was occupied by the Romans back before the time of Christ. Julius Caesar was responsible for conquering the whole region, and his *Gallic Wars* gives a vivid account of his expeditions. In his day the land was called "Gaul", and the expression "Gallic" is still used to refer to anything French. Whenever the Romans occupied an area, it meant more than just having a few legions around to keep order. It meant that the Latin language, together with Roman legal and political institutions, came along with them. This was especially true of France. The French language is one of several European languages derived from Latin. French legal practice stems from Roman law. There are many Roman ruins still left in France, and some of them are in Paris. One is at the Abbey of Cluny, where traces of Roman baths can be seen. Paris also has an old Roman arena, the Arènes de Lutèce.

The French are as unique as the land they live on. They're incorrigible individualists, and even their individualism is unique. It's not exactly the rugged and sturdy individualism of the Tyrolese in Innsbruck. Nor is it quite the sober and serious sort of individualism in evidence around Lucerne. It's an individualism which combines seriousness with gaiety, tradition with radical innovation. If anything, French individualism is a paradox. For example, French national unity has seldom been seriously threatened by separatist movements based on regional loyalties. But it has been threatened from time to time by the idiosyncracies of different individuals, each with his own ideas about the destiny of his country.

The seating arrangement in the French National Assembly, for example, is altogether different from the seating arrangement in the British Parliament. In the latter, the Tories sit one one side of the room, glowering at the Laborites, who sit on the other. This encourages party solidarity, and puts a damper on any erratic displays of individualism. After all, when a deputy shares a bench with his colleagues in a political party, he tends to identify himself with their cause. All of his energies go into challenging the other side. In the French National

Assembly, on the other hand, the seats are arranged in a fan shape, much like the U. S. Congress. There is no center aisle. The psychological effect isn't difficult to guess. The sort of party solidarity familiar in the British Parliament simply doesn't exist. Each deputy is a party unto himself. He doesn't face an opposition on the other side of the room. All he realizes is that there is a deputy on his right and another on his left, and that he's squarely in the center. This makes him much more independent (not to say unpredictable) than his British counterpart. By the way, this is where the political terms "Left" and "Right" come from. They originally referred to the place where this or that deputy sat on the floor of the French National Assembly. The conservatives were seated on the right-hand side of the room, the liberals and radicals on the left and far-left sides respectively.

French individualism isn't something new. Francis I loved hunting, so he strewed the countryside with hunting chateaux. He ordered his soldiers to participate in mock wars while he sat back and enjoyed the spectacle. Sometimes these mock wars were all too real: battering rams, bows and arrows, and cannons were used. The casualties were real too. But then the king simply went in for military spectacles. And, of course, no one could complain. Louis XIV, the famous "Sun King," is the most important ruler in French history, next to Napoleon. Louis XIV thought of himself as a Roman conqueror, and for a long time he was. He won one victory after another, extending the boundaries of France to the northeast. He also patronized the great playwrights and artists of his day, including Molière, Racine, and Le Brun. But his greatest triumph was the huge palace of Versailles, just outside of Paris. It took 40 years to build, and cost a fortune. He had lived in Paris so long that he could no longer endure the sight of it. He wanted a different view outside his window, so he ordered the building of Versailles. And again, no one dared complain. The king was no more extravagant in his individualism than many of his countrymen. If they had had the chance, they would have done the same thing.

Then there is Napoleon. He kept the continent of Europe in constant flux for 15 years. After 10 years of spectacular exploits, he found himself at the helm of an empire stretching from the English Channel to the Russian border. But he was more than just a conqueror; he was a political genius of the first rank. He completely re-organized French law along Roman lines. The result was the famous *Code Napoléon,* which is still the basis of French legal institutions. In fact he re-organized practically every aspect of French life, from education to commerce, and centralized it all in Paris. He made the city a bureaucrat's paradise. Everything in France was from that time on controlled from Paris. This, to a large extent, was what the student riots of 1968 were all about. The students were demanding that the French educational system be decentralized, and that each university have greater control over its affairs. France is now beginning a process of political and economic decentralization which spells the end of the system Napoleon constructed in the early 1800's. But the very fact that his innovations persisted for so long a time reveals a great deal about the man who made them. Small wonder that France experiences periodic "Napoleon revivals" in fads and fashions, in spite of the fact that the Napoleonic system is being gradually dismantled. Napoleon's portrait, as a matter of fact, is still on the 100 franc bill.

Paris goes back to Roman times. The name comes from "Parisi", a Celtic tribe which lived along the Seine when the Romans conquered the area. The Romans called one of the towns Lutetia. Later it acquired the name of "Paris." At first it was a village on an island in the river. That island is now the most expensive real estate in the city. It's actually two islands: the Ile de la Cité and the Ile St-Louis. The Romans made a military stronghold of it, and made additions over the centuries. Wealthy Roman merchants settled in the town and built sumptuous mansions, parks, and public baths. The ruins of one of these baths have been discovered under the monastery of Cluny.

In the Middle Ages, Paris became a great trading center and a cosmopolitan city. Huge fairs were held here, attracting merchants from all over Europe. The University of Paris was founded in 1253, and soon became one of the largest and most influential of all European universities. For a time, its only rival was the University of Bologna. Today it stands on a par with Oxford and Cambridge. Paris really came into its own in early modern times. Such kings as Francis I and Louis XIV scattered magnificent palaces, public squares, and formal gardens throughout the city. Most of the palaces are still standing. The Louvre Museum is one of them. The visitor can see for himself what it was like to be a French monarch in these times. The largest and most impressive of all is Versailles.

For the moment, however, the visitor might keep all this in mind as he scouts around the city on his own, remembering especially the individualism of the French before wading into the traffic charade around the Place de la Concorde, where every Citroën stakes its reputation on outguessing and outmaneuvering all the others; or before trying to point out to a painter at Montmartre that his masterpiece really isn't worth more than 10 francs; or before expecting a waiter in a café to come bounding over to the table the minute a customer snaps his fingers. It's the better part of virtue and prudence to refrain from chewing out a French shopkeeper. After all, this is the land of Francis I, Louis XIV, and Napoleon, and in the veins of every Frenchman flows a bit of their blood. Each person is used to doing things his own way. If the visitor is tactful enough and willing to learn, Frenchmen may show him how to do things their way too.

Where to Find it in Paris

Paris is only half as large as London, but it's still the largest metropolis on the Continent. It's not always easy to get from one part of town to another. The telephone system is overburdened and sometimes unreliable. But the Parisians manage to survive. In fact they often joke about the city's problems.

The Paris métro (subway) is the best way to get around. Instead of buying individual tickets (cost: 1 franc), one does well to buy books of ten tickets. A "book" of ten tickets *(un carnet deuxième)* costs only 8 francs. The fare is always the same regardless of the distance traveled. The Paris métro is made up of 14 crisscrossing lines. Each line has two names, depending on the direction the train is heading. Going one way, the line is named for the last station in that direction. Going the other way, it's named for the last station in *that* direction. A métro map can be obtained at any of the outdoor newsstands. One often has to transfer once or twice to get to a given destination. Some stations have an ingenious electronic map. There are buttons for every stop. Push the desired one and the route that should be taken will be indicated by colored lights on the map. When the train comes in, one of the middle cars will be a different color from the others. This is the first-class car for which one is supposed to pay extra. The doors on the trains must be opened by hand, but they close automatically. Several lines now have rubber tires instead of steel wheels on the cars. It's amazing how silent they are.

Paris buses are much more scenic than the subway, but they also cost more. The tickets are identical to subway tickets, but their cost varies according to the distance. Each bus stop has a list showing where each bus goes. One has to use a map to read it.

Paris telephones, like Italian telephones, operate on tokens. Tokens can be bought in post offices and cafés. The system works exactly like

the one in Italy. Even the names of the tokens sound alike. In Italian it's *gettone,* in French *jeton.* Long-distance calls from Paris are very difficult to make, and may require a whole afternoon of waiting. It makes more sense to send telegrams. This can be done at any post office. To find a post office, look for the sign "P&T". Stamps may be purchased at *tabacs* — cafés which sell cigarettes, stamps, and other products of the government monopolies. Some cafés having these items display a red, cone-shaped marker outside.

By the time the visitor reaches Paris, he has become familiar with the Belgian franc and the Swiss franc. His task now is to get to know the French franc. It's worth 18¢ Five and a half to the dollar (written 5.5, 50 NF). Ten dollars is 55 NF. The franc is divided into 100 centimes. Five centimes are worth about a penny. There are banknotes for 5, 10, 100, and 500 francs. Coins go as low as 1 centime and as high as 5 francs. (The five-franc coin is called the "French silver dollar", now worth 90¢.) Caution: it's easy to become confused by rather cheap-looking coins that have "10 francs" or "20 francs" on them. Contrary to one's immediate expectations, they're not worth $2 or $4. They're worth 2¢ and 4¢. These coins go back to the days of the "old franc." There are even some coins which go back to the German occupation of the 1940's. Instead of "Liberty, Equality, Fraternity," these coins say "Work, Family, Fatherland." A picture of an axe takes the place of the Goddess of Liberty.

Suggested Activities in Paris

Just exploring Paris on foot is enough to keep anyone busy for many months. It's a city that pulls the visitor along, making him *feel* the excitement which so many generations of previous visitors have felt. But one has to start somewhere. The following suggestions will help the first-time visitor to share the Paris of the native Parisian. After the first few days he has already seen the essentials of Paris: its major neighborhoods, monuments, and famous boulevards. This is the time to sally forth on one's own and discover the Paris that belongs to oneself alone.

(1) *The Arch of Triumph* (métro-stop: Etoile) puts the visitor on top of some of the world's most expensive real estate. From the top (cost of entry: about 2.50 NF) one can look all the way down the Champs-Elysées to the Place de la Concorde and visualize the victory parade which marched down the Champs-Elysées at the Liberation of Paris in 1944. From the arch it is a short walk to the *Drugstore des Champs-Elysées,* the only place in Paris which sells corn on the cob. It's

one of five "American drugstores" in Paris.

(2) There are many excellent department stores in Paris. The best is *Aux Trois Quartiers*, next to the Madeleine church. Behind the Paris Opera are two larger and less expensive stores: the *Galéries Lafayette* and *Au Printemps*. All three stores can be reached on foot from the Opera métro station. Depending on the type and amount of one's purchase, it's possible to get a refund of the French sales tax by paying in travelers' checks. The discount can amount to as much as 20%.

(3) On any day except Monday one can visit the *rue Mouffetard*, the most colorful shopping street in Paris. Housewives and grocers have been haggling over prices here for 700 years. There are throngs in the street, buying everything from fine French cheeses to peaches. Two hours before lunch or dinner is the time to be there. (Métro stop: Censier-Daubenton)

(4) From the métro station Saint-Michel it's a short walk across the Seine to the Ile de la Cité. Through the big iron gate on the left is the *Sainte Chapelle*, built in the 1240's. It's famous for its exquisite stained-glass windows, the most beautiful blue and red glass this side of Chartres. Admission: about 1 franc.

(5) The *Louvre* is easy to find, and is the most renowned museum on the Continent. The building is a good ten blocks long and has its own métro station. Just a short walk away, on the Place de la Concorde, is the Jeu de Paume museum. The Jeu de Paume features lovely examples of impressionist painting from the early 20th century. Both museums are closed on Tuesdays. On Sundays the entry charge is suspended.

(6) One can follow the footsteps of Renoir, Picasso, and generations of American expatriate painters by walking up the incredibly steep stairs to *Montmartre*. (Métro: Anvers) Montmartre is really a tiny village, removed from the clamor of Paris, and is a perfect place to spend a relaxed afternoon. It is pleasant to browse among the paintings on display in the central square, to sit down at one of the cafés, and to watch painters daubing away.

(7) Bookstalls are an important part of the Parisian landscape. Some have unusual items, including rare first editions. The best browsing areas are along the quays of the Seine (especially around Notre Dame) and in the tiny streets just east of the Place Saint-Michel.

(8) Café-sitting is also an important pastime in Paris. Near métro station Saint-Germain-des-Près are several of the best. The customer can stay at the café as long as he likes. The price of a glass of wine includes the right to relax and observe other people for a while. Most visitors

wind up staying much longer than they had planned. In Paris, taking it easy in a café is considered an activity all by itself. The waiter would be insulted if someone bolted in, gulped down his drink, slapped a franc or two on the table, and dashed out.

(9) Gothic architecture buffs and those who just like excitement should return to Notre Dame for a more extended visit. (Metro-stop: Saint-Michel.) For about 1 franc, one can climb up the 325 steps to the top of the towers, where Quasimodo the Hunchback rang the church bells in Victor Hugo's novel. The gargoyles on Notre Dame have a bizarre presence all their own.

The Week in Paris

It has often been said that Paris is a state of mind, not just a place. The visitor has to work his way into it little by little. Paris is subtle, coy, even deceptive. It doesn't show itself all at once. It's necessary to play hide and seek with it the first few days. Then one begins to feel at home. And once that happens, the visitor will never be able to leave. He'll take Paris with him.

As in London and Rome, a city sightseeing excursion is about the best way to get a general idea of the city. Local guides usually begin with the Boulevard Saint-Michel and pass through the Latin Quarter, where students have lived since the Middle Ages. Today, many of them still subsist in tiny garret rooms for $1 or $2 a day. The district is called the "Latin Quarter" because the instruction at the University used to be in Latin. The whole area was full of students jabbering in Latin — or so it is said.

Nearby is the old Abbey of Cluny. Underneath the building and around the grounds are ruins of an ancient Roman building. No one knows exactly what it was used for or who built it. The abbey itself was put up in the Middle Ages by the monks of Cluny. Later, around 1500, it was greatly enlarged, and became one of the most luxurious buildings in Paris. French royalty would stay here from time to time. Inside is a famous collection of tapestries and other works of art dating from the Middle Ages. Parts of the original collection of tapestries were brought to the U.S. and are now on display at the Cloisters Museum in New York City.

Then there are the Luxembourg Gardens. Originally, the Romans built a camp on the site. In the Middle Ages, another order of monks, the Carthusians, built a monastery here. During the Renaissance, Queen Marie de Medici (who was of the famous Medici family in Florence) built the palace and gardens which stand there. The hedges and flowers here are incredibly beautiful in the summertime.

The gardens are near the heart of the Left Bank. The Sorbonne is a block away. This institution goes back to the Middle Ages. There was a struggling student by the name of Robert de Sorbonne. He managed to survive his examinations, and he became an influential priest. In 1253 he persuaded Louis IX (St. Louis) to finance a college in which penniless theology students could live and pursue their studies. The term "Sorbonne" refers only to the complex of buildings down in the Latin Quarter. They were built in the 17th century, largely by Cardinal Richelieu. It's amazing how the architects managed to squeeze over 20 theaters, 20 lecture rooms, 40 offices, a library, 2 museums, and several hundred laboratories into such a small place. Around the Sorbonne, one will notice that the streets have been repaved recently. In 1968, student insurgents tore up the cobblestones to use as weapons against the police, and de Gaulle had the streets coated with asphalt in reprisal a few weeks later.

Any sightseeing excursion stops for a look inside the great cathedral of Notre Dame. It stands on the Ile de la Cité, one of the two small islands in the river Seine. The cathedral was built between 1163 and 1345. There has been a great deal of restoration work on the building recently, as well as on many of the other important monuments in the city. It's all part of a massive clean-up operation begun by de Gaulle in order to polish up *la Gloire de la France*. The Louvre also looks almost new again. In sprucing up Notre Dame, though, the workers had to be careful with the old and brittle statues. Sandblasting would have destroyed them. Instead, they've been using small brushes, even toothbrushes.

Across the river from Notre Dame and slightly to the left is the Louvre. It's a fabulous palace, built by Francis I. Napoleon added on to it, and several other additions were made in the 19th century. Today, it is one of the most famous museums in the world. The *Mona Lisa* is there, along with the *Venus de Milo* and a treasury of other works. It also has a large collection of ancient Egyptian art, including a small temple which the visitor can walk into.

Behind the Louvre are the Tuileries Gardens. Originally, there was a palace nearby where Napoleon lived. Unfortunately, it was destroyed in the riots of 1871. But the gardens have been restored. In these gardens is a miniature of the Arc de Triomphe. Straight through the arch one can see the obelisk in the center of the Place de la Concorde, and beyond that, about a mile away, the real Arch of Triumph. All three are lined up perfectly. This in a nutshell is the French approach to landscape design. Everything is perfectly geometrical, orderly, logical.

The Place de la Concorde is a huge square right next to the Seine. In the center is the tall obelisk, brought from Egypt in 1833. It weighs 150 tons, and the inscriptions sing the praises of the Pharaoh Rameses II, whom many archeologists regard to be the "Pharaoh" with whom Moses had to deal in order to free the people of Israel. The square was originally laid out by King Louis XV in order to highlight a statue of himself in the center. During the French Revolution, the square was renamed "Place de la Révolution." A huge guillotine was erected and thousands of heads began to roll, including those of King Louis XVI and Queen Marie Antoinette. After all the blood and violence, the square was renamed as the "Place de la Concorde." It was more a wish than a fact.

Around the square are many statues representing some of the cities and provinces of France. On one side is the Jeu de Paume Museum. The name refers to the tennis courts which used to stand here. It was in these tennis courts that the French Revolution really began back in 1789, when a group of radicals banded together with the "Tennis Court Oath".

Across the Seine from the Place de la Concorde is the French National Assembly, which houses the French parliament. Nearby is a small hotel where Voltaire had a room back in the 1700's. He had a fantastic view of the city outside his window, and wrote at his desk as he looked over the commotion and bustle below, scoffing and laughing to himself at the follies of mankind. The scene is re-created on the 10-franc bill, including Voltaire's ironic smile.

Further up the river is the Eiffel Tower. It looms over the whole city and is clearly visible for miles away. Many visitors are surprised the first time they see it. Their impression of it is derived from photographs. But the Eiffel Tower is notoriously difficult to photograph accurately. Most photos make it look grayish blue. Actually, it's a reddish brown. It was designed by Gustave Eiffel and built for the Paris World's Fair in 1889. Eiffel wanted to demonstrate the new principles of engineering he had developed. He insisted that iron could be used. Ordinarily, iron is very brittle, and is difficult to use effectively in scaffolding or trellis-work. But Eiffel showed that by using very thin pieces and the technique of multiple bracing, iron could be made as strong and flexible as any other metal. The tower itself is extraordinarily light. The weight at the bottom is only 56 lbs. per square inch, about the same as the weight of an average-sized man. If one were to make a scale model of the tower a foot high, using the same metal, it would weigh ¼ of an ounce. When it was built, the major custodians of culture were outraged at the thing. They thought it would destroy Paris' classic skyline. Plans were made to tear it all down at the end of the World's Fair. But the Parisians soon became fond of it, and demanded that it be left intact. It's 1006 feet high. Today, it's used as a radio and TV transmitting station. There's a restaurant on the second level.

The Arch of Triumph is in the center of the Place de l'Etoile. The square was given the name *Etoile* (star) because of the many streets radiating out from it. Many of the oldest and wealthiest Parisian families have homes along the tree-lined streets and shady parks of this area. The Avenue Victor Hugo is especially elegant. The Arch of Triumph itself was built by Napoleon to celebrate his victories in Europe.

Near the Eiffel Tower is the Hôtel des Invalides. It was originally a military hospital. Later, Napoleon was buried there in a huge marble sarcophagus. Visitors must view the sarcophagus from a balcony above. This forces the viewer to bow his head while looking down at Napoleon's tomb. Some say Napoleon planned it that way.

There are many other things the visitor can do on his own during a week in Paris. A walking tour through the winding streets of Montmartre is a delight. Montmartre is an area of Paris up on a hill to the north of the Seine. Nearby is the Basilica of Sacre Coeur. There is a park where many artists set up their easels in the shade. Outdoor cafés with pastel awnings line the edge of the park, and the color contrasts in this area of Paris are particularly vivid.

Most visitors to Paris take a trip to the Palace of Versailles. It's just outside the city to the southwest. In 1660 it was a sleepy town on the edge of a boggy marsh, surrounded by a huge forest. By 1700 it had become the most luxurious palace in the world. It started when Louis XIV announced that he was tired of Paris. He preferred the restful woods around Versailles and wanted to build a palace which would rival the monuments of his predecessors. It was a stupendous undertaking. Vast marshes had to be drained and ground had to be cleared. Tons of earth had to be brought in to level it off. The workers lived in huts on the edge of the marshes. Eyewitness accounts tell of malaria and other epidemics carried by mosquitoes. But the work went on, and forty years later the King had his dream house.

He moved in with his queen in 1682, and 20,000 guests moved in with him. Things became a bit crowded, so the King had to limit his house guests to about 1000 "great nobles" and 4000 servants. The rest moved into estates around the town. 9000 soldiers kept salesmen away from the front gate.

But to get an accurate impression of life at Versailles, one has to understand the way things were done at the French court in the days of the "Sun King". Everything was regulated by a strict code of etiquette. There was a right and wrong way to scratch one's ear, cross one's legs, button one's coat, or even yawn. For example, if the Duc d'Alembert were chatting amiably with Lord and Lady Mercier, admiring the King's latest exploits abroad, and began to feel tired, he could not simply go off to bed. Monsieur Le Duc's inclination might be to stretch a few times, heave himself out of his chair, and make his exit toward the door, muttering *Bonsoir* to the others. But this was not permitted at Versailles, where, if the Duke was about to leave the room, he had to announce his intentions far in advance. He would work up to the point cautiously and with elaborate euphemisms. Perhaps he would begin by observing how wonderfully balanced nature is, and how the amount of time required to get work done is compensated for by an equal amount of time devoted to rest. Then he would bring this down to the immediate present, throwing in a few choice lines from *another* Moliere play, but that's out of the question. The King was not amused by that play; it was a flop. No one even whispered about it. After these twistings and turnings — by which time he was wide awake again — the moment of exit finally arrived. He would stand up, take a graceful bow, utter a few sweet nothings to Madame Mercier, and then tiptoe out of the room.

There was nothing private about the King's day-to-day life. Everything was done in the presence of noblemen whom the King used as his personal valets. In this way, the 1000 great lords actually earned their keep. The King couldn't wash his face without being surrounded by a flotilla of chamberlains. Then there was the famous ordeal of the King's rising in the morning. He actually rose twice each morning. His actual rising was rather unpretentious, and known as the *Petite Lever* (Small Rising). After this, the King went to a much larger room, his official sleeping chamber. He changed into his official pajamas and crawled into the huge bed. Then the doors opened and a hundred noblemen filed in. This was the *Grand Lever* (Great Rising). With this, the day at Versailles officially began. Among the attendants were the greatest poets and playwrights of the day. They were there at the crack of dawn, well before the King's heavy eyelids snapped open and his large black eyes started searching out the room for the appropriate faces. There was someone to hold the King's washcloth, another to fasten his garters, and someone else polishing his shoes. Out in the anteroom, a chamberlain was ready with the Royal

Snuffbox. These noblemen had no choice but to live at Versailles. It was the center of French political, social, and cultural life. All patronage came from the King. If a man was at all interested in a political position, in social climbing, or in getting a play produced, he had to be at Versailles to attract the attention of the King.

Once inside the palace, today's visitor is taken through the royal apartments, and the many salons, reception rooms, and large halls where Louis XIV and his noblemen danced with the demoiselles. There is the King's bedroom, where the *Grand Lever* took place, as well as the Queen's chamber and the council rooms where Louis XIV deliberated with his ministers. Some of Marie Antoinette's personal effects are on display, including the famous painting of her with her children. The velvet wallpaper and the tapestries on the wall were done by the famous Gobelin works in Paris. But the most spectacular room in Versailles is the Hall of Mirrors. It was here that the Versailles Treaty was concluded in 1919, bringing World War I to a close. It was also here that President Kennedy visited de Gaulle back in 1962. The palace was pillaged several times during the French Revolution, but was restored in the 19th century. After World War I, John D. Rockefeller made a large donation to finish the job.

The doorway out of the palace leads to the formal gardens outside. Every shrub and hedge is clipped and sculptured into shape. Everything that grows, grows according to plan. They say that even the bees have been trained to follow the right azimuths. In the distance is a perfectly rectangular artificial lake. The King used to amuse himself by having gondolas paddle back and forth on the water.

A short distance from the formal gardens are the Trianon Gardens. There are two small palaces on the edge of the gardens. One part of the gardens is formal, but the other is very informal: things actually seem to grow out here. Little trails wander off through the woods, and tiny bridges arch over the canals. There is a grotto where Marie Antionette hid to escape a mob of revolutionaries. The *Hameau* (Hamlet) is nearby, where Marie Antoinette and her maids played at farming. This was quite common in her day. It was a sentimental glorification of peasant life. There were cows and goats, and the Queen herself would hoe in the garden from time to time. The hamlet sits on the edge of a lake. It's the most peaceful spot in all of Versailles.

Much more is going on in Paris than one can see by simply walking around Montmartre or looking inside Versailles. Paris is the busiest capital on the Continent. It's a watershed of new ideas and new developments in painting, drama, and science. The visitor won't feel that he's really been in Paris until he finds out a little more about them. At the Cité Universitaire, one can hear some students and professors discussing the role of the student in the French university. The visitor can see who wants what when he hears students and professors debating these issues in the dining room of the Maison Internationale, in the tiny cafés across the Boulevard Jourdan, or in the bookstores which line the boulevard. Both have strong opinions, and will keep the place jumping a good hour or so.

Paris is a city of art. There is enough in the Louvre and Jeu de Paume Museums alone to fill a thick textbook. The Jeu de Paume is a treasure house of Impressionist art. The Impressionists thought they could make a science out of color and light effects, giving the viewer an experience of a lake or a cathedral more vivid than he would obtain by actually seeing them. It was ambitious, and they enjoyed more than a measure of success. There are other paintings beside those of the Impressionists at the Jeu de Paume. Van Gogh's famous self-portrait is there, and some of Rousseau's primitivist paintings are an eerie sight.

The real character of the French is revealed most of all in their literature. A general familiarity with modern French letters and the French way of life will answer many of the questions the visitor is bound to have puzzled over. Exactly what is the individualism of the French? Where does one look for it? There is so much going on in Paris that it's easy to miss the important things, such as the French *ésprit critique* (the critical attitude). The critical attitude is simply the way that the French use their common sense. There's nothing especially tricky or cynical about it. The French simply want the best out of life. To get it, they must know what is worth having and what isn't.

There are many other things to do in Paris. Like lunch downtown at one of the cafés in the vicinity of the Madeleine. Or an evening at a tiny café on the *rue du Pot de Fer* (Iron Kettle Street). One can get fresh fruit at the outdoor markets along the rue Mouffetard. The Mouffetard is a narrow lane winding its way up a hill. Every square inch is jammed with fruit and vegetable stalls, and thrifty housewives jostle each other for the freshest items. Many Parisians still don't have refrigerators. So they do their shopping twice a day, just before lunch and before dinner. That is why there are so many small fruit and vegetable markets all over Paris. They add a special color to the city.

Any evening is perfect for a *Bateaux Mouche* excursion under the bridges of Paris. The word "Mouche" here is simply the name of the man who has been operating the excursions for over 25 years. They're a regular institution in Paris. One proceeds down to the Seine and gets on board one of the boats. The boat glides lazily along the river, under one bridge after another. A guide tells about each bridge and major building as the boat comes to it. One bridge has a large "N" on it. That's one of Napoleon's contributions to the city, and he wanted everyone to know it. Another one is the bridge over which the victims of the Revolution were carted on their way to the guillotine.

Then there's the most famous bridge of all: the Pont Alexandre Trois. This is the one most often featured in perfume or fashion ads. Its wrought-iron elegance matches anything else in Europe. The Bateaux Mouche excursion is a nice way to get to know the Seine. The boat sails all the way from the glamorous bridges and pleasure boats around the Place de la Concorde to the river barges and smokestacks of the industrial suburbs. It's the whole city at a glance, and from a very unusual angle.

One thing on the Boulevard des Capucines is a "must". One of the Paris "drugstores" is down here — "le Drugstore Opera." Paris drugstores are not exactly like the Rexall's on the street corner back home. They're the Parisian interpretation of the American drugstore, department store, snack shop, beauty salon, shopping center, and newsstand all rolled into one. If one wants to know how a Frenchman sees America, he should take a look inside this place. It is brand new, and crammed with gleaming stainless steel and glass showcases, uniformed salesmen, coffee bars, and elegant restaurants. Anything and everything is available, including Texas-sized hamburgers.

In Paris, one must leave plenty of time for simply loafing. This isn't really loafing; it is the most effective way to learn. Paris is always throbbing with excitement. It *has* to be the busiest place in Europe. But if the visitor is just as busy as everyone else, he'll miss the whole thing. One has to sit back and relax from time to time in order to see what's going on. Once he has penetrated the real Paris, he'll bring a good bit of it back home with him.

Chartres-Châteaux Country Field Trip

The most common mistake Americans make on their first trip to France is to spend *all* of their time in Paris — as if everything France has to offer were stuffed, like eggs, into one basket.

Things aren't that simple, of course, and there's no reason why they should be. French history and culture are as fascinating and complex as the land itself. One can't see it all by staying in Paris. The real France must be sought out. An ideal way to do it is to head south of Paris to the cathedral of Chartres, and then travel along the Loire River

Valley to see the castles on either side. It's a journey back in time to the France of yesterday – to the days when cathedrals were everywhere in Europe, and when French kings and nobles decked the countryside with hunting estates and amused themselves by holding jousting tournaments.

The road south to Chartres passes through the industrial suburbs which ring the city. They're called the "Red Belt" because many of the workers living there regularly vote for the Communist party.

The route follows a fast highway which begins just outside the city. It's not exactly an Autostrada or an Autobahn, but it's quite adequate for its purposes, and in any case very appropriate to the rustic scenes we're looking for. Before long the Cathedral of Chartres comes into view. Its twin towers can be seen for miles around. The cathedral sits majestically on a hill. Chartres is generally considered to be the best and purest example of Gothic architecture in Europe. The spires are a bit puzzling at first – they don't look the same. One is fairly plain. It's the newest one, although it's called the "Old Tower". The other one is much more elaborate. It is called the "New Tower", even though it's actually 'older. The rich decoration was added in the 1500's. Every visitor to Chartres has to go through this confusion. The statues in the main doorway of the façade are among the oldest and best preserved in Europe. Christ is seen in the center, surrounded by Apostles and other saints. It's amazing how vivid and realistic their faces are. Their bodies, however, are stiff and lifeless. This paradox is one of the most noted features of Chartres. In carving the faces, the sculptors used prominent lords and bishops of the day as models.

One of the most interesting aspects of the cathedral is the way it was built. By this time, the visitor is used to hearing that such-and-such a cathedral took 100, 200, or even 600 years to build. Notre Dame in Paris, for example, took almost 200 years. Here at Chartres, though, it's just the opposite. The cathedral was built in the short span of 25 years.

Building a cathedral in 25 years, using medieval engineering techniques and hand labor, is an incredible feat. It was an astounding achievement. How was it done? To begin with, there was something special about Chartres from the very first. The spot on which it stands had always been sacred ground. Even before the days of the Romans, there was a pagan temple on the site. It was used by the druids, a class of priest-magicians who held enormous power among the Celtic tribes living in France. They venerated a small well in the area, where mysterious spirits were supposed to congregate. The well has been unearthed under the floor of the cathedral. The Romans followed in the druids' footsteps and built a temple in honor of a mother-goddess. After the Celtic people had been converted to Christianity, the townspeople around Chartres thought that the Romans must have had a foreknowledge of the Virgin Mary. They consecrated the pagan statue and moved it into a new basilica. From that time on, it became a special feature of each succeeding building on the site. It was called "Our Lady Underground", because the statue was kept in a crypt below the floor. Pilgrims came from miles around to venerate it. Unfortunately, it was destroyed during the French Revolution. In 1857, a new statue was made, and it still stands in the crypt of the cathedral, which is opened every hour on the half-hour. (Admission: about 2 francs.)

Chartres has always been a center of intense devotion, in spite of several disasters. In 1194, the old cathedral was almost totally destroyed by fire. (It was the fifth cathedral built on this site.) After that, the townspeople decided to build a new one. This was to be the biggest and best one of all, and it would be built to last. It became a surging community project. Everyone pitched in, from the king and his lords down to the masons, carpenters, shopkeepers, and simple peasants. Dukes donated a stained glass window or two. A fruit vendor kept the workers supplied with apples and pears so that they could stay on the job.

The result is priceless. Because of the short time in which it was built, Chartres has a unity of architectural style practically unparalleled in Europe. When it takes 300 years to build a cathedral, there are bound to be changes in style and fashion along the way. One end of the building might be Romanesque, the other Gothic. Or one part Gothic and the other Baroque. Not so at Chartres. The whole building is pure 13th century Gothic. It is more than a building. It's the whole medieval world at a glance.

After proceeding inside, the visitor is astonished at how wide the building is. In fact, it has the widest cathedral nave in France (52 feet). The rose window is breathtaking. The big round window of a cathedral was called the "rose window" for two reasons. First, the design rather resembles a rose. Petals of ornate glasswork radiate out from the center. Second, this window was always dedicated to the Virgin Mary, and one of her emblems is the rose.

The walk continues around the ambulatory. The ambulatory is the circular walkway which goes around the altar. The floor around the ambulatory is uneven. It was designed that way. When pilgrims came to

Chartres, they came by the hundreds. There were no accommodations for them to stay in, and so they slept on the floor of the cathedral. The next morning, the custodians came by with large buckets of water to swish over the floor. The builders were quite familiar with these customs, and made the floor slope so that it would drain off the water.

The glass windows in Chartres are the most famous cathedral windows in the world. They were made by craftsmen who spent their whole lives getting just *those* shades of color. Notice the blue in particular. It's the famous "Chartres blue". Modern glass-stainers have found it impossible to duplicate.

On the left side of the altar, against the outer wall, is a much-revered statue. It's the "Virgin of the Pillar" dating from the 1500's. It has been the object of many a pilgrimage.

Chartres is the supreme achievement of religious faith. It's also a very human sort of thing. Think of the hundreds of people crowding into the cathedral on any good saint's day. Or the throng of townspeople outside, buzzing around the market stalls at the base of the cathedral. Melons and cabbages stacked six feet high; oxcarts full of headless chickens, ready for the pot; an old gypsy selling religious trinkets or fake relics; a fishwife hawking odorous salmon; a well-attired squire fresh from the manor dismounting his frothing steed, while waving away a beggar. In the Middle Ages, cathedrals were centers of *activity.*

The castles of medieval France lie straight ahead to the south of Chartres. The first on our route is in Blois. Like most of them, it's perched on top of a rocky bluff. And like the others too, it was built in various stages. The part which is visible from the front was built at the end of the Middle Ages by King Louis XII, who reigned from 1498 to 1515. The red brick blends in perfectly with the dark stone; added to this is a handsome black and white checkerboard design, formed by different colored marble. Inside, the rooms are only sparsely furnished, and some not at all.

The most gruesome event in the life of the castle occurred in 1560. This was during the Reformation, and France was plagued by religious strife. A Protestant by the name of La Renaudie and some followers plotted to enter Blois in small groups and then reassemble. Their plans are not known for certain, but many historians assume that they were after King Francis II, who was a Catholic. (His young wife was Mary Queen of Scots.) The plot was discovered, and the participants were seized as they arrived in Blois. They were hanged from the balconies or beheaded or thrown into the Loire in sacks. Legend has it that on certain nights a low, soft wail can be heard from the top of the battlements. These are said to be the wails of the plotters, lamenting their failure and its tragic aftermath.

Our route continues southwest along the River Loire. It drifts lazily along to the left of the road, heading for Amboise, another castle-town, where Leonardo da Vinci is buried. But first, a few impressions of the countryside around it. This is "Loire country". It has a person-ality all its own. The whole region seems years away from the glamour and throb of Paris. The Loire valley is known as the "garden of France", and rightly so. The climate is perfect: a breeze blows in from the Atlantic.

The wines around here are some of the best in France. Near Blois they're red. Soon the road enters white-wine country. *Pinots* are the specialty here. It took the people a long time and a happy accident to discover the art of pruning the vine. Monks used to be the best vine-growers and wine makers in the Middle Ages. One day some donkeys plowed through the fence of their corral and romped through the vineyards. They nibbled off the leaves and sprigs. Only the stalks were left. The monks gnashed their teeth and bewailed a lost crop. But next spring, the grapes were the most succulent they had ever seen. The donkeys had taught them a lesson about vine-pruning.

Everything about this region is gentle and peaceful. The soil is fertile, growing everything from fig trees to mushrooms. The people, lulled into nonchalance by the climate and rich harvests, have always espoused a serene and mild philosophy of life. Legends tell of beggars who refused to be cured by the relics of St. Martin because it meant they would have to go back to work again. But some not-so-idle people hail from this area. The great French philosopher Descartes was from Touraine, and two writers — Rabelais and Balzac — were also from the area. This is said to be the heart of "Old France", where the best traditions of the people were born. The purest French is said to be spoken here. In many ways, this is to the French what the area between Florence and Rome is to the Italians: the nation's hearth, its showpiece.

The people here love their wines. They often drink their wine out of special glasses which have no base. There is no way to set them down. Thus, they assure themselves of sipping away the whole glass, down to the last drop. The wines are kept in dark cellars. Attendants fuss around them for years and years until they are properly aged. Then they're removed from the protective straw and shipped to various parts of the world. Cheaper wines are aged in casks and then bottled. Often, they're mixed with wines from other areas. It has been said that all the wine which is actually produced in Beaujolais in a year wouldn't be enough to keep the city of Paris in Beaujolais for a day. Beaujolais is diluted with other wines (1 part Beaujolais per 4 or 5 parts from other areas) and then exported as "Beaujolais". The same is true for the famous vintages of this region. To get 100% pure Pinot, for example, one has to come to the Loire Valley itself, unless one is willing to spend $10 or $20 a bottle in Paris or New York.

The visitor may be surprised to see how low the River Loire has become at this point. It's usually this way in the summer. In the winter and spring, however, the rains bring the water level up to the top. A long time ago large sailing ships would ply the waters of the river, making full use of the breezes. Here and there one might spot an old windmill.

Then the road reaches Amboise. The castle is visible on the left as one approaches the town. The castle looms up from the river, which is the best spot from which to view it. Much of the castle was built on orders from King Charles VIII, who reigned from 1483 to 1498. He was the sort of person who was used to getting what he wanted when he wanted it. He wanted his castle built as soon as possible. To get it done, his builders had to continue the work at night, by torchlight. Even the winter frost didn't deter the king. The workers simply held the building stones over a fire to melt the ice.

Once he had his castle, King Charles looked around for other things to do — such as an invasion of Italy. He succeeded in his invasion in 1496, and brought back to Amboise all the booty he had collected, including gold and silver utensils, paintings and sculpture, tapestries, and furniture. Amboise was his Versailles. While in Italy, he had been impressed by the Italian gardens and resolved to spruce up his castle along the same lines. Again he wanted it done right away. Back came the torches at night and the fires for winter work. Charles' expedition into Italy inaugurated the long Italian influence on French art. In fact, it really introduced much of the Italian Renaissance into France for the first time. Charles' later successors like Louis XII and Francis I continued this trend. Louis XII, for example, made an expedition into Italy in 1500 and captured Leonardo da Vinci in Milan. He brought him back to France, where he died in 1519.

But Charles VIII was only a prelude to the fun ahead at Amboise. King Francis I arrived, and left his indelible imprint on the castle. Francis I reigned from 1515 to 1547. He came to Amboise when he was only six years old. In fact, he was educated here, and the Italian influence brought in by Charles VIII and Louis XII had its effect. He acquired a taste for art and culture, on top of his original taste for hunting and women. Court life at Amboise was full of tournaments, balls, festivals, and animal hunts. Artists were retained to work for the king. Francis was the one who finally brought Leonardo to Amboise, where he died.

From Amboise we head south, away from the Loire for a while. Our route takes us to the castle of Chenonceaux, which is well worth an inside visit. In the meantime, the visitor might well imagine what it must have been like to live in one of these castles in the Middle Ages. For one thing, it is important to remember that the king didn't have any fixed capital city. Paris was an important trading center, but the king spent only part of his time there. Most French kings fell in love with the region of the Loire, and wanted to spend as much time there as possible. They owned some of the castles themselves. Others were owned by great noblemen. The king supported himself and his court by sponging off them. He and his retinue would travel from chateau to chateau staying as long as he liked. There wasn't much a particular lord could do about it, especially if the king happened to be someone like Francis I.

The castles were large and they cost a great deal to keep up. Added to this was the expense of a royal visit. Many nobles went broke, and had to sell their estates to pay off their debts. The king often stepped in and obligingly took the property off their hands. In this way, the castles were passed back and forth from one owner to another. Often the king financed his military expeditions by selling off some of his castles. At present, most of them are owned by the state, and have been converted into museums. But Chenonceaux is still in private hands. It is owned by a French chocolate magnate, who lives upstairs. The first floor is open to visitors.

Life in the castles underwent many changes over the years. At first the stone buildings were very rough and crudely furnished. There was one central room in which everyone slept, including the dogs, goats, and sheep. All possible precautions were taken against intruders. There was no front door, only a small opening reached by a ladder. Nor was there central heating in the winter; even the huge fireplace wasn't enough to keep ice from forming on the stone walls. There were no rugs and no tapestries on the walls. Instead, straw was strewn on the floor to keep it a little warmer. The meals were plain, but usually substantial. Spices from the East were valued because they covered up the flavor of spoiled meat.

It must have been boring in the castle during the long winter, and even the tiniest diversion – a wandering minstrel, a pilgrim on his way to Chartres, a hunt, even an occasional war now and then – was welcomed by everyone. It was their only contact with the outside world.

Things gradually improved over the years as the Crusaders brought back luxury goods from the East, and as trade brought in greater wealth. The castles were augmented and the one central room gave way to several rooms with different functions. The Great Hall became the medieval equivalent of our living room. Official gatherings were held here, including banquets, courts of law, and trade bargainings.

Near the Great Hall was the Room, where day-to-day life went on. Harsh winter winds were kept out with shutters or windowpanes. Tapestries or paintings took the place of damp stones. Carpets or mats replaced the musty straw. Furniture improved too. Carved chairs, chests, tables, and mirrors were used. Some of these items were brought in from Italy, especially Venice. Venice was the major point of contact with the East. Beds took the place of rough mats, and often boasted a canopy. No one really knows the origin of the canopy, but some historians have surmised that they became popular in medieval castles because they protected the peaceful sleeper from any loose stones falling down from the ceiling. The canopies were made of heavy wood, presumably with this purpose in mind. Caged birds, including parrots, were kept to amuse the ladies or reveal their secrets to the men.

There were various other rooms, including the wardrobe – the origin of our closet. Then there was the kitchen. It was kept at a long distance from the other rooms so that the smoke from the open fire wouldn't get the tapestries and other furnishings sooty. This often meant that the food was cold by the time it reached the lord's table, but one must keep in mind that hot food was a trivial luxury compared with the cost of replacing the tapestries. In Louis XIV's time, for example, the kitchen was in a different building from the dining salon. During the winter, it was not uncommon for the *asperges* and *haricots verts* to arrive with frost on top. About the only silverware in these days was a knife for cutting fruit. The rest was eaten with the fingers. A 16th century etiquette manual, for example, explains the most graceful way to put a morsel of food in one's mouth with the tips of the fingers. It also mentions that a guest is more likely to win the respect of his host if he refrains from throwing food across the table.

All have heard the Middle Ages referred to as "a thousand years without a bath." Contrary to popular belief, people in the Middle Ages were quite properly concerned with personal cleanliness and bodily care. In the 1200's, for example, there were 26 public baths in Paris. By the time of Louis XIV and the "golden age" of Versailles, there were only two. In the Middle Ages, every great house had its tub. Sometimes the lord would entertain friends while swimming around in his pool. At other times, he would invite them to test the merits of his bathtub before joining him for dinner in the Great Hall.

All this was done away with in the late Middle Ages by various revival movements. Great preachers walked from city to city denouncing the care of the body. They stressed instead the care of the soul. In the Middle Ages, the two had gone hand in hand. But later the scales were tipped, and asceticism reigned supreme. This brought about a natural reaction during the Renaissance, when a scorn for everything medieval set in. But the Renaissance writers blamed the Middle Ages for excesses it didn't really commit. The very expression, "a thousand years without a bath," dates from the Renaissance. But it is the Renaissance, and not the Middle Ages, to which it applies.

Next on our route is the chateau of Chenonceaux. The castle is separated from the town by a large forest. It's an incredibly peaceful spot. Small wonder that many nobles quarreled over it. All one sees at first are the woods. Then, as the bus pulls up to the parking lot, one can make out a wide pathway leading up to the castle. At the end of it is the front façade. The white stone glistens in the sun.

Chenonceaux is built out over the River Cher, a tributary of the Loire. It's one of the newest of the chateaux, having been built in the 1500's. It lacks some of the heaviness of the medieval castles. Instead, it's small, light, and elegant. As one walks along the avenue toward the front gate, it is easy to imagine the reception given the visitor in the time of Charles IX (1560-74). Ladies would stand in the shallow trenches on either side, dressed as mermaids and nymphs. Once inside the visitor was wined and dined with the best the valley had to offer.

One's entrance today is somewhat more modest, but no less spectacular. It's beyond anyone's capacity to describe the peace and serenity of this place. There is nothing else around but the castle, the formal gardens, the woods, and the river, which mirrors the whole scene as one looks down at it. A young scion born and raised here would find it difficult indeed to appreciate what the revolution and violence in Paris were all about in 1789. It would seem like a tale from another planet.

A guide takes visitors inside and explains something about the major personalities who lived at Chenonceaux. The emblem of a salamander with a crown on its head is very prominently displayed near the entrance. It's the coat of arms of King Francis I. The guide invariably relates a tale about Diane of Poitiers. She was the mistress of King Henry II, who reigned from 1547 to 1559. Henry gave her Chenonceaux as a present. One of the rooms inside is decorated with wallpaper on which there is a design in which the letters "H" and "D" are interlaced. They stand, of course, for "Henry" and "Diane". She loved the place and never wanted to leave. But she was forced to do so in 1559, when Henry II died. His wife, Catherine de Medici, took over as Regent of France, and she took her revenge for having been thrust aside for Diane. She evicted Diane and took the castle herself. No doubt the first thing she did was to have the room repapered. It has since been restored.

Catherine de Medici made a number of improvements in the castle. She had the formal gardens laid out. They are the largest of the two gardens which are visible today. She also did something with the bridge which had been used to connect the castle with the other side of the river. Catherine had two stories built on top of the bridge, thus doubling the size of the chateau. The first story is a large ballroom. During the First World War, it was used as a field hospital.

Before leaving Chenonceaux one should be sure to walk through the two formal gardens. The smaller one is a bit away from the castle. Looking away from the castle toward the woods, one sees several pathways radiating out from this point. They're as straight as a ruler. One can't see the end of them; after a while, they simply blend into the forest. It's really an amazing sight to see these pathways diverging off in slightly different directions, like spokes in a wheel. The geometry is perfect.

We're back on the road now, and heading for the Loire. Before long the river comes into view. We follow it for a while, duplicating our earlier course down the river, but going the other way and on the other side. The road passes by Blois again; one can glimpse the castle on the hill across the river.

A bit later we turn right and head away from the Loire. The road approaches the last chateau on our itinerary, Chambord. This is the largest of them all. The road approaches it through a forest. As one looks ahead, rows of dark green trees appear on either side of the road. Beyond them is an opening, but one can't see anything yet. Then, suddenly, the trees disappear and a positively gigantic white castle appears out of nowhere. Large lawns and gardens are spread out around it. The late-afternoon sun covers the castle with a radiant gold.

Chambord was built by the pleasure-loving Francis I. He was penniless at the time. His two sons had been kidnapped and were awaiting ransom in Spain. His treasury had a deficit. But he wanted a new palace so he raided the churches and monasteries, plundered the silverware and jewelry of his nobles, and somehow got all the money together. At first he wanted to divert the Loire River so that it would flow in front of the castle. But that proved to be too ambitious an undertaking. He had to rest content with a smaller river.

Off again, and following the River Loire. Further on, the road approaches Orleans, the largest city in the area. The most famous events in the life of Orleans took place when Joan of Arc lifted the English seige of the town in 1428-29. The English under Lord Salisbury were threatening to take Orleans. With unflagging zeal, and at great personal sacrifice, the "maid of Orleans" urged her troops on until the town was relieved.

Orleans is an ideal place to stop for dinner and to sample the local specialties with all the trimmings. After all, this is the "garden of France".

The Return Home

One's last day in Europe is always one of mixed emotions. The visitor finds that his thoughts are on both sides of the Atlantic at once. Memories of his European experience mingle with expectations of the return home.

Once the plane takes off, it will be following the sun. Indeed it races the sun across the Atlantic. The westbound flight takes a bit longer than the flight over because of the prevailing winds. It takes seven hours or more. But the five-hour time difference between New York and Paris means that the difference in *local* time may be as little as two hours.

Many visitors waste both time and nervous energy worrying about the formalities of immigration and customs in New York. The following suggestions are intended to simplify the whole procedure.

Immigration involves showing two documents upon arrival: a passport and a yellow smallpox vaccination certificate. If by any chance one has lost either one, he must report this to the U.S. Embassy and receive a temporary replacement. In fact, it's best to check these things a few days in advance. That's it for immigration.

Customs procedures in New York are even simpler. Depending on the arrival time, a small percentage of suitcases and hand luggage will be spot-checked. The majority of people now go through customs at J.F.K. without having any of their luggage checked.

During the immigration procedure, passengers are asked the value of all the goods purchased abroad and carried with them. "With them" in this case includes both items in their luggage and the items they're wearing, such as the sweater or watch they might have purchased in Lucerne. Passengers may also be asked about gifts which they mailed home directly from Europe. Generally speaking, such gifts should not exceed $100 in value. The customs officials will ask the value of these gifts, and it's up to the passenger to make a declaration of their estimated value.

As long as one has less than $100 in merchandise bought overseas, there is no need to fill out a customs declaration. It is unwise to attempt to bring into the United States any illegal items such as switchblade knives, drugs, or firearms. Only adults over 21 years of age are allowed to bring in alcoholic beverages. They are entitled to 1/5 of a gallon of spirits duty free.

Once the passenger has all this squared away in his mind he can relax and enjoy the flight back across the Atlantic.

TO THE READER.

THIS FIGURE, THAT THOU HERE SEEST PUT,
IT WAS FOR GENTLE SHAKESPEARE CUT;
WHEREIN THE GRAVER HAD A STRIFE
WITH NATURE, TO OUT-DO THE LIFE:
O, COULD HE BUT HAVE DRAWN HIS WIT
AS WELL IN BRASS, AS HE HATH HIT
HIS FACE; THE PRINT WOULD THEN SURPASS
ALL, THAT WAS EVER WRIT IN BRASS.
BUT, SINCE HE CANNOT, READER, LOOK,
NOT ON HIS PICTURE, BUT HIS BOOK.

BEN: JONSON.

ORIENTATION ESSAYS

Essay 1.

THE BRITISH EXPERIENCE

> This scepter'd isle,
> This happy breed of men, this little world,
> This precious stone set in the silver sea,
> This blessed plot, this earth, this realm, this England,
> This teeming womb of royal kings . . .

Compare the picture evoked by these words of Shakespeare to (say) Twiggy in a Union Jack mini-skirt, or to Princess Anne swinging (clad) with the cast of *Hair.* Maybe there's some truth to what David Frost (now of late-night American TV) and Anthony Jay wrote in *The English*: "In England nothing is what it appears to be . . . The English are the most peculiar people on God's earth!"

But some more random impressions: a skyscraper partially blocking out St. Paul's dome; Prince Charles crowned under a plastic canopy within a crumbling castle in Wales; Lord "Screaming" Sutch, titled pop-singer, running on the Teen-Age party ticket against Harold Wilson; Beatle George Harrison setting up housekeeping in a Gothic nunnery; the Duke of Bedford staging a hippie weekend at Woburn Abbey, his ancestral pile; a 21-year-old female M.P. (Member of Parliament) fighting in a Londonderry street riot; an ultra-modern cathedral set amidst the bombed-out ruins of old Coventry . . . Perhaps these are the sorts of sights that British Travel had in mind a few years ago when it beckoned, "Come to Britain — Ancient and Mod."

In the following pages we'll sketch out a few of what we consider to be the major characteristics and institutions of the English. Some are ancient, some very contemporary; most are both.

I

Who *are* the English? Not an easy question. We're not asking whether they're "really" Celts, Angles, Saxons, Normans, or Swedes — yet, have you ever thought of Britain as a melting-pot? All of us, of course, . . . heard in the first grade that *America* is the melting-pot — and proud of it! But consider the following: the first English martyr, St. Alban, was a Roman soldier; Beowulf, hero of the Anglo-Saxon epic that never mentions Britain, was probably (if he ever existed) a Swede; Henry VII, the first Tudor king, was a Welshman (and Welshmen are *not* English —

just ask Richard Burton!); James I and the other Stuarts were Scots (also *not* English!); Victoria and Albert (of Saxe-Coburg-Gotha) were very German; Winston Churchill was part Iroquois Indian, etc. Elizabeth II is, of course, also of the Victorian house of Saxe-Coburg-Gotha (but now that's anglicized to "Windsor"); her mother is a Scot and her husband a Greek — and whatever does that make Charles, Prince of Wales? Perhaps we should re-word the question.

All right, what are the English *like*? Each of us has his own "image", no doubt; as the case may be, a glittering (or unglittering) generality, a prejudice. But first, let's hear some (so-called) Englishmen tell us what the English are like.

E. M. Forster: "It is not that the Englishman can't feel — it is that he is afraid to feel. He has been taught at his public school that feeling is bad form. He must not express great joy or great sorrow, or even open his mouth too wide when he talks — his pipe might fall out if he did!"

David Frost and Anthony Jay: "England is immeasurably the best place in the world to live. Its people are more tolerant and more talented then even they believe."

George Bernard Shaw: "An Englishman thinks he is moral when he is merely uncomfortable."

And Winston Churchill, speaking after the Battle of Britain: "When I warned (the French) that Britain would fight on alone, whatever *they* did, their generals told their Prime Minister: 'In three weeks England will have her neck wrung like a chicken.' Some chicken. Some neck."

Most of us have probably inherited the stereotype that the English are smug, or at least cold — the traditional icy hauteur, and all that. Let's just say that they're a bit more *reserved* than we — or Europeans — are in general. But we have yet to meet a cantankerous or unfriendly one; just don't expect much jolly backslapping on first acquaintance.

The best short analysis of British reserve that we know is one by Leo Rosten:

> The English are proud; the French are vain.
> Italians weep; Englishmen wince.
> Germans bark; Englishmen murmur.
> Spaniards sneer; Englishmen frown.
> Americans enthuse; the English sigh, "Quite."

Not that Englishmen don't enjoy life. Relieved finally of an empire, they can now afford to loosen up a bit. Duty and stiff-upper-lip aren't *all!* For instance, the English are great lovers of sport and of pets — perhaps even more than we Americans are. Of consuming interest is Association Football (or "soccer"). You probably won't be able to see a soccer game in London during the summer, but you might perhaps be able to see a cricket game. Cricket, Britain's national summer pastime, is played on Saturdays at Lord's, just west of Regent Park. Also during the summer: the Henley Regatta, the Ascot Flat Racing (as distinguished from Steeplechase), greyhound racing, and the Royal International Horse Show. If you think that American fans get fanatic, you should see the English.

Coupled with British sport is betting, which may be the *real* national sport! Crockford's of London (reportedly) does a two-billion-pound-a-year business; and it's all quite legal, but like drinking in a pub, it's hedged about with the most elaborate restrictions. Which suggests that the English — at least those of the Establishment generation — are somewhat puritanical about their pleasures; fun you can have, but only if you're inconvenienced or taxed to death!

Their enthusiasm for pets suggests another side — they're a bit sentimental. There's the Queen, of course, with her Corgis. (Corgis are marvelous little shepherd dogs from Wales; if you can visualize an improbable combination of German shepherd and dachshund, you've got the picture.) A wholesome, homely touch to royalty. Less endearing was the announcement a few years ago that the royal household, to economize, would sell its worn-out horses for hamburger. The outcry was enormous — and the horses were retired to a country stable.

British pets enjoy an exalted legal status. "It is surely not without significance that as long ago as 1822 Parliament passed the first law making cruelty to animals a crime," said *Punch* recently, "whereas it took ... another sixty-seven years to get around to making cruelty to children also an offence." One Middlesex couple's marriage ended in divorce because the husband accidentally kicked their dog; and the judgment was revealing: "It is no use telling ... the court that a dispute over a dog is a matter of little importance. Few could be graver." As some wag or other once quipped: "All the world loves a lover, but the British prefer their animals."

Finally, before we go on to discuss British institutions, a word about tradition and the English: The stereotype, no doubt, is that they're "hide-bound". This is all tied up with institutions like monarchy and religion — subjects of Part II of this essay. For now, just two general statements. First: As Americans, we tend to place little real value on tradition generally. If anything, our traditions are frills — nice, but not very useful. (We leave the Fourth of July parade, for example, mostly to the American Legion or the D.A.R.) Perhaps part of the reason is that the American experiment isn't very old. In this connection, it's interesting to note that the British celebrated the 350th anniversary of the Pilgrim Fathers' departure, with elaborate festivities. And not primarily, we think, as a tourist gimmick. In any case, we never heard much about the Pilgrims' anniversary over here! Our point is that, until recently, Americans have had a "pioneer mentality"; we've had to work so doggedly just to develop the land that we've had little leisure to celebrate our history. (It's not only our present generation that's been a "Now" generation.) Probably many Britons — particularly youth-minded Britons — would agree that most traditions are "irrelevant", Perhaps they'd even agree that the *idea* of tradition is irrelevant. But the second statement, one by Lord Cobham, Governor of the Bank of England at the time, gives another side — one more characteristic of the English:

> The handling of tradition is an art at which this country excels. We know how to keep what is old and useful and to add in each century what is new and useful. So that in the end tradition is not just an archaic form, but a plant, with its roots in the past, with a history of continuing development, and with a lively present. (*The National Geographic,* June, 1966.)

Bear this idea of tradition as an art in mind as we examine British institutions.

The English are more — much more — than we've described. We've merely tried to suggest some broad outlines. Your own observations can do much to fill in details, highlights, and color. We go on now to a few institutions. What we hope to convey aren't facts nearly so much as "feel".

II

(1) *Class and Education*

British society is (officially) classless. Rock stars from Liverpool are entertained at Buckingham Palace and are awarded the Order of the British Empire. A Yorkshireman with a working-class accent was her Majesty's Prime Minister — the youngest one in memory. Fashion has shifted from Savile Row to Carnaby St. and Chelsea. Oxford and

Cambridge, those "hoary seats of excellence and privilege," are open to workingmen's sons. Royalty swings with the masses, and egalitarianism is "high camp". But let's back up: "In England, nothing is what it appears to be ..." Is Britain classless? Yes and no. There are still Royal Highnesses, Graces, Worships, and Right Honorables. The House of Lords, somehow, endures. Empty titles? Stage masks? Yes and no.

One of the ironies of British life is the gap between politics and society. It would appear that the England that led the world toward political equality is nevertheless incurably class-conscious. And some pundits are arguing that the class-divisions are really deeper now that they have become almost invisible.

Pardon our sounding almost undemocratic, but there's not a little to be said in favor of class. It gives every man his pigeonhole; he performs (or fails to perform) according to set expectations; he has no "identity-crisis"; he knows his lines. If he fails, he can always blame it on the dead-end system instead of himself. And, without question, the class-system has produced some towering individuals. The aristocaracy has been given — and often has fulfilled — an enormous responsibility in public service.

You perhaps were wondering why we entitled this section "Class and Education." Why *and*? Is there a connection? Consider the American public school. What is its real reason for being? To produce excellence? Isn't the public school's real function to put everyone on an equal footing, to provide "equality of opportunity"? Isn't it really meant to be an instrument for democracy rather than excellence? Aren't most Americans basically suspicious of private schools?

In *some* ways the British situation is analogous. The majority of British students are in unselective, state-operated "secondary modern" schools, and liberals generally (officially at least) consider these schools instruments for furthering classlessness. The Labor government once pledged to "nationalize" British schools. At the same time, most conservatives in Britain (roughly equivalent to the wealthy, but with not a few exceptions) really believe in the "Public" Schools — and that's where they differ from most Americans. Most Americans probably consider it "unhealthy" to send their sons away to boarding school — and would continue to feel this way even if they could afford the luxury. So liberals harp about inequality and snobbism, and conservatives about educational excellence — but the hidden issue is class. In point of fact, the secondary modern school is often a social deadend: it leads only to the factory, office, and kitchen. It's the "Public School" that leads to Parliament and the executive suite.

The Duke of Wellington once said that "the Battle of Waterloo was won on the playing fields of Eton." He could just as well have said that the class battle is won there. Or, as *Time* once put it, "To run England's Eton is to tutor England's Establishment." If you saw the movie *If*, you've got a picture (warped) of an English Public School. It's austere — in fact, the more exclusive the more austere. The headmaster of Eton only a few years back called beating "useful". Useful it is when it leads to the top — and not a few liberal politicians choose the likes of Eton for their sons.

(2) *The Monarchy*

Said Disraeli: "Everyone likes flattery; and when you come to royalty, you should lay it on with a trowel." Probably many Americans consider monarchy a put-on — in Muggeridge's phrase, "royal soap opera." What good is a constitutional queen; isn't she *just* a figurehead, and an expensive one at that? Some Englishmen would applaud, though probably not most. Whether Elizabeth II be "a Brittanic Majesty presiding over a non-existent Empire" (Muggeridge again) or not, apparently most Englishmen love her. And symbols have their uses.

Nor is the Queen powerless; her prerogatives are considerable. She officially appoints Prime Ministers, for example, and she has veto-power. (Not that it's often used, but by refusing to sign a "money" bill, she could conceivably force a general election.) Prerogatives aside, she is probably better informed — by right — on major issues than anyone else in Britain; and while she must remain relatively aloof of mere politics, she is, when she speaks, a voice listened to.

The crowning of Prince Charles a while back brought to the fore the question of the monarchy's future. Will there be — better, *should* there be — kings when the generation of today takes control? In an open letter published in *Time*, a Cambridge student put it to Charles: "If you are to be a king at all, you must be *our* king." Who can guess what *that* will mean twenty years hence? Perhaps, at the very least, it means, "You must symbolize us."

As we said, symbols have their uses. The following words, spoken by an Englishman of the Establishment, say better than we can what we're trying to get across:

> There is nothing quite like (the Queen) in your country . . . Here our sovereign — particularly in times of national emotion, such as war — is the living symbol of all the patriotism and feeling that we have for our homeland. She is the very embodiment of our national existence in a way that

no politician can be. In your country I think only your flag quite assumes that national identity and elicits that response. (*The National Geographic,* June, 1966.)

(3) *The House of Lords*

"The House of Lords is useless, and dangerous, and ought to be abolished" — rather an avant garde notion for 1649, but one recommended by the House of Commons in that year. Many today would share that sentiment. They would add, perhaps, that the Lords today are quite impotent. Well, not quite: their powers have not yet been summarily lopped off, though certainly they have been trimmed. But, despite the trimmings, the Lords serve — and some would say usefully. At the very least, they put on a good show.

Imagine a congregation of the titled of the realm — dukes, barons, bishops — all furred out in ermine and crimson, and with their jewels fairly glittering. Trumpets blast, and then the Queen's Majesty herself appears — all in white but for the blue sash of the Order of the Garter.

Of course, every day isn't State Opening. More usually the red leather benches are a quarter filled: numerous old men, using the hearing-aids thoughtfully provided; somebody asleep; somebody else speaking; a bishop or two; and on the Woolsack, the Lord Chamberlain, the only one now in robes and wig — impassive. About seventy-five come every day (i.e. Tuesday through Thursday); perhaps 150 come several times a month; the rest of the thousand lords, infrequently. Most of those who come are old. Younger lords haven't the time for a duty that carries almost no remuneration. And a young lord with political ambitions would do better in the Commons, although he would need to renounce his title; more than one has. Each lord represents only himself — not necessarily any party-line or constituency. And he has a few special privileges: he is immune from civil arrest, for example, and may wear his hat before a judge; and until capital punishment went out, he could be hanged with a silken cord.

The chief power of the Lords is mostly to postpone — currently for a full year — any bill from the Commons that it vetoes. Considering that the Lords are mostly conservatives, this power can be quite a thorn in a liberal government's side. Accordingly, the last liberal government proposed two changes: (1) to reduce the postponement to six months, and (2) to limit voting to "created" peers, i.e., those who have earned rather than inherited their noble status. (Those with inherited titles would only "advise".)

What would be the effect, were the liberal proposal to become law? Our guess is that the House of Lords would become a committee of the favored — favored not by birth but by the government. (The Queen awards the titles, but the Prime Minister does most of the nominating.) We wonder if there isn't at least one advantage to the traditional set-up: that a hereditary peer is beholden to no government and no party, and is therefore free to do his own thing.

Just a sampling of the personalities in the House of Lords: Lord Mowbray, holder of the oldest barony in England, who, when sued by his wife, claimed a lord's traditional immunity; Lords Dewar and Guinness, who operate breweries; former Prime Ministers Baldwin, Attlee, and Eden; the two Archbishops and twenty-four other bishops, called "the Lords Spiritual"; Lady Clementine Churchill, aged 84; "Boofy", Earl of Arron and free-wheeling anti-Establishmentarian columnist; and the lone Communist, the Baron of Milford.

(4) *The Church of England*

"What a pity it is," once mused the Reverend Canon Sydney Smith, 19th century cleric and wit, "that in England we have no amusements but vice and religion." Many Englishmen would agree that the Anglican Church is an amusement, not least Malcolm Muggeridge (since a convert), who once prophesied that, were the Church to be disestablished, it would surely cease to exist. What is this curious Church of England? It can probably be expressed best by a chemical analogy: it is an unstable (but enduring) catholic-protestant-fundamentalist-liberal compound, bonded together either by the *Book of Common Prayer* or sheer inertia! Surely it is a prime example of the British genius for compromise — an arrangement that dates back to Elizabeth I. Many would call it an irrelevance; others would say that it's the national expression of basic and historic Christianity.. Basic and historic it certainly is, but not yet broad enough to embrace the Methodists!

Its uncommon personalities are lively. Foremost, of course, is the 100th Archbishop of Canterbury, the Most Reverend and Right Honorable Michael Ramsey — hoary, craggy, erudite, witty, and beloved, the spiritual head of the world's 40 million Anglicans. Dr. Ramsey has supported unity with the Methodists and is currently working on the Vatican. His predecessor, Lord Fisher, was more of a bureaucrat, but broke a 400-year-old tradition by visiting the then Pope John XXIII; to boot, he invited Billy Graham to campaign in Britain. Another yeasty churchman, the "Red Dean" of Canterbury was long a center of controversy for his Marxist views. But perhaps Britain's swingingest cleric is the

Bishop of Woolwich, the Right Reverend John A.T. Robinson, author of the best-seller, *Honest to God*. Robinson attacked the idea of "God-out-there" and proposed a "religionless Christianity"; he was denounced even by Canterbury himself, but a bishop he remains.

If you want to see the Church of England at its best in London, try Westminster Abbey or St. Paul's. Their services are often splendid; the preachers, provocative.

(5) *The Welfare State*

The Welfare State idea makes plenty of people, and not only Americans, see red: something about womb-to-tomb socialism grates against the rugged individualist's grain. (Sean Connery, for example — the ex-James Bond — has inveighed against it on occasion, not to mention Prince Phillip.) Welfare, certainly, is nothing new — it used to be called "charity". What is new, among other things, is the idea that governmental assistance is in many aspects of life proper.

It should be understood that the Welfare State idea does not necessarily preclude a free enterprise system. Very little industry in Britain has, in fact, been nationalized. Free enterprise is regulated, however, to insure maximum employment and employment benefits, high living standards (including housing), full medical coverage, and free (or highly subsidized) education. In Britain it's an expensive way of life, just as our "War on Poverty" was expensive, and it's surely not brought on a Millenium.

Critics, perhaps not unjustifiably, attack not only its expense, but also the loss of freedom and the bureaucratic inefficiency which almost inevitably result from such a system. On the other hand, it can be argued that the Welfare State promotes equality of opportunity, universal education, and gives everybody at least the same chance at the good life. Furthermore, one can say that the Welfare State in Britain seems to pose little threat to personal liberty; for instance, though medicine is socialized, a patient may choose his physician, and the physician his patient; and prescriptions, while no longer free, cost a pittance. After twenty years of socialism, Englishmen seem to be about as free as any people on earth — free, that is, except of taxes. Nonetheless, most people in Britain have managed to adjust to the Welfare State, and it certainly hasn't been without benefits.

(6) *The Good Life*

"Take Courage!" admonish billboards everywhere. A national Moral Rearmament campaign? Positive Thinking? Recall: "In England, nothing is what it appears to be ..." No, "Take Courage" is just an ad for a brand of beer named "Courage".

Logically, perhaps, a discussion of the Good Life belongs with Welfare. Certainly, not a few liberal politicians would consider the two ideas synonymous. The Welfare State, though, is more concerned with bare basics. In these last few paragraphs, we'll outline just a bit about British food, drink, and the conviviality that comes with them.

Let it be said, first, that British food has, until recently, gotten short shrift. (Or perhaps it was simply abysmal.) In either case, even *Gourmet* magazine has now worked out a gastronome's tour of Britain. But let's be clear: it's not so much that Continental *haute cuisine* has arrived; it's that British food itself has come into its own.

Real English food is simple and hearty, starting with breakfast. No continental crust-of-bread-with-coffee here; rather, bacon and boiled eggs and tomatoes and stewed prunes and kidneys and kedgeree and fried bread with marmalade and coffee and tea with milk. Slight exaggeration, perhaps, but it makes the point. A spread like that should get any sluggard going.

Luncheon is lighter, but then tea-time's at about four. The "Ploughman's Lunch" is hardly *haute*, but certainly typical — not only for ploughmen but also for city office workers who like to retreat to a pub during the noon-hour. Order it almost anywhere and you get: freshly baked bread sliced thick, a wedge of Cheddar, a pint of foaming bitter, and probably a couple of pickled onions — for considerably less than a dollar.

Everybody knows that the English are great beef-eaters. Really, though, in most families roast beef is reserved for Sunday "lunch". Usually the pink roast is complemented with horseradish, greens, turnips, potatoes, Yorkshire pudding, and a bit of sherry. (No elaborate sauces for the English, and few frills.) The humblest probably substitute mutton for the beef, but the rest is the same, and any leftovers go into Monday's "Shepherd's Pie."

Fish-and-chips probably aren't eaten every weekday in every household, but many a factory-employed mother sends one of the children regularly down to the corner "chips shop." (One might say that fish-and-chips is the national ordinary-day dish and that roast beef is the national Sunday dish.) There are other seafoods, of course: eels (delicious "jellied"), and cockles-and-mussels ("alive, alive, oh!") in cider-and-milk soup — fantastic!

Varieties of cheeses seem endless — each little country district seems to have its specialty — so just a few names: Cheshire (also Blue Cheshire, Farmhouse Cheshire, and Red Farmhouse Cheshire), Blarney (pseudo-Swiss from County Cork in Eire), Double Gloucestershire, Orange Leicester, and Derby Sage.

But on to drink, and again we quote the Rev. Sydney Smith: "What two ideas are more inseparable than Beer and Britannia?" The English do drink other brews, but when the English barmaid asks, "Your pleasure, gentlemen?" the answer is most often, "Bitter". Bitter is a medium-dark draft beer, strong and yeasty, and served at cellar temperature. The name pretty well describes the taste sensation; a taste for it is only acquired. Another popular drink is "stout" ("Guinness is good for you!" say the signs — and it's sometimes part of the diet in hospitals); stout, a malt liquor, is black and very heady.

Cider — really a form of wine — should be mentioned because many Americans think that this means Hallowe'en apple-juice. Not so! Cider sounds innocent, but it's sometimes 8% and can pack quite a wallop to the unwary.

We could wax on and on, but this is supposed to be a mere introduction. Honeymead (about which there's considerable lore) virtually went out soon after Beowulf. Suffice it to say that, despite his venerable, paradoxical, and highly-taxed institutions, the Englishman has his consolations: beef and bitter. The Good Life in Britain is good, and apparently improves with age.

Essay 2.

LONDON

London is the epitome of our times.
— Ralph Waldo Emerson

When a man is tired of London, he is tired of life;
for there is in London all that life can afford.
— Dr. Samuel Johnson

In a very real sense, the history of London is the history of Britain — at least it's a mirror-image of Britain's larger history. How and when did London begin? We can only guess; the earliest we know about is the Roman town of "Londinium", and about that we're not very sure. But diggings in and around other Roman settlements in Britain give us some clues. Bits of the city wall, a temple's ruins, perhaps a bath, some mosaic pavement, and part of a letter scratched onto a tablet are about all of Roman London that we have to work with. It must have been about a mile square, the square mile that is now "the City," the financial center of London. Ruins of the old Roman wall can be seen in St. Alphege's church-yard in Wood St., which runs north from Cheapside, not far east of St. Paul's Cathedral. We know that Londinium was not one of the chief Roman cities, though it must have been a valuable port. Apparently there were six principal cities, each built on the Roman checkerboard plan and heavily fortified. These included Gloucester, York, and Colchester, the capital, the walls of which remain remarkably preserved after 1900 years.

The Romans were great road-builders, and Londinium was located on one that stretched nearly to Wales. Its old English name has stuck: Watling Street. Probably the docks of Londinium were an important supply point on that route. We have no way of knowing for sure, but it is probable that life in Londinium was prosperous and relatively quiet. Most of the skirmishing between Romans and Britons took place up north. After 410, the town started to decline, for the Romans were gradually withdrawing their "protection". So for nearly 200 years, there's a gap in the record. Was Londinium abandoned? When did the Saxons move in? We haven't a clue. Yet there was some life in evidence there in 604, because Augustine, who had come to Canterbury seven years earlier, consecrated a certain Mellitus to be Bishop of London, the first of two bishoprics which Augustine created. There's another gap until King Alfred's time. In the ninth century, Danish Vikings were camped there, perhaps using London as a base for raiding operations.

Strange to say, somehow a hundred years later London had become the largest city in Britain, and Westminster (just outside the walls to the west) was fast becoming the royal seat. In 1066, William of Normandy defeated the Saxons at the town of Hastings, near the sea, about 60 miles east of London. William the Conqueror, really surnamed "the Bastard", was crowned on Christmas Day at the brand new Westminster Abbey. Almost none of that 11th century building remains now, though the Abbey Museum is in the basement of the old church. It is filled with old royal wax funeral effigies and other memorabilia. To awe Londoners with his presence, William built a fort, now called the "White Tower" — the beginning of the Tower of London. A formidable and impregnable fort it was; indeed, the Tower of London has never in its 900-year history been taken.

We know considerably more of the city's appearance a hundred years later. London was now able to boast many stone buildings. (Unlike the Romans, the Saxons had built mostly with timber and wattle; and most of these Saxon buildings were leveled by the fire of 1136.) Principal streets were paved now. A new London Bridge — this time of stone   was completed in 30 years; and there was even an open sewer system. (Almost certainly Londinium would have had a covered sewer; the Romans knew far more about sanitation than did their medieval successors.) Thirteen monasteries and over 100 parish churches were carrying on the work of prayer. Guilds were burgeoning — pre-eminently the Weavers' — and new docks would soon be built to handle the thriving import trade.

A big moment had come in 1135: the citizens of London had chosen a King of England. Henry I had died, and Mathilda should have succeeded him, but the Norman barons couldn't stomach the idea of a female sovereign. After considerable politicking, the City of London was asked to decide, and it chose Stephen I. Later Mathilda raised an army and even took Stephen prisoner, but his loyal Londoners forced her to flee. Stephen, unfortunately, wasn't much of a king: he was gullible and over-generous — and a king in medieval Britain could afford to be neither.

Yet, fortunately for Londoners, Stephen granted the city considerable independence — or perhaps the city simply took it. In any case, by 60 years after his death, London had its own Lord Mayor. In 1215 the guilds elected the first one, and the guilds still do so today. Now, there are 82 guilds, sometimes called "livery companies" because each has a distinctive — even gaudy — "livery" or uniform. New guilds develop occasionally, such as the Scientific Instrument Makers (1964). Most prestigious today are the Grocers, Mercers, and Fishmongers, but of course they're no longer made up of grocers, mercers, and fishmongers, but of bankers and business executives — a good example of how British traditions update themselves. But back to the Middle Ages.

A merchant middle class was gathering strength all over England, but its strength centered in London. The prosperous homes of the merchants were a conspicuous sign of their increasing political and economic muscle. Related to this was the development of Parliament, including the "Commons", which was now meeting in the Chapter House of Westminster Abbey. The middle class was strong enough to force nobility to start listening.

Geoffrey Chaucer, prominent civil servant and after-hours poet, was living in rooms atop one of the city gates — a natural observation deck. From that vantage he saw streets teeming with haberdashers, food-vendors, friars, and minstrels. He watched royal and religious processions, and heard the squabbling over prices and the lusty tavern songs, such as this one:

> Twice two full quarts we lawyers need,
>   To fill a legal jug.
> With one, we're gay; with two, we teach;
>   With three, we prophesy!

He knew well the rat-infested sewers and garbage heaps, and small wonder it is that medieval London wasn't much harassed by the plague — not until the 17th century. But he also saw the glory of the city: on Ludgate Hill, St. Paul's Cathedral, being enlarged in the latest Gothic style — the third largest church in Christendom. Its new spire, 489 feet, was the loftiest in the world at that time. Nevertheless, London pilgrims journeyed to a more ancient and storied shrine, to the mother church of England, to Canterbury, the tomb of Becket. Chaucer saw those medieval pilgrims, at their best and their worst, and preserved them to all generations in his *Canterbury Tales*.

We skip now more than a hundred years, to Henry VIII, who reigned from 1509 to 1547. Henry is best known, of course, for his amorous exploits, as the reader will recall if he saw the film, *Anne of the Thousand Days*. Perhaps more important historically, however, was his dissolution of the monasteries in 1532, for he started with religious establishments in and around London. It wasn't that Henry rejected monasticism on principle; it was simply that his exchequer was low. One of the interesting ironies is that little of the booty ended up in the king's coffer. Anyway, these old monastic properties became the king's "liberties". Royal encroachment! In order to appreciate what this meant for London at the time, recall how the city had gradually gained its cherished independence. Even today, Queen Elizabeth must *ask* the Lord Mayor's permission to enter the City — the ancient square mile in the center of town. Inconsequential perhaps, but once it represented an important right. So Henry encroached. But it was a partial blessing in disguise for fifty years later Elizabeth I was allowing theaters to mushroom in those "liberties" — and the puritannical City Fathers be damned! Had she been less adamant, a young country fellow named Will Shakespeare might never have gotten into acting — and therefore, into playwrighting.

Elizabeth I's London had some real problems to solve: crowding and sprawl. There were now perhaps 200,000 Londoners — not all squeezed into the "City's" square mile, of course, but squeezed. The fens and fields outside the walls were being "developed", and even an unsavory marsh on the south bank, called Southwark, was sprouting tenements. The wealthy were fleeing to the suburb of Westminster and were building their classical townhouses along the Strand. But it was a lusty, rollicking, swinging London under Good Queen Bess — much to Puritan dismay! Its spirit must have been a lot like today's London, but with a difference. Britain under Elizabeth was *leading* the world in exploration and trade; its *joie de vivre* was grounded in really justifiable optimism.

Only a few physical reminders of Elizabeth's London remain: most notably, parts of the Guildhall, and all of the Tower, Westminster Abbey and Hall, and the Palace of St. James'. In 1666, the Great Fire devoured most of the rest, even old St. Paul's. Eighty-seven churches and over 13,000 half-timbered dwellings burned down. Barely 20% of the city's buildings escaped the holocaust. Samuel Pepys, the great diarist, standing in All Hallows Barking tower, described the inferno: ". . . as far as we could see up the hill of the City, . . . a most horrid, malicious, bloody flame." The damage to property was incalculable — and this on top of the previous year's Great Plague, which had claimed 75,000 of London's nearly half-million citizens.

That fire, which started in a bakery shop in Pudding Lane, made possible the look of London today. Houses of brick soon replaced wooden ones. Streets were straightened and widened, with little squares laid out to give the city color and space. The greatest mark, though — a mark of utter genius — was Christopher Wren's: 49 new parish churches and a new cathedral, all in his elegant yet restrained Baroque. The crown of his genius was, and is, St. Paul's. Wren's epitaph could hardly have been more apt: *Si monumentum requiris, circumspice* — "If you want to see his monument, look around!"

With the rebuilding of London, the character of the City (the ancient square mile) changed. It had always been a business center, of course, but soon it was to become *the* center of the nation's big business. Centered in the Bank of England (established in 1694) and in the reconstructed Royal Exchange, and enriched by the East and West Indian trade, the wealth of the City became a force to be reckoned with by any government. The rest of London was, by comparison, a series of connected villages. There was virtually no cooperation in the planning and administration of Greater London at that time. (The city didn't have a central police force until 1829.) The popular picture we have of that London is of Samuel Johnson, Oliver Goldsmith, and David Garrick, all chewing the fat at the Mitre, the "Club," or the Cheshire Cheese — and duly reported by James Boswell. In a sense, it was indeed the "Age of Johnson." He and his fellows gave the period its color and wit, but those who pulled the real strings were in the banks and the Exchange.

Since 1800, population explosion and industrialization, with their attendant dilemmas, have forced extensive building and re-building. Great modern cities simply cannot operate efficiently with flickering oil-burning streetlights and outdated facilities. Likewise, horse-drawn trams were doubtless leisurely and comfortable, but railroads eventually had to be built. The advent of the automobile, of course, brought a whole new set of problems to a city never designed for it. All this may seem perfectly obvious, but consider the sheer magnitude of such problems for an already large metropolis like London.

London has always had its poor, but by Charles Dickens' time, poverty in such a wealthy empire was a national disgrace. He epitomized it in *Hard Times* and *Bleak House:* vermin and filth and moldy bread and child abuse and debtor's prisons. The hovels and the sweatshops have vanished, of course. But fortunately, the townhouses of affluent Mayfair and Hyde Park still grace the town, and no doubt still shelter latter-day Forsytes. Much of London was very comfortable indeed, and some parts were incredibly wealthy. The rest was neatly segregated off, and therefore invisible. But on the whole, Victoria's was a Golden Age, and Victorians could afford to be snobs.

Today's London is a bustling metropolis, full of all sorts and conditions of men. The young are highly visible, not only for their numbers (2½ million or so, many camped in and around Chelsea), but for their dress. Not since the Renaissance has such plumage brightened the scene. But look for the less flamboyant too. London today isn't only — or even mostly — Carnaby Street. Notice that politician of furled brow and stiff upper lip, walking smartly with a bowler on his head and an umbrella in his gloved hand. (Mod London's gone frivolous, but not he!) Or that gray-mustached bureaucrat, all decked out in formal morning wear, heading a long bus queue. (Not quite upper-class, but still trying!) Or that clergyman in gaiters — those tight leggings which reach from ankle to knee (Obviously "C. of E." — Church of England!). Watch these people — they're Britain's Silent Majority.

London has continued to sprawl, so that now its area is twice that of New York City. But the two cities are quite different. London is beginning to get a few near-skyscrapers, yet one can walk down its busiest streets without feeling that he's at the bottom of some canyon. New buildings there are, certainly, but Englishmen are wiser than to replace their best antique edifices with towers of stainless steel and glass — and New York is only now beginning to learn that wisdom. London, in fact, faithfully reconstructed many of its fine old buildings after the World War II blitzes, and at enormous cost. Britain knows the value of its heritage. A few of the newest buildings are truly distinguished, though we don't single out the Post Office Tower for kudos. Rather, we have in mind such buildings as the new Royal Festival Hall, located on the south bank near Waterloo Bridge: gaunt, even brutal, but distinguished.

London has now stretched itself to the outer limit and beyond. A 20-mile wide "Green Belt" surrounds the city — a strip of unspoiled English countryside. That belt is sacred; new developments are being built only beyond it. And one can *breathe* in London! Parks are everywhere and always green, and the city is full of little windowboxes. One comes across patches of green and flowers in the most unexpected places. Now if London could only do something about precipitation . . .

Essay 3

THE WORLD OF WILLIAM SHAKESPEARE

The facts about Shakespeare are rather meager. Nothing like the scientific biography existed in his time, and the first attempt at writing down his life came in 1708, nearly a century after his death. Yet we know more for certain about him than about most of the other famous personages of his time. The first item of evidence is rather trivial: in April, 1552, a certain John Shakespeare, living in Henley Street, Stratford, was fined 12 pence for failing to remove a garbage heap from in front of his house. This John Shakespeare, a glove-maker who later served as "high bailiff" (mayor) of Stratford, was almost certainly the John Shakespeare recorded as Will's father. In 1557, he married the daughter of a wealthy landowner, Mary Arden. The baptism of Will is recorded in Holy Trinity Church in Stratford as April 26, 1564. The date of his birth is not known, but it is popularly celebrated on the 23rd, the day on which he died, 52 years later, and appropriately St. George's Day, the feast of England's patron saint. We can assume that Will attended the free grammar school, though there is no record of this.

In 1582 there is recorded a request for a special dispensation for the marriage of Will to Anne Hathaway during Advent. (Marriages were usually prohibited during Advent and Lent.) But there is no record of the ceremony. The first child was baptised six months later. Anne was 8 years older than Will (he would have been 18). Very possibly the two had entered a "pre-contract" (engagement) earlier. Pre-contracts were legally binding in Elizabethan England; if one had entered such an engagement and married someone else, his marriage would be considered bigamous and both would be subject to excommunication. So Will's marriage would have been considered perhaps ill-advised — he was a minor — but hardly scandalous. We don't know when he went to London and entered the theatre — perhaps about 1588. But we do know that he was both an actor and a playwright by 1592, for he was attacked in print as an "upstart crow", and a "tiger's heart wrapped in a player's hide". In 1599 Will finally got the coat of arms that his father had been refused. The motto: *non sanz droict,* "not without right". In 1597 he bought New Place, the largest house in Stratford, which would indicate considerable financial success and local social prestige; and later he made several other large investments. Shakespeare made his fortune as an actor, not as a writer; even the most prolific writers could barely support themselves. He probably retired from the stage about 1612. Just before his death in 1616, he made his will. His wife was left only "the second best bed with the furniture". London law automatically would have given the widow at least one-third of the estate, but London law didn't much affect practice in the country districts. Will had hoped for a male heir to perpetuate his name, but his son Hamnet had died as a youth; he wanted to leave his estate to some future grandson, but none was ever born. He was buried in Stratford Church (Holy Trinity), and it was unusual that his wife wasn't buried in the same grave. Perhaps "Curst be he that moves my bones" — the last line of the epitaph he had composed for his tombstone — had something to do with it?

Stratford-on-Avon

Stratford-on-Avon in Will Shakespeare's time must have had about 2,000 or so inhabitants — a rather large community, considering that it was off the beaten track. London itself had less than 200,000, and it had grown rapidly in the previous 30 years; Bristol, the second largest city in Britain, had perhaps 30,000.

Stratford is considerably larger today, but the layout of the town is basically the same: three streets running about parallel with the river Avon and three streets crossing them at right angles. First we cross the old bridge, built just before 1500 by Sir Hugh Clopton, a local boy who made a fortune in trade and became the Lord Mayor of London. He also gave the town the guild chapel and hall, where Shakespeare undoubtedly attended the free grammar school; it's still used as a school today. It must have been a good school, for it paid the unusually high stipend of £20 and hired graduates of Oxford.

The main street was, and is, Bridge Street, running up to the old market square and crucifix (since torn down) which stood at the intersection of Henley and High Streets. Shakespeare's birthplace is in Henley; the prosperous merchants lived on High — the Quineys and Sadlers and Rogers. Rogers, the apothecary, sold not only the usual potions, but such New World novelties as sassifras and tobacco. His house is called "Harvard House", since his grandson gave the library that became Harvard College. Farther down, High Street becomes Chapel Street, and here, across from Clopton's Guild Chapel, stood "New Place", the largest house in Stratford, built by Sir Hugh, which Will Shakespeare bought in 1597. An 18th century clergyman who owned the place was so plagued by sightseers that he had it torn down; only the foundations and formal gardens remain. And on down the street in "Old Town" is "Hall's Croft", the house in which Will's daughter Susanna lived with the prominent physician, Dr. John Hall. The parish church, Holy Trinity, stands by itself near the river. Here Will and his family were baptized and here they lie buried. The church stands on the site of a Saxon monastery, and is an interesting mixture of architectural styles: Norman, Early English, Decorated, Flamboyant, and Perpendicular. Besides the grave, the elaborate Renaissance Clopton monument, the chained Bible (King James version), old baptismal font (used for many years as a flower pot!), the door knocker, and "misericords" (makeshift back rests, carved with grotesques) are worth seeing. The stained glass is modern, the originals having been broken by Puritan enthusiasts.

The principal industry of the town was "malting" (i.e. brewing). Otherwise, Stratford was, and is, a market town; the annual "Mop Fair" and ox-roast survive from the Middle Ages. The liveliness of the little town was considerably increased by religious dissension, a sport open to all. Bloody Mary had burned a good quota of Warwickshiremen during her gloomy regime, and a sizeable number of recalcitrant Catholics chose to pay heavy fines during Elizabeth's reign rather than "conform". In Elizabethan England, religion and politics were inextricably mixed, and a subject was loyal to the queen only if he were loyal to her church. And since such loyalty wasn't always quite spontaneous, Stratford citizens were fined if they didn't attend church every Sunday. Besides, government commissioners were continually on the prowl to see that the law was enforced. The pulpit itself was a handy mouthpiece for government propaganda, and the ready-made sermons that Parson Bretchgirdle had to read must have been of great assistance in preventing anybody from making up his own mind about any subject whatsoever!

The England that Will Shakespeare grew up in may have been "Merry Old England", but the town of Stratford was a tight little community. The Renaissance came to Britain late and had little effect outside London. The townspeople were jealous of local trade especially, and strangers were suspect. There were hundreds of regulations on the books, each with an appropriate fine. You were fined if your dog went unmuzzled, if your duck wandered from the house, if you played forbidden games, if your children were out after 8 o'clock at night in the summertime, etc. Occasionally wandering minstrels and troupes of players came to entertain, but they were suspect, being regarded as vagrants — and their show had to be censored by the town council first. For a boy like Will Shakespeare, London, not Stratford, would have been where the action was.

The Theater in Shakespeare's Day

Acting, in Shakespeare's day, was no easy profession. It took rigorous training and had little of the glamor the stars in show business enjoy today. Remember that the audience was close to the stage; the Globe Theater was probably only about 80 feet in diameter; the penny-paying crowd in the pit could stand right up to the stage, and the most expensive seats were often on the stage itself. And the London audience liked to see blood! It was necessary to find some way to run a sword through an actor's body or to tear out his entrails without ruining him for the next day's show. The audience wanted blood and it got *real* blood. Ox blood was too thick, so sheep's blood was generally used. The one to be stabbed would be equipped with a bladder of blood under his costume; when he was stabbed, he would arch himself and the blood would spurt forth quite realistically.

The Elizabethan stage represented a universe that was literally "three-layered". The stage ceiling (heaven), painted with sun, moon, stars, and signs of the Zodiac, had numerous pulleys and ropes, and whoever played Ariel in Shakespeare's *Tempest* would need to swing from rope to rope and simultaneously speak his lines. "Hell" was under the stage; the stage floor had several trap-doors, and spirits, ghosts, and witches would arise through clouds and sulphur fumes.

Shakespeare's acting experience gave him a considerable advantage over most of his rival playwrights. He knew his fellow players better than his own brothers; not only did they work long hours together, but the membership of his company was constant over several years. He worked with a few of the same men for over 25 years. Shakespeare's company was a "share company". The members of the company owned shares, and so each day's "take" went into the common pot, out of which expenses had to be paid. As Shakespeare became a more accomplished playwright, he probably held a "writer's share", i.e. he was paid mostly for writing, though he still acted minor roles. Tradition has it that he played roles of kings and Hamlet's father's ghost.

The London Council opposed theaters out of sheer spite: the playhouses were located in "liberties" outside their control (i.e. outside the City proper). In Shakespeare's time, play-going was a great national pastime. Plays were performed in the afternoon, so apprentices would leave their shops early after lunch. Since theaters were outside the City it might take an hour to get there. This meant that they would be late in getting back to work. The Council also objected to the theater because it received no revenue from the acting companies. Furthermore, any large gathering was suspect, unless for prayer or sermonizing, because crowds bred rebellion. Her majesty's government shared the same fear. The Earl of Essex once used a political play to foment a short-lived riot.

But on the whole the theater's greatest supporter was the Queen herself. She allowed players to build their theaters in her "liberties" (i.e. areas not subject to the authority of the London Council), especially on the south bank of the Thames. The most famous of these "liberties" was the "Liberty of the Clink". (The "Clink" was an ancient penetentiary; hence our current expression.) And she gave actors extra revenue by having them perform at Court. Elizabeth's tastes were rather bourgeois, and she enjoyed the lusty humor and the patriotic fervor of a Shakespeare as much as did the common Cockney.

Shakespeare's Grave
    Shakespeare's famous epitaph reads:

> Good friend, for Jesus' sake forebear
> To dig the dust enclosed here;
> Blest be the man that spares these stones
> And curst be he that moves my bones.

Shakespeare's grave, in the chancel of Stratford church (Holy Trinity), is right next to a door, the door that led into the "charnel house" (demolished in 1799). Charnel houses, once common in England, were storage houses for old bones dug up when the churchyards got overcrowded. Very possibly young Will Shakespeare once saw old graves being dug up to make room for new ones. Such a gruesome sight would have made quite an impression! The Stratford churchyard dated from the 9th century at least, and few of its inhabitants enjoyed a permanent tenure. Even though, as a "lay rector", Shakespeare was entitled to burial in the chancel, he apparently wanted to take no chances. His grave is said to be 17 feet deep! When he was buried, the chancel was in disrepair; in fact it had been boarded up by the Puritans, who thought that sermons were more important than sacraments. It has since been restored and can be seen for a few shillings. You can also buy a large rubbing of Shakespeare's epitaph.

    The grave has never been opened, though not too many would be deterred today by the curse on his gravestone. The London *Times*, however, did report some time ago that a group has petitioned church authorities to open the grave. Perhaps they expect to find a confession that it was Sir Francis Bacon who *really* wrote the plays? So what if the diggers shovel down 17 feet to whatever's left? Just what might they hope to find — a confession note to the effect that Bacon (or Elizabeth or whoever) was the *real* writer behind the Shakespeare "front"? And what if they did? Would such a revelation destroy Shakespeare? Perhaps Shakespeare the man; but would Juliet be any less poignant, Falstaff less hilarious, Hamlet less problematical? The plays don't stand or fall with Shakespeare the man (or myth). "Shakespeare" lives so long as his plays live for us. As Ben Jonson (no friendly critic) wrote of him:

Thou art a monument without a tomb,
An art alive still while thy book doth live.

The miracle of Shakespeare is that he seems to be ever new. Eighteenth century classicists tamed him and "corrected" his works, making him properly classical. Romanticists saw in him the wild revolutionary, and raised him almost to deity. Victorian moralists expurgated not a few lines (they missed some of the better ones!) and discovered the great moralizer. And today? Well, we have modern-dress productions with a long-haired Hamlet, and Julius Caesar as a South American dictator. Romeo and Juliet are the tragic lovers of *West Side Story*. (Or, played straight, they make it a smash hit film, as contemporary in theme as *The Graduate*.) And doubtless generations yet unborn will discover new relevancies. But again, Ben Jonson said it best: "He was not of an age, but for all time."

Essay 4.

THE GERMAN EXPERIENCE

One of the most striking developments on the German national scene in recent years has been the protest movement of the younger generation. Heaven knows, protest movements as such are nothing new. Everywhere these days, it seems, young people are restless and impatient, voicing dissatisfaction with many aspects of the societies in which they live.

Only ten or fifteen years ago, observers found German youth astonishingly indifferent to political issues. Youngsters were immune to political slogans and to ideologies; they were reluctant to show enthusiasm for anything that wasn't hard-headed, realistic, or pragmatic. German youth at that time were dubbed "the skeptical generation". They avoided any commitment to causes outside their own limited sphere of interest. Typical of a young German was the well-adjusted student or apprentice who worked hard to obtain the type of education and training which he required for his career. It was the hard-working skeptical young man and woman of the post-war generation that the older generation trusted to bring democracy to maturity in Germany. Hard-headed realism, after all, is what you would expect of a mature citizen. It was the skeptical generation who helped rebuild the German economy, bringing about what Germans call the *Wirtschaftswunder* (Economic Miracle).

The situation has changed radically. Although the majority of German young people still spend a good part of their time and energy building their careers, a new type of young person has come on the scene, and he has caught the public eye to such a degree as to dominate the image of the German youth today. This new type is the student involved in organizing demonstrations, publishing and distributing leaflets, and participating in marches and teach-ins. More than likely, he regards himself as a member of what he calls the "extra-parliamentary opposition", or in German: "ausserparlamentarische Opposition" (APO).

The movement continues, and of particular interest for us is the fact that these young people, while professing to represent an entirely new phenomenon, display in a striking manner some very traditional German traits. A brief discussion of them will help us to understand much of the thinking and philosophical attitude of the German people as a whole. One of these traits is an extreme difficulty in viewing a political adversary in proper perspective, in appreciating the valid and beneficial parts of his program while recognizing the precise point at which his thinking diverges from one's own. Connected with this is a tendency toward intolerance of one's opponent, and a refusal to cooperate with him on programs where agreement is possible. Instead, an opponent is simply dismissed as evil. Politics is thus emotionalized, and the public tends to be polarized toward one extreme or the other.

This emotionalism runs parallel to another trend which distinguishes Germany from its neighbors in Europe: a tendency toward the unclear, the mysterious and mystifying – in a word, toward mysticism. Whether this trend should be traced back to the mood prevailing in the vast, gloomy forests in which the ancient pagan Germans lived, hunted, and worshipped – a mood which filled them with a fear of something they felt but could not define – or whether the trend derives from the heritage of the Celtic Druids and Nordic sorcerers with their esoteric rites, witchcraft, and magic symbols, is something I leave to the historian or anthropologist. This trend, at any rate, sometimes expresses itself in a fatalistic attitude which renounces any attempt to fathom the forces which shape human destiny. It sometimes leads German writers to blame an anonymous fate for things which are actually due to all-too-human acts or omissions. The predilection for the mysterious reveals itself in many works of German literature: for example, the stories of E.T.A. Hoffmann, Wilhelm Hauff, and other writers of the Romantic period. We even find it in the works of contemporary writers like Günther Grass. It constitutes one of the fascinating factors in the style of Caspar David Friedrich, one of Germany's great painters. In religion, there are the writings of Jakob Boehme and Meister Eckhard, two famous mystics. But this trend can be traced back to the German language itself.

More than any other language, German lends itself to poetic expression: to indication without clear statement, to vague suggestions which excite the reader's imagination but leave it to him to interpret their exact meaning. The German language grants a tremendous degree of freedom to the writer: he may form new words out of old ones, place an article before any type of word and use it as a noun, or transform a noun into a verb or adjective. In short, he may develop his own brand of German. This may be fine in poetry, but it can be hazardous when public issues are under discussion.

German students, too, have developed their own special brand of German usage. Not only do they use Marxist terminology, but they also use English words borrowed from the field of sociology. At one conference recently, many German commentators found it easier to understand these young people by mentally translating their statements into English. The students realize that they use a language which is hard for outsiders to understand, but it doesn't bother them. Instead, they seem boastful about the fact that they possess a secret language which makes them an elite apart from the rest of the people. Rather than seeking a dialogue with persons of different persuasions, they appear to be satisfied with monologues. It's an old Germanic vice: instead of communication they prefer self-expression.

Both factors — the vagueness of the German language in general, and the use of an esoteric brand of it — can affect practical politics, because language is something more than a vehicle of communication; it is a total way of thinking which can have very real effects. In debates between German and American students, for example, the American partner often flounders helplessly in desperation because the German debater's statements are too long-winded and too complicated in sentence structure and logic. The German student will introduce new definitions, refer to authors the American could not possibly have read, cite quotations from poems or essays which are beautiful but not quite to the point — in short, he neither replies to a question nor asks straightforward questions of his own. What he does is to give a relatively brief lecture on a topic only distantly related to the original theme of the discussion. This makes it impossible for his American partner to find out what he wants to say and where the debate should be headed. Furthermore, a German debater is often content merely to classify the problem he's dealing with by defining its place in the field of ideas. The practical solution to the problem ranks last. People who express interest in getting the problem solved are dismissed as "social engineers" or as practitioners of "merely" applied knowledge. And there is a slight undertone of arrogance and disdain in the way these expressions are pronounced.

The emphasis on theoretical ideas is sometimes so pervasive that practical experience is disregarded outright if it becomes inconvenient for the theory being elaborated. A charming illustration can be found in a poem by Christian Morgenstern. The poem describes a traffic accident involving Palmstroem. Palmstroem is an imaginary character invented by Morgenstern, an odd person who takes proverbs literally, probes into the meaning of everyday expressions, develops his own brand of logic — in short (to use Morgenstern's own words), a person "non-existent in the sense that he is ruled out by bourgeois convention." Palmstroem, having been hit by a car at a street corner and badly bruised, studies the local laws and traffic regulations. To his surprise, he finds that cars are not permitted to drive around that particular corner, and Palmstroem concludes that his experience must have been a dream, for how could something happen in fact if it was not possible in theory? The poem concludes: "And he comes to the conclusion/His experience was an illusion."

This is a trait which is typically German. The Germans' attitude toward their own history is full of contradictions. One of Germany's characteristics as a nation is a strong commitment to the value of tradition, which parallels the people's awareness of history. Some thinkers go so far as to describe this consciousness of history as a kind of ethical imperative — for example, the author Reinhold Schneider, who once wrote:

> We come from the most distant times, are the sons of countless generations and heirs to what they did. It is imperative for us to carry them with us in our conscience. Since man is the one who stands in history — 'between sin and salvation' — he cannot be what he ought to be unless he is aware of the roads that have been walked, and of those who walked on these roads.

Like other Europeans, many Germans are forced to turn to history simply because the things around them remind them so vividly of the past: churches, castles, works of art, names of places, the Slavic, French, or Scandinavian names of many persons, even the looks of people — in fact, there are German citizens who have slanted eyes and high checkbones, German redheads, blondes, blackhaired people, tall and short people, stout and slender types! History somehow holds the explanation, and the very word "history" fills the German with awe and respect.

Yet there is no accepted national interpretation of history, and for a good reason. Germany became a nation in the modern sense quite late. In 1871, the German princes, at Bismarck's behest, elected the King of Prussia Emperor of Germany. There had been a German empire before, the so-called "Holy Roman Empire", but that was never more than a relatively loose patchwork of princes with divergent interests and frequently conflicting aims. Each of these princes jealously guarded his rights, and indeed he had to in order to stave off the territorial ambitions of his neighbors. The emperor could rely only on his own principality for support, unless he was able to exploit occasional disagreements among his vassals. A self-confident middle class was able to use the financial difficulties of the princes to gain greater independence. In this way, a number of autonomous cities developed, the so-called *Reichsstädte* (Imperial Cities), which did not belong to any principality.

In the opinion of some observers, a feeling of nationhood began to arise only in the late 18th century at the court of Carl August, Duke of Weimar. The Duke summoned the greatest men of letters to his capital: Johann Gottfried Herder, Johann Wolfgang Goethe, Friedrich Schiller, Christoph Wieland, and others. The achievements of these classic figures of German literature and thought inspired the German people with a feeling of national pride and self-confidence. Awareness of national accomplishment in the cultural field gradually created a feeling of belonging together, of a common cultural heritage, and culminated in a desire for national unity. This feeling was intensified during the Napoleonic wars — although it must be stated that Bavaria and some other German states fought on Napoleon's side against their countrymen. In 1806, Franz of Hapsburg, the last ruler of the Holy Roman Empire, resigned and henceforth called himself Emperor of Austria. But the national movement continued, and was carried on mainly by students and intellectuals. It was suppressed temporarily after the abortive uprising in 1848, but finally triumphed in 1871. Yet seen from the viewpoint of national unity, it was a false triumph, for the Second German Reich which Bismarck created excluded the German part of Austria.

For all these reasons, it is understandable that the word "history" has come to mean one thing to a citizen of the once powerful city-state of Hamburg, something completely different to a Rhinelander, and yet another thing to an East Prussian — not to mention the famous differences of outlook between Bavarians and Prussians. The traditions which influence the political attitudes of German people vary not only with their place of birth but with religious and cultural affiliations. To take the most obvious cases, a Catholic's view of the Reformation will differ from that of a Protestant; a farmer's attitude is bound to differ from that of an industrial worker who can look back upon generations of union membership; craftsmen differ from intellectuals in their assessment of the major problems facing Germany today, and so on.

But to return to the question of national unity: While the type of patriotism displayed under Bismarck and Wilhelm II seems to us today to have been arrogant, aggressive, and rather empty, the Second Reich nonetheless helped tear down some of the barriers which separated German groups from each other. A process of internal integration began, along with industrialization, social legislation, and coordination of education, and it was supported by the cultural achievements which were considered the common property of all Germans. Philosophers, composers, poets, scientists, inventors, and writers worked for the benefit of the entire nation — and in a wider sense for all mankind — rather than for their small social or religious or local groups and communities. True political and cultural unity appeared to be within reach.

But the failure of the policies of Wilhelm II, and Germany's defeat in the First World War curbed the rise of national unity, even though the common experience of war had created a feeling of solidarity among war veterans. As the war ended, separatist tendencies emerged in various parts of Germany, particularly in the Rhineland and in Bavaria. Part of the attraction which the National Socialist party held for many people was its appeal to the desire for national unity. In fact, the complete collapse of nationalism after World War II seemed again to confirm the opinion of those elements in Germany which placed state, city, community, social, or religious interests above the national interest.

A return to provincialism was prevented mainly by another dramatic result of World War II, namely the influx of 13.7 million East German refugees into the Federal Republic. This caused an upheaval in the entire social system. Protestants moved into areas which had been predominantly Catholic for centuries, and vice versa. The establishment of new industries caused a migration of tens of thousands of workers to new homes; artisans and farmers who had lost their means of subsistence took new jobs in other sectors of the economy. Many of them went into industry and introduced new elements of tradition and thought into the ranks of industrial workers, with telling effect on labor union policies.

Yet these welcome repercussions, following a period of national collapse, have not succeeded in creating a sense of national solidarity. The Federal Republic is an artificial structure created, not by the free will of its citizens, but by the decisions of the Allied powers. As such, it has little appeal to popular sentiment. In spite of this, great economic strides have bolstered German self-confidence. Germans pat themselves on the back when speaking of German efficiency, German skill, and German precision work. There is complacency aplenty, but little patriotism. "A good German cannot be a nationalist," said President Heinemann in a speech on July 20, 1969, commemorating the unsuccessful plot on Hitler's life of 1944. "Today, a German who wants to be conscious of his nationality must think of himself as a European first." The failure of the National Democratic Party to win seats in recent elections for the Federal Parliament indicates that nationalist ovations have lost their appeal for the great majority of the voters.

Let us return to our earlier statement about inconsistencies in the German attitude toward history. While Germans cannot help being reminded of historical developments which influence the present, some of them succumb to instant amnesia when the years from 1933 to 1945 are mentioned. They have not yet learned to incorporate that period into their national history. And since the Germans have a tendency to place theory above reality, they apply it here in the form of escapism. Some Germans speak of "overcoming the past", a vague expression which is bound to be as puzzling to foreigners as the attitude behind it. What it means, bluntly stated, is that many Germans simply refuse to accept the facts about this period of their own history. Somehow they know the facts to be true, and they also know that what happened during those twelve years should never have happened to a civilized country. Like Palmstroem, however, they hope it really did not happen, and sometimes they say so. The events simply do not fit in with the theoretical image of their nation. Consequently many Germans evade the facts, expelling them from memory, secretly hoping to awaken one day to see the image of the "Land of Thinkers and Poets" restored to its traditional, lost glory.

In part, this attitude is due to the attempt made in the early post-war years to hold the individual citizen responsible for the atrocities of the National Socialist regime. The thesis of "collective guilt" implied that the people had been active accomplices of the regime, instead of victims or naive supporters. Seeing themselves in the role of defendants, the people instinctively pleaded "not guilty" and implicitly denied the guilt of their co-defendants, the Nazi rulers, as well. Furthermore, many Germans had cooperated with the regime because it represented governmental authority; and how could the authorities have been guilty of criminal acts? Indeed, there has always been a tendency among the German people to accept unquestioningly whatever decisions were made by the authorities — the city magistrate, state administration, or national government. In recent times, this trend has declined noticeably. It had arisen gradually throughout the course of German political history. Until the middle of the 19th century, most German states were monarchies governed by absolute rulers. Parliaments did not begin to play an active role until the second half of the 19th century. Prior to that, the German people were powerless subjects of their monarchs instead of voting citizens eager to defend their rights. At the very time the United States fought its war of independence, the Count of Hesse sold young men into the service of the British. Quite a few of these mercenaries died in a strange land defending the claims of the British crown. The very idea of protesting this ill-treatment at the hands of their sovereign would have been unthinkable.

On the other hand, German docility made for an excellent civil service. Generally loyal and efficient, and immune to bribery, the civil servants took charge of the day-to-day administration of the country. They enjoyed considerable influence and public esteem, and even though the Germans often poke fun at the narrowmindedness and pompousness of some *Beamten* (officials), they have to admit that civil servants seldom abused their power for personal gain, and that they have always been one of Germany's major assets.

Both factors, then — the subject position of most German citizens over the centuries, and the efficiency of the civil service — have tended to prevent the ordinary wage-earner from taking an active interest in governmental affairs. Even today, though the government may come in for criticism now and then, most people are content to let the civil service run things, as long as they're left in peace to mind their own private business with a minimum of interference. In *this* respect, the activities of the radical students constitute a departure from tradition indeed!

Another characteristic of the German people which results from both geography and history is its much-touted industriousness, a quality in which Germans take pride but which has not enhanced their popularity with other European nations. It is this quality, plus American aid, which brought about Germany's economic recovery after the war. Without the Marshall Plan the Germans would not have been able to achieve what they did, but without their industriousness and efficiency, American aid would not have been put to as good a use as it was.

What makes the Germans all that industrious? Speaking only half in malice, one could say that they are industrious only because they have to be and only as *long* as they have to be. Germany is a country rich in natural resources, minerals, forests, lakes and rivers, and fertile soil. It is a country which richly rewards effort. But it is a country which yields nothing *without* such effort. Ancient writers described Germany as a region of dark woods, extensive bogs and moors, with a rough climate, long and cold winters, rainy and often foggy summers. It required hard work to cultivate such a terrain. Woods had to be cut, fields drained, and meadows cleared of stones. An old German parable illustrates this situation. A vintner told his sons on his deathbed about a treasure hidden in the vineyard, but he died before he could give its exact location. Eager to unearth the treasure, his sons immediately began to dig up the vineyard, leaving no stone unturned, sifting every grain of soil — but without finding any trace of gold or jewels. In the fall, however, they were amazed to see that the harvest was twice as abundant as it had been the previous season. It was then that they understood their father's advice: the vineyard would make them rich if they worked hard enough.

Further inducement to work came with the wars which swept the country over its long history, destroying whole cities and villages. Again and again the people had to rebuild their homes and recultivate fields which had been devastated by passing armies. Hard, incessant work was the price of survival, and it became habitual.

Even today, Germany's main asset is her working capacity. There is not enough arable soil to feed the entire population, and it is necessary to export industrial products in exchange for the food it needs. Many Germans regard work not merely as a necessity but as a moral obligation.

A clergyman once visited a dying woman and asked her whether she was confident of her salvation. She replied, "Oh Herr Pastor, I am sure I will be saved. I have worked hard all my life." This attitude is typically German. It is the tendency to elevate a mere necessity to the status of a moral duty, to do something not merely because it has to be done but to glorify, idealize their doing it. The action is thus invested with a higher meaning; a practical matter is lifted up to the realm of ideas. And this helps us understand the German youth movement today. To quote from *Der Spiegel*, the protesters " . . . are characterized by an emphasis on ideology instead of politics, by the attempt to find a new morality in ideological engagement alone."

This is the German experience as it has been lived thus far and as it continues to be lived today. Our review has attempted to point out that while attitudes are changing because they constitute a process rather than a rigid structure, the interplay of inherited traits with new developments has revealed the presence of some constant features. A better understanding, and in some instances a transformation of these features will be required if Germany is to cope successfully with the problems of the present and to lay the foundations for the future.

Essay 5.

THE ITALIAN EXPERIENCE

Anyone traveling in Europe almost invariably remembers his entrance into Italy as a pleasant experience, although it may be complicated by some things he doesn't expect. Among the latter is the protracted waiting at the border and the rigamarole of customs — with much stamping of carnets, papers, passports, and other documents. But the surprises awaiting the traveler usually outweigh these distractions, and the customs officers in Italy are courteous, correct, and sometimes downright friendly. They smile and exchange pleasantries — especially when dealing with some *belle ragazze* (pretty girls). When the visitor notes the friendliness of the border guards, he may be sure that he has arrived in Italy.

Once one has settled down in Venice, Florence, or Rome, it is important to understand certain aspects of Italian life. Appreciating regional differences and the attitudes that go with them, the ritual of bargaining in shops, the Italian penchant for flirting with foreign women, and the Italian's love of art, can add immeasurably to any stay in Italy. Regional differences, for instance, are probably more pronounced in Italy than in any other modern nation, and regional rivalries follow close upon regional differences. The Milanese have a saying: *Milano lavora, Napoli canta, e Roma mangia tutto* (Milan works, Naples sings, and Rome eats everything up). The Venetians refer to *i toscani sarcastici* (the sarcastic Tuscans). Florentines are given to repeating, *L'Italia si termina a Roma e l'Europa si termina a Napoli* (Italy ends at Rome and Europe ends at Naples). And on it goes.

Many Italians still speak their local dialects within the family or among friends; this is especially true in the South and in Sicily. Each region of Italy has its own dialect, and a Sicilian from Palermo speaking his dialect would not be understood by a Venetian speaking *his* dialect. The Neapolitan dialect contains a liberal sprinkling of French and Spanish words, borrowed from these languages when the city was under Angevin (French) or Aragonese (Spanish) domination. For instance, the titles *don* and *donna* in Italian come from Spanish via Neapolitan. Moreover, a sizeable literature exists in some dialects. Goldoni, the famous eighteenth-century playwright, wrote most of his comedies in Venetian dialect, and a group of Sicilian poets kept up the tradition of dialect poetry for a number of centuries. Of course Dante also wrote in his Tuscan dialect, but he established his dialect as standard Italian, since he was the first great author in Italy to write in the vernacular.

In much the same way, Chaucer established the Midlands dialect of English as standard English in the late Middle Ages.

The above considerations notwithstanding, all contemporary Italians — even those in remote areas — speak and understand standard Italian. Mass communications and mass education in Italy have taken their toll of the dialects; but dialect theatres flourish in various Italian cities, catering to regional pride. The most important point here is that the traveler should attune himself to the phenomenon of regional pride in each part of Italy. Above all, he should avoid making unfavorable comparisons between Italian cities (for example, "Naples is so much noisier than Florence") within earshot of local Italians, many of whom may understand what he says. Instead, he should enjoy what each area has to offer. Certainly, each area has more than enough to charm its visitors.

Cooking is also a regional affair in Italy. One of the most difficult things to impress upon travelers in Italy is that there is no "Italian" cuisine. There is Tuscan cooking, Roman cooking, Neapolitan cooking, Bolognese cooking, Sicilian cooking, but no "Italian" cooking. Generally speaking, macaroni products (called *pasta*), olive oil, tomato sauces, fresh cheeses (such as *mozzarella*), and pizza predominate in the South, while rice or cornmeal (*polenta*), butter, cream or meat sauces, cured cheeses, and seafood predominate in the North. Some regional specialties well worth trying are Florence's *bistecca alla fiorentina* (charcoal-grilled T-bone steak, served with a wedge of lemon), Rome's *saltimbocca alla romano* (veal cooked in butter and white wine), Venice's *scampi fritti* (fried shrimp), or Naples' *vermicelli alle vongole (pasta* with clam sauce). Remember, however, that nowhere in Italy are *pasta* or rice served as main courses as they sometimes are in the U.S. They are meant as introductory courses, and take the place of soup.

The best way to explain these regional differences in Italy is to emphasize the relative youth of the country as a national entity. Italy has been united for only 110 years. Before that time, stretching back for more than a thousand years, Italy was divided into small, independent city-states, including the Republic of Venice, the Republic of Florence, the Papal States, and others. Each of these states developed an intense commercial rivalry with the others during the Middle Ages, often involving open warfare. Marco Polo, the prominent Venetian explorer, was captured by the Genoese during one of their wars with the Venetians over control of the lucrative shipping lanes to the Middle East.

When we speak of commercial rivalry, we touch upon one of the keystones of Italian history — the rise of the merchant, urban middle class. Banking as an institution began in Florence in the early Middle Ages. Our word "bank" derives from the Italian *banca*, or the table over which banking transactions first took place. Today, the game aspect of commerce is as keenly felt as it was centuries ago. There are still shops, especially in southern Italy, where shoppers are expected to bargain, and Italians can drive a hard bargain on an international scale as well. The Fiat automobile company is building a billion-dollar plant in the Soviet Union.

There is *one* characteristic which may be considered universal in Italy, quite apart from regional differences. That characteristic, of course, is the Italian male's fascination with women. Nowhere the female tourist travels is she apt to attract so much solicitous attention as in Italy. She will be followed, clucked at, spoken to — even, in some cases, pinched. Any Italian male between the ages of 9 and 99 is apt to try his hand at skirt-chasing.

An incidental word about violence in Italian urban centers: it simply does not exist at all. There are two good reasons why it is safe for men (or for women with escorts) to walk the streets of any Italian city at any hour of the day or night. First: Italians, as they become more affluent, tend to move in toward the center of the city. There is no "flight to the suburbs" in Italy. Consequently, Italian city centers are not deserted by the civic-minded middle class. In fact, the Italian urban center remains a spectacle of beauty, unmarred by slums and factories. The latter are usually relegated to the industrial zones on the edge of town. The happy result is pleasant streets along which to walk — and walking is a favorite Italian pastime. Second: the Italian's legendary volatile temper explodes at almost any provocation, especially at minor traffic snarls. The first time this happens, it may seem a bit frightening or confusing to the American visitor, who is used to calmer methods of dealing with minor crises. However, verbal anger never leads to physical violence in Italy. The shouting acts as a safety valve, allowing all excess steam to escape. These crises and their attendant outbursts of temper are just as instantaneously forgotten. As a result, frustration and anger do not build up in quite the same way as they do in other cultures, releasing themselves in spectacular acts of physical violence. The Italian rids himself of his anger immediately; the American often harbors it and adds it to a mounting store of hostility and resentment.

Finally, a word about the Italian's attitude toward art. The American tourist, raised in tremendous awe of "culture" often cannot understand the Italian's rather casual attitude toward art, music, and literature. His casual attitude is, in fact, a very natural way to respond; it does *not* mean that he is insensitive to his cultural heritage. After all, he has been raised in a country which amounts to a gigantic outdoor museum. He might attend a church whose altarpiece was painted by Giotto; or he may have played as a child in the Piazza Navona, whose major fountain was designed by Bernini and whose major church was designed by Borromini; or he may drive to work every day around the Ponte Vecchio in Florence or the Duomo in Milan. He may even live in a town, such as San Gimignano outside of Florence, which has been designated a national monument. He whistles operatic arias as people in other countries whistle pop tunes. In short, he has spent his life surrounded by art, and may therefore be forgiven if he tends to take it for granted. But this does not mean that he loves it any less; one takes one's parents for granted in the same sense.

For the Italian, art is not a thing set apart. It surrounds him, it pervades his life. Indeed, perhaps more than anywhere else, the living of life itself becomes an art in Italy. It is no accident that Baroque art (and its musical handmaiden, opera) began in Italy in the late sixteenth and early seventeenth centuries, for Baroque art reflects the vibrant zest for the spectacle of life inherent in the Italian personality. It is an attitude still imbedded in the contemporary Italian — an attitude which the visitor might well savor, and in due course come to share himself.

ROME
The Eternal City

Rome is probably the most fascinating of all European cities. Paris may be the most beautiful, London the most "swinging," but Rome has the grandeur of almost three millenia of history packed into it. Rome simply overwhelms the visitor with a sense of timelessness. But Rome is more than just one city; it is many overlapping cities in one. There is ancient Rome, Christian Rome, Renaissance Rome, and modern Rome. A brief look at each of them will furnish at least a hint of what this giant of a city has to offer.

Ancient Rome

The ancient city, which can still be viewed in the impressive ruins strewn liberally around Rome, was the throbbing, vital heart of an empire which covered almost all of the known world. The Romans owed their empire not only to their formidable military skills, but even more crucially to their administrative and engineering abilities. Without Roman roads, Roman administrators, and the Roman system of law, the empire could never have held together for over four centuries. The technical achievements of the Romans are just as impressive today as they were in ancient times. Roman plumbing, sanitation, and central heating techniques were not equalled until the twentieth century. One can still see the remains of water pipes and central heating ducts embedded in the walls of the ancient ruins of Ostia (near Rome) and Pompeii (near Naples). The Romans had hot and cold running water, flush toilets, and a forced-air heating system — luxuries unknown in Europe until the 19th century.

Roman architecture was monumental. The Romans developed the use of the arch and the dome to aid them in building huge, complex edifices. One of the most awesome sights in Rome is still the immense ruin of the Baths of Caracalla, where outdoor operas are now performed in the summertime. Try wandering through the Imperial Forum along the famous Palatine hill and see the awesome remains of grand public buildings and majestic triumphal arches. There is of course the Colosseum, where all sorts of public spectacles were held. The real name of this famous structure is the "Flavian Amphitheatre", so called because it was built by one of the Flavian emperors, Vespasian. It is called the Colosseum because it was built on the site of a colossal gilded statue of Nero, which was torn down after Nero's downfall. In this amphitheatre, 70,000 spectators could witness gladiators in combat. The Romans even staged mock naval battles in the arena by flooding it. After the fall of the empire, the amphitheatre degenerated into a mere repository of large marble blocks for other buildings. This destructive procedure continued until an early Renaissance pope declared the edifice a sacred monument to the memory of the early martyrs, making it a crime to remove any more building stones. An altar and crucifix were set up inside. (Actually, most of the Christian martyrs lost their lives at the nearby Circus Maximus, not in the Colosseum.)

Another prominent structure of ancient Rome is the Pantheon, a temple dedicated to all the Roman gods, which was converted into a Christian church in the early Middle Ages. The painter Raphael is buried inside, along with the kings of Italy. Yet another imposing ruin is the Basilica of Maxentius. It is interesting to note that early Christian churches were modelled architecturally after the Roman basilicas, which were courts of law or shopping arcades, rather than after the pagan temples. That is why most of the major churches in Rome are still referred to as basilicas, chiefly St. Peter's.

Christian Rome

Very early in Christian history, Rome established its central position as the capital city of Christendom, and the Bishops of Rome, who eventually became the popes, exercised supremacy over the other bishops. Through the centuries, the popes gradually consolidated their power, though at the expense of a split with the Christian Church in the East, which was centered in Constantinople. Rome became the center of Christianity in the Middle Ages and remains the center of Roman Catholicism to this day. Located inside of Rome is the smallest independent state in the world, Vatican City, which is ruled directly by the Pope. From this tiny state, the Pope directs the religious activities of the world's Roman Catholics. In fact, the four major basilicas of Rome happen also to be the four major churches of the Catholic world. Devout Catholics who come to Rome make a special point to visit all four of them. They are St. Peter's (San Pietro), St. Mary Major (Santa Maria Maggiore), St. Paul's Outside the Walls (San Paolo fuori i muri), and St. John Lateran (San Giovanni in Laterano). The last-named church is the Pope's official parish as Bishop of Rome. There are, of course, dozens of other important churches in Rome, including Santa Susanna, the Church of Domine Quo Vadis, and St. Peter in Chains.

The very heart of Christian Rome is the Piazza San Pietro (St. Peter's Square). Bernini's famous colonnade envelops the square, and towering over everything is St. Peter's Basilica, designed primarily by Bramante and Michelangelo, though involving other architects as well. Its dome can be seen from almost anywhere in the city. On Sundays at noon (except during the summer, when he is at Castel Gandolfo), the Pope appears and addresses the crowd assembled to hear him.

Renaissance Rome

In the 1500's, Rome became the chief artistic center of Italy, and four popes were instrumental in accomplishing this artistic revival — Alexander VI (1492-1503), Julius II (1503-1513), Leo X (1513-1521), and Clement VII (1523-1534). They patronized the greatest artists and architects of the day, including Michelangelo, who transformed the city almost overnight. One should really speak of Renaissance *and* Baroque Rome, for the two artistic periods, at least in Rome, are inseparable. The major artistic figure of the sixteenth century, Michelangelo, served to bring about a transition from one to the other. It is almost impossible to mention any spot in Renaissance Rome without recalling his name; he left his touch on everything. For instance, he had much to do with designing St. Peter's and he built the Piazza del Campidoglio, the most perfect architectural expression of Renaissance Rome. The Piazza del Campidoglio is on the Capitoline hill, behind and to the right of Italy's Monument to the Unknown Soldier (popularly known as "The Wedding Cake") and in front of the Imperial Forum. The imposing Palace of the Senate dominates the square, flanked on either side by identical smaller buildings.

After Michelangelo, the most important architects and artists of Rome were Bernini and Borromini, both Baroque artists. "Baroque" is a word which is used frequently in connection with Italy, and it might be best to explain it here. It comes from an Italian word meaning "in poor taste," which is what early Baroque art was considered to be. But within a very few years, it came to refer favorably to the quality of the art itself, which had by this time gained wide acceptance. The primary characteristics of Baroque art are its exuberance, extravagance, and theatrical appeal. The painting, sculpture, and architecture of the Baroque period (roughly 1580 to 1720) all exhibit a preoccupation with the dramatic. In painting and sculpture, strange convolutions and daring curved designs abounded. In architecture, unusual planes were used in the facades of buildings in order to create a theatrical play of light and shadow as the sun changed position during the day. It was in this period also that many of the great fountains of Rome were built; it was felt that the interplay of light and water could be used to highlight the dramatic effect of the sculpture in the fountain.

Probably the most exciting Baroque monuments in Rome are the Piazza Navona, Bernini's Colonnade in St. Peter's Square, and the Church of San Carlo alle Quattro Fontane. The undulating facade of the

Church of San Carlo assures a changing play of light on the building as the day wears on. And the curved Bernini Colonnade in the Vatican furnishes a dramatic view of St. Peter's Basilica. However, the Piazza Navona, built on the site of the ancient Roman Hippodrome (made famous by the chariot races held there), is probably the best representation of the style of Baroque art and of the idea behind it. The Fountain of the Four Rivers (everything seems to come in fours!), also in the Piazza Navona, was designed by Bernini. Bernini also submitted an architectural design in connection with a competition for the commission to build the Church of St. Agnes, which was to face the fountain. Bernini was awarded the contract for building the fountain, but was dismayed to learn that his rival, Borromini, won the contract for the church itself. Nevertheless, Bernini had his Baroque — that is to say, theatrical and dramatic — revenge. He waited until the church was completed before finishing the Fountain of the Four Rivers. Then, he altered one of the figures in the fountain so that it faced the front of the church and held up its hands, as if in horror, and turned its head away as if to say, "I can't bear to look at that ugly thing." Such was the Baroque manner of revenge.

Another reason for the exuberance and vitality expressed in Baroque art may be found in the politics of the 16th and 17th centuries. It was a period of authoritarian rule and strict limitation upon individual freedom. Religious austerity and moral rigor were characteristics of both the Protestant Reformation and the Catholic Counter-Reformation. Burnings for witchcraft or for heresy were a common occurrence. In the political arena, kings became autocrats, holding powers of life and death over huge populations. It is no accident that Philip II of Spain and Louis XIV of France both ruled in this period. Under such conditions, with almost every phase of life regulated by the authorities, art was the one area left more or less free — at least as regarded color and design, if not subject matter. Consequently painting, sculpture, and architecture expressed an exuberance and joy which were denied in almost every other sphere of life. At this time too, opera, the most Baroque form of music, was born. In opera, the morally suspect (but extremely popular) theatre could be united with sublime music and thus pass religious muster, especially if the subject were religious or edifying.

As the Baroque period unfolded, art became more and more flamboyant until it began to deteriorate into sheer excess. Partially in reaction to this, *rococo* art began, evolving from the Baroque but stressing playfulness, elegance, refinement, and smallness of size as opposed to the monumentality of the Baroque. But that is a whole new story, and it affected France and Austria more than it did Italy.

Modern Rome

Contemporary Rome can be seen everywhere, but especially in the newer residential quarters of Parioli and Monte Mario. The apartment buildings in these areas are among the most modern in the world. In addition, the railroad station (Stazione Termini) is generally admired for its tasteful modern lines, as are the E.U.R. center in the south of Rome and the Olympic area in the northwest part of the city.

Italy, along with Scandinavia and Brazil, has become an important architectural center since the Second World War. It counts among its great architects Pier Luigi Nervi, whose use of reinforced concrete has revolutionized modern architectural design. Needless to say, the different "cities" of Rome are not neatly divided into sections or zones, but incorporated into the city proper. Stazione Termini, for instance, symbolizes this unity in a beautiful way. This modern building, constructed after World War II, is located on the site of Roman fortifications from the 5th century B.C. Parts of the ancient wall still stand in the plaza in front of the station. No one in Rome seems to find the contrast too unusual. This very ease in integrating the remnants of so many different periods of history into one cityscape has always been Rome's most striking feature. The native Roman is perfectly at home when he looks out the window of his modern high-rise apartment and sees an old Roman tower standing across the street. To him, it's all part of his magnificent city.

Essay 7.

SWITZERLAND AND THE PATTERN
OF EUROPEAN DEMOCRACY

No doubt one hears a great deal about Swiss democracy, and is anxious to see for himself how it works. But before visiting Switzerland, one should ask himself a few basic questions. How typical is Switzerland of European democracy? What, exactly, *is* European Democracy?

Begin with the second question. The word "democracy", like many of our most important words, comes to us from Greek. It means "rule by the people." In a truly democratic society, people participate directly in making the decisions which influence their lives. But this ideal has rarely been attained in history. Like the work, Western democracy itself goes back to ancient Greece, and especially to the "Age of Pericles." Aristotle's classic work Politics sums up the Greek experience during these times. But all *was* far from perfect. Athens was supposedly the most democratic city-state, but few of its inhabitants were allowed to vote. Many were slaves. The same problems beset the Roman Republic while it lasted.

Western democracy also goes back to the Germanic tribes which swept over Europe in the 5th century. They usually elected military leaders for their administrative and tactical skills. The Norse Vikings at first had the same custom. The oldest modern democratic constitution — still essentially in operation — dates from 930 in Iceland. There, all farmers, who were descendants of the Vikings, would gather every year in a common meeting-place to settle matters of law and justice.

But the Greek, Roman, and Germanic democratic traditions virtually died out in the Middle Ages. Monarchies became hereditary, and each feudal lord became a monarch unto himself. The modern concept of human rights was all but unknown, since legal justice was centered around the notion of contractual obligations, and these contracts were binding primarily among nobles, not between nobles and serfs.

Still, all was not undemocratic. Independent communes grew up in the 12th and 13th centuries, especially in Italy and southern France. These were towns whose people raised the money to buy their freedom from the feudal lords. They formed municipal governments and elected their own officials. But soon these communes were taken over by powerful families. In Florence, for example, though nobles were excluded from the town government, a family of wealthy bankers and merchants, the Medicis, became all-powerful in the 15th century.

One great medieval advance toward democracy was the *Magna Carta.*

King John of England was forced to grant this "Great Charter" to his barons in 1215. It reaffirmed the old idea of the "fedual contract." This idea construed civil government as an agreement between king and subject for mutual benefit. Thus subjects had the right to agree or disagree with their king's policies if they felt that these policies were injurious to the common good. The *Magna Carta* set forth principles which have since become familiar to us: taxation only with representation, trial by a jury of one's peers, and so on. These principles shaped the development of the English parliamentary system. They also inspired the political thought of John Locke, which in turn influenced our own founding fathers as they drew up the Constitution. Also, recall that England became a *republic* for several years in the 17th century. Cromwell and his followers executed King Charles I and Parliament took over for about 10 years. Even when the monarchy was restored, the power to make laws remained in the hands of an elected Parliament, as it is today.

But except in England, the era of modern nation-states did little at first to advance democratic institutions. Renaissance political theory is represented by the Florentine writer Machiavelli. He believed that a prince should be invested with virtually unlimited powers. In the 17th century, Louis XIV of France, the "Sun King," became the model of the absolute monarch. The king possessed unlimited power, appointing all officials and making the whole of France his personal bailiwick. As one visits the palace and gardens of Versailles, he finds it easy to visualize this spot as the center of political and cultural life in France in the 17th century. Thousands of nobles and attendants at court were carefully watched for any signs of dissent from Louis XIV's policies.

The 18th century replaced the concept of the absolute monarch with that of the "benevolent despot." This idea goes back to the notion of the "philosopher king", as expressed in Plato's *Republic.* It was assumed that a monarch of unlimited powers, such as Frederick the Great of Prussia, would do his best to promote the welfare of his people. This was sometimes the case, but more often it was not. Consider Catherine the Great of Russia: a despot indeed, but far from benevolent.

The failings of the "Old Regime" produced widespread discontent. Ideas about human equality and legal rights were proclaimed by philosophers and political writers, and began to spread to the ordinary citizen. In 1789 the French Revolution broke out. Its ideals of "Liberty Equality, Fraternity" stormed through Europe and brought in a whole new era of history. In the first few months of the French Revolution, a constitutional monarchy was retained, though dependent on a popularly elected national assembly. Soon, though, Liberty was forgotten, and the "terror" began. The King and Queen were guillotined, and people of dissenting opinions on all sides were imprisoned and executed. Thousands were forced into exile. Local revolts were suppressed by the army. Administration was concentrated in the capital. In France, town mayors were left with little authority of their own, and "prefects" (who correspond on a smaller scale to our governors) were appointed from Paris, not elected. (This system has persisted to the present day.) Military and economic mobilization for 25 years of war caused the French Republic to return to the same strong central government that the monarchy had built. Federalism, a loose union of semi-independent regions, was quickly abolished. Soon the French Republic went the way of the Roman Republic. Three "consuls" assumed broad powers, and in 1804 Napoleon Bonaparte, a successful general and "first consul," established the French Empire.

Democracy in our modern sense was instituted in Europe only in the late 19th and early 20th century. Kings were put back on their thrones after 1815, though their power was vastly curtailed. Even today, some European countries, such as Spain, Portugal and Greece, cannot really be called democratic. Since 1789, France has had a series of five republics (each with a different constitution), two monarchies, another empire, and a "French state" (under the German occupation). The present Fifth Republic, founded by de Gaulle in 1958, is basically a presidential system similar to ours, although it has dozens of small political parties instead of just two main parties.

In England, gradual reforms throughout the 19th and 20th centuries brought about a "constitutional monarchy," in which laws are made by an elected assembly. This is also the form of government in Belgium, Holland, Sweden, and, theoretically at least, in Spain. The German and Austrian Empires lasted until 1918. Italy was a monarchy until 1946. These countries (again excepting Spain) now have systems more or less similar to that of France. But nothing is unchanging, and in Europe democracy is still very much in flux.

This historical background gives the reader some idea of the problems confronting modern democracy. Centralism (strong central government) has tended to win out over federalism (weaker central government, with more regional independence). However, democracy is not easily adapted to the many social, economic and military tasks facing the modern industrial state. For example, the "welfare state" requires that everybody be taxed to provide services which some need more than others, such as social security, medical care, even education and food. Another problem (especially in South America) is that in times of war or crisis a government can easily be taken over by military leaders or by a single

dictator supported by the army. Also, growth in populations has made democratic processes more and more awkward to apply. It is hard to determine and respect the "will of the people" in a nation of 50,000,000, which is about average for the chief countries of Western Europe. Finally, any mass society finds it easy to neglect the rights of minorities in the name of "majority rule."

All these problems have virtually been solved, if indeed they ever existed at all, in Switzerland. The Swiss have always had a long tradition of local government. Even today, the male inhabitants of some smaller cantons gather each year to discuss laws and taxes, much like a New England town meeting. These meetings are known as *Landesgemeinden*. The smallest political units consist of *communes*; these elect town mayors and councilors, who are figures of great local importance. Swiss political life is based on families, not individuals. Only in 1970 were women granted the right to vote. The theory was that each woman has a chance to influence her husband, who then casts the family vote.

Distrust of strong government goes very far back in Swiss political history. Most Americans have heard the legend of William Tell, or seen his likeness on Swiss stamps. Think of Tell while driving through the quaint medieval town of Altdorf ("Old Town"), where he is supposed to have defied the Austrian governor. As his punishment, he was forced to shoot an apple on his son's head. Later, his assassination of the Austrian governor helped inspire the Swiss to revolt and establish their own confederation in 1291. Tell's revolt was as much against central government as against foreign oppression. Whether his story is history, legend, or folklore, he has become *the* Swiss national hero, and his protest against strong central government still influences Swiss political life.

Switzerland is Europe's only *federal* state, though West Germany is technically called one. It can be compared to our own system just after the War of Independence, when the states were reluctant to give up any of their powers to the central government. Switzerland's cantons have their own elected governments and traditions, many of them going back to the early Middle Ages. In 1291 an alliance was made among three small cantons — Uri, Unterwalden and Schwyz. The last of these three names became the basis for the name of the country. These cantons, plus that of Lucerne, the next to join their confederation, formed the geographical and historical heart of Swiss democracy. They are located in the center of Switzerland, around the "Lake of the Four Forest Cantons" (*Vierwäldstattersee* in German), also known as Lake Lucerne. From the original three cantons, the Swiss Confederation grew to 13 cantons by 1513, and in 1815 to today's 22 cantons.

Democracy can be endangered by too strong a central government. Switzerland has never had this problem. Swiss laws are made by an elected Federal Assembly with two Houses similar to our Senate and House of Representatives. But any law it makes can be vetoed by a referendum in which all citizens can vote. Thus the Swiss, unlike us, can always overrule their lawmakers. Also, the Federal Assembly is composed of members from many different parties, as in France and Italy. This means that the most varied opinions can be officially expressed and represented in Swiss political life.

The Federal Assembly is the legislative branch of government. It in turn elects the executive branch, called the Federal Council, which carries out the laws. The Federal Council is composed of seven men, and is responsible for foreign affairs, finance, justice, and defense. The Swiss dread the possibility that a strong personality will assume a dominating political position. As a result, the president of the Federal Council is elected for only one year and has extremely limited powers. It has long been an international joke that the average Swiss citizen hasn't the slightest idea who he is.

Another problem which has not plagued the Swiss is that of a strong "military establishment." The Swiss army is made up entirely of local militia, and in peacetime it has neither a professional officer corps nor a commander in chief. A long tradition of neutrality has kept Switzerland out of European wars since 1815, and the military has never had the opportunity to influence the government to any appreciable degree.

This, then, is a sketch of how Swiss democracy works. But the most important question, whether one is trying to understand the present or the past, is not "what" but "why." Why has Switzerland developed the unique political system which has kept it free of domestic turmoil and foreign military involvement for over 150 years? Naturally the venerated traditions we have been talking about have something to do with it, but they too must be explained.

Geography and climate explain a great deal. Even in summer, Swiss mountain communities are often isolated. Village and town customs still make up much of Swiss life. This is true even of towns like Andermatt and Göschenen, which are on the great communications route which crosses the St. Gotthard Pass. Imagine how isolated these mountain towns, and hundreds like them, must be especially in the wintertime. Many of them can be reached only by train, and even rail service comes to a halt when the mid-winter avalanches take over. Winter snows divide Switzerland into several areas which are nearly impossible to reach. Ticino, the Italian-speaking canton, is in touch with the rest of the country only by the St. Gotthard tunnel. Graubunden ("Gray League," the canton in the southeast where Romansch is spoken) can be reached only by the upper Rhine valley. And the canton of Valais has only one important road, which follows the upper Rhine valley. When it's out, only rail traffic is possible. It is natural, then, that isolated mountain communities should cling to their own customs and traditional political institutions.

Another explanation for the success of Swiss democracy is the small population. Recall the problems that large populations pose in France, England, Germany, and Italy. Switzerland, with a little over 5 million citizens, finds it much easier to sound out and respect popular opinion. Also, the Swiss' religious tolerance encourages respect for the views of their fellow citizens in other areas as well. This is essential in a democratic society. The same effect is brought about by Switzerland's legal recognition of four national languages — German, French, Italian, and Romansch. Switzerland is actually about half Catholic and half Protestant, and about the same proportion holds true for German and French-speaking citizens. These differences in religion and language encourage a strong regional life which is so distinctive a feature of Swiss democracy.

Let us turn back now and try to answer the questions we asked at the beginning. Can we say now why Swiss democracy is unique? Of course it is — because Switzerland *itself* is unique. Its special set of traditions (including local government, regional life, and a distrust of strong government) blend with the natural conditions of its environment, including the isolation of its regions, the diversity of its religious affiliations and language, and its small population.

But how, then, can Switzerland be incorporated into the history of democracy as we sketched it earlier? Switzerland as a whole, and its cantons and communes in particular, remain in the political tradition of the Greek city-state and the medieval commune. Switzerland comes as close as any nation in the modern world to the ideal of one of its famous sons, the 18th-century philosopher Rousseau, who proclaimed that "That government governs best which governs least."

THE FRENCH EXPERIENCE

Ask any European which country he considers the most "European" of all and he'll probably answer that it is France. Thomas Jefferson knew France well, and never lost his affection for it; he dubbed it "every man's second fatherland." How then, can it be that one also hears so many negative comments about the French — i.e. that they're rude and unfriendly, narrow-minded, inefficient, or even promiscuous? — though they seem to be falling behind the Scandinavians in this last line of criticism. We ourselves have often been unsure what to think of the French: we've seen a cab driver and a motorist argue for five minutes over just who dented whose fender in a Parisian traffic snarl, and then laugh the whole thing off as they both double-parked, sat down at a cafe, and argued about who would treat whom to a vermouth. It's only normal that most of what one reads about France tends to abound with adjectives like paradoxical, ambiguous or just plain baffling.

Obviously, to understand *any* foreign country, one has got to keep his mind open, but this is especially true of France. Variety, individualism, and a love of liberty are keys to the French way of life, and it takes about as open a mind as one can muster to appreciate them. Take the sheer variety of things in France. The country produces over 350 distinct types of cheese, more than the rest of the world combined. Each Frenchman has his favorites, and of course no two persons agree on which are the best. France is the only European country which touches the Mediterranean, the Atlantic, *and* the North Sea. The population of northern France is ethnically close to the Danes. Most people in Normandy can trace their ancestry back to Scandinavia. People in eastern France are more Germanic, and many actually speak German. In the south, life is sunny and relaxed, much like it is in Italy or Spain. The people in western France are Bretons and speak a language similar to Gaelic and Welsh. Then there are the Basques, whose language and culture are a complete mystery to experts, and unlike anything else in Europe. Imagine all this variety in a country roughly the size of Texas — about 20 times *smaller* than the U.S. French individualism shows itself at every turn, indeed at every intersection. Motorists, pedestrians and even bus-drivers interpret the traffic rules in their own way. If one goes into a bakery, a cafe, or any shop, the salespeople won't act like robots. Before the customer can give them a request, they may start talking to *him* about high taxes or their brother-in-law's case of neuralgia. In the U.S., a telephone operator has a set of about eight fixed phrases which she is supposed to use when talking to customers. In France, operators are alternately cheerful, irritable, or just plain indifferent, depending on how they feel when one talks to them. One of them may even tell a joke, or may admit that the phones aren't working too well and that it might be better to send a telegram.

The Frenchman's love of independence is possibly his most misunderstood trait. It consists of a general attitude which makes a prime virtue of minding his own business and expecting others to do the same. The visitor won't be in France for long before he spots the characteristic shrug of the shoulders, which is the Frenchman's reaction to all startling or shocking news. A remark of General de Gaulle illustrates this. When the news wires everywhere were crackling with the disturbing announcement that Premier Khrushchev of the U.S.S.R. had been deposed, de Gaulle was asked for his reaction. His answer: "So? The earth will not stop turning." It's easy enough to misunderstand the Frenchman's tolerance for rudeness or indifference, but it is still a mistake. Frenchmen don't believe in being extra-friendly toward total strangers, preferring instead to reserve their warmth for family and friends. The French are basically courteous, but instant friendliness is considered in bad taste. The French also have a great sense of discretion. French newspapers, for example, seldom if ever discuss the family, personal life, or religious beliefs of nationally-known figures. Few Frenchman know whether the French President is Catholic, Protestant, Jewish, or a nonbeliever, and they feel it's none of their business to find out.

It should be clear that generalizations about such a people can be extremely hazardous. Nonetheless there are certain features which unite the French. One is a deep pride in France as a nation. France is, after all, the modern world's oldest unified nation of any size. For centuries it was the most influential country in Europe, and it still is probably the center of the European artistic and intellectual life. The French have suffered great losses in the twentieth century and are understandably sensitive to the fact that France no longer plays so great a role on the world stage. The humiliation of four years of German occupation in World War II has left them with a strong desire to re-establish French influence in the rest of the world. The visitor has no choice but to respect their sensitivities in this regard.

Another unifying factor is the universal French respect for intellectual distinction. The French probably read more than any other people. The leading intellectual figures of the day receive the same kind of attention which heavyweight champions or television celebrities get in the U.S. The French are great believers in solving problems through rational analysis, and they look to the pronouncements of novelists and philosophers for guidance in everything from politics to love. The French educational system is one of the best in the world, in fact the envy of many other nations. President de Gaulle was recognized as a great contemporary master of French prose; President Pompidou started out as a literature teacher, and has published a fine anthology of poetry. The essence of this emphasis on the intellect is what the French call the *esprit critique* — the critical attitude. Every Frenchman is taught from earliest childhood to examine and analyze ideas for himself, and not to take anything for granted. The Frenchman dreads being hoodwinked more than anything else. This may have some unwanted effects on French political life, but it probably makes French conversation the most stimulating (and best-informed) anywhere. France and especially Paris is also proud of its role as a haven for some of the best minds in Europe. On Paris campuses, for example, there are students of every nationality preparing for leadership in their own countries. Artists who felt shackled in their home countries have often come to Paris to sample its heady atmosphere of creativity and freedom. One thinks of Hemingway, James Baldwin, F. Scott Fitzgerald, and James Joyce, or of the Spanish artists, Picasso and Casals, who found refuge in France. Two of France's leading playwrights are both foreigners who write in French: Samuel Beckett from Ireland, and the Roumanian, Eugène Ionesco.

But there is always the other side of the coin. The visitor to France must expect a fair amount of inefficiency, and it's obvious that France, while prosperous, is not quite as modern-looking as some other European countries, notably Germany. The Brilliant French intellectual record is not matched by industrial achievements, and France still exports "prestige" goods like wine and perfume instead of really profitable items like steel, computers, or automobiles. Many Frenchmen simply don't accept such modern conveniences as washing machines. (Washing machines, they believe, damage clothes.) But somehow, in spite of the slow rate of progress, the French seem to be reasonably happy with their way of life. They would rather spend an extra hour and a half over lunch, discussing politics or poetry, than rush back to the adding machine at the office. The best part of the French experience comes when one realizes that this may not be such a bad idea after all.

Essay 9

PARIS
The City of Light

It is said of many places that they are a "state of mind." The first one who said this must have been talking about Paris, because it's practically a documented fact that when pretty girls reach Paris they just "feel" prettier, painters can hardly wait to start in on their next masterpiece, and everyone instinctively knows there's something important afoot here, something absolutely and overwhelmingly unique. If anyone cared to, he could explain all this wonderment in terms of the city's history. There is the café where Voltaire held forth nightly, just across from the theatre where Molière gave of his life and wit. And there is a very special street which is always dark at night and which keeps getting narrower as one walks along; this is the street that generations of famous lovers have taken as they whiled away a Parisian evening, gazing into the Seine and into each other's eyes. There is no end to such examples, because every street in the center of Paris is charged with this kind of reminiscence. But the visitor to Paris need not think about Voltaire or anyone else to sense all that is special about this city. He can see the spirit of Paris just as it used to be, because the character of the city has changed little with the years. Today's Parisian is still very much the character he's always been — strong, temperamental, a bit eccentric — but basically as generous and as sensitive as anyone else.

Parisians are a distillation of everything in the French character; no other city in the world so dominates the country it is in. Parisians realize that in a real sense they are carrying all of France on their shoulders. One can spot this attitude in the exuberant Parisian fishmonger, hawking her trout and mollusks at one of the sprawling open markets, and shouting to passers-by to come smell how fresh her fish are and take advantage of the special price she's offering today. It's equally visible in the smart, snappy gestures of the Parisian café waiter, immaculate in his white jacket and handlebar moustache. He manages to pass out aperitifs, take orders, and flirt with a handful of girl customers, at one and the same time. Paris is beautiful enough, but it's best to see it as a gigantic stage-prop for a special way of life that goes on in the streets, alleys, cafés, and innumerable apartments of the City of Light.

The visitor can't help but notice a great many different kinds of Parisians, each one standing out in his own way. Paris is a crowded city, the cost of living is high, and the city is not noted for its modernity or conveniences. What redeems it all is the *style* of the Parisians, and the manner in which this style infects everyone who comes in contact with it. We can recall visiting Paris once with a middle-aged businessman who had just flown in from the U.S. He was unhappy with Paris. It was his opinion that all the old buildings should be pulled down to make way for air-conditioned hotels and shopping centers. We hope that before the end of his stay, he did get to visit at least one of those tiny neighborhoods of Paris where life may be a bit old-fashioned, but where *people* somehow prevail. Policemen, bankers, little children in dark blue smocks, old ladies all in black, — all can be seen lining up at midday outside the bakery to bring home the three-foot-long loaves of bread for lunch. People don't just walk into the bakery and grab a loaf; they go through an elaborate ritual of asking the baker's wife how her children are doing in school, whether her sister is feeling better, and what the weather looks like for tomorrow. There are quicker ways to distribute bread, but this personal, human style is what makes Paris so distinctive.

No two neighborhoods are quite alike, however, and the visitor should try to get to know several of them. The right bank of the Seine tends to house offices and the apartments of the well-to-do, but in the middle of the right bank in the plateau of Montmartre, a quiet, isolated section which is inhabited mostly by musicians, artists, and show people, and which claims to be a separate "republic," independent of the rest of France. In the central area of the right bank are the glamorous districts which correspond roughly to New York's Fifth Avenue — the fashionable shopping area around the Opera, and the elegant cafés of the Champs-Elysées, just around the corner from the headquarters of Dior and the other major designers. Many offices have moved into this neighborhood, and it is hectic by day though relatively calm at night. Probably the most typically "Parisian" quarters are on the smaller Left Bank. The hub for this part of Paris is the Latin Quarter, which has been the center of student life since the founding of the University of Paris in the thirteenth centruy. Just adjacent to the university sector are Montparnasse and Saint-Germain-des-Près, both gathering places for writers and journalists. At any one of the cafés here one is likely to overhear an animated conversation between two economists from the university faculty, see a well-known starlet sipping coffee with a contro-versial young newspaper columnist, or come across a painter, one of the thousands in Paris, sketching away as he watches the passing crowd. The surprising part of these neighborhood experiences is that the very smallness of the area makes the visitor feel instantly that he's a *part* of what is going on. All one needs is a bit of curiosity and imagination.

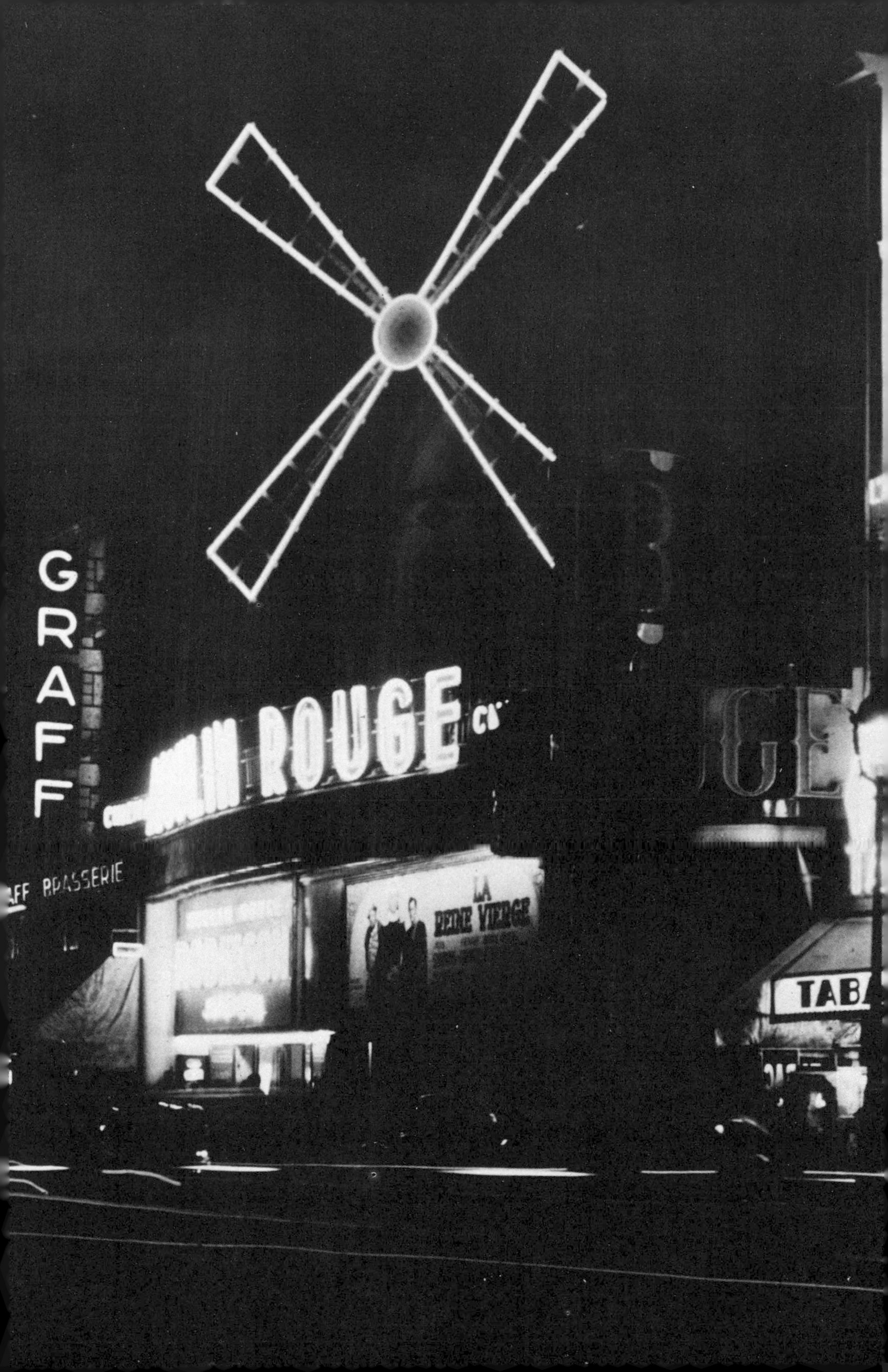
GRAFF
ROUGE
BRASSERIE
LA
REINE VIERGE
TABA

It's tempting to allow the many tiny delights of life in Paris to charm one into forgetting the many places that one really *should* see in order to understand the life of the city. Notre Dame cathedral must certainly be first on the list; it's best to walk there one quiet afternoon and slowly take it all in — the way one might read a book. Paris is also a city of monumental public squares, such as the Place de la Concorde, the Etoile (with 12 avenues all radiating symmetrically from one central traffic circle), and the massive Place de l'Opera, surrounding the world's largest indoor theater. Art-lover or not, one should devote a good part of at least one day to the Louvre, and we also recommend the Jeu de Paume museum for those who are attracted by French Impressionism — which turns out to be most everybody. If one can understand French and happens to like the theater, he should try attending a performance at the Comedie Française; student rates are about $1.50 for good seats. In all cases, the visitor should get into the habit of walking casually around Paris, letting Paris take him where *it* wants to. He'll soon discover that Paris has a life all its own: it wants to tell him its secrets, making a Parisian out of him bit by bit. He shouldn't be surprised if he ends up uncovering a Paris that only he knows about, made up of the singular sights and emotions he experienced while unwrapping Paris' treasures one by one.

Essay 10

CHARTRES
A Microcosm of Medieval Belief

Introduction

Chartres Cathedral is generally considered to be the most stylistically consistent and purest representative of all the great medieval monuments. Chartres, like any medieval cathedral, is a book, and Chartres in particular provided medieval man with what was then a liberal education. Indeed, for the common man, it was his *only* education. Chartres' 10,000 pictures in glass and sculpture were the encyclopedia of what man should "know and believe to his soul's health", namely the history of the world from Creation, the history of redemption, the dogmas of theology, the good examples of the saints, the hierarchy of virtues and vices, and finally the range of the sciences, arts, and crafts.

For medieval man, art had to be didactic. The medieval view of art was worlds away from that, say, of a Renaissance man of letters like Benvenuto Cellini. Medieval art was not primarily meant to give pleasure to the eye or to "express" the personality of the artist, but to give symbolic form to an edifying idea.

For the medieval mind, the cathedral was a microcosm of the world — not just the visible world, but more importantly the invisible. It was the invisible which gave significance to the visible. The building itself was laid out in the form of a cross, summarizing the idea that history is redemption and that all the works of man are to be a testimony to that redemption. The cathedral faces the east, the rising sun, symbol of birth and resurrection. For the medieval mind, salvation always comes from the East, i.e. the Holy Land. The north, in contrast, is the realm of cold and darkness. This idea comes from late ancient times, when the "North" stood for hosts of unconverted Germanic tribes. Thus in the liturgy, before the Gospel is read, the reader moves the book from the southern to the northern, i.e. from the right to the left, side of the altar, symbolically proclaiming it to those most in need of it, i.e. the Germans. This custom still survives in the Roman Catholic Mass.

The north side of the cathedral is usually reserved for representations of the Old Testament figures: i.e. the Law and the Prophets and the history of Israel. The idea was that before the Germanic tribes could begin to comprehend the subtler truths of the Christian Gospel, they first had to have instilled in them a sense of law in general, which would restrain their chaotic plunder and wanderings. Hence the stress of the Law and Prophets on the north wall of the cathedral.

The south, in contrast, is warm and bright. The southern wall of the cathedral is festooned with pictures representing the Gospel stories and the legends of the saints. The west wall, especially the façade on the outside, is usually filled with pictures and statuary representing the final doom: the Last Judgment, etc. For the medieval mind, the west was the region of gloom, old-age, and death, symbolized by the dying sun. Hence the preoccupation of the west wall with themes of death and judgment.

Whenever sculptured figures are grouped in a collage, the more important figures stand on the lesser ones. For example, Moses is supported by the golden calf, Balaam stands on his mule, and the Apostles ride piggy-back on the Prophets' shoulders.

Numbers, like objects of nature, always had a symbolic significance for medieval man. The four-and-twenty elders of the Apocalypse correspond to the numerical sum of the twelve prophets and the twelve disciples. The number seven, above all, held a special importance; it stood for the complete (i.e. redeemed) man, and symbolized his dual nature (four=the body; three=the soul). There were the seven ages of man, the seven deadly sins, seven virtues, seven sacraments, and the seven planets which govern man's destiny (one governing each of man's seven ages). There were the seven tones of the Gregorian chant, expressing the harmony of the heavens. The number five also had great importance. There were the five foolish virgins, representing the five senses, and five wise virgins, representing the five forms of religious contemplation.

Medieval art was highly stylized. Along with their craft, medieval craftsmen learned a way of representing sacred figures. Peter, for example, always had to have curly hair, a tonsure, short beard, and keys. Paul had to be bald with a long beard. (See Albrecht Dürer's portrayal of Paul in his famous painting *The Four Apostles.*) The Virgin Mary had to wear blue, her traditional color, a veil (symbol of virginity and of the religious life), and wear shoes.

Pagan legend and myth were also given a place. One can see signs of the zodiac, Greek dieties (often depicted as vices or virtues), pagan philosophers, the phoenix (a mythical bird representing resurrection), the unicorn and the maiden (unicorn=Christ, maiden=Virgin Mary). Outside the cathedral, where fancy could run wild, one finds grotesques and gargoyles to fend off evil spirits.

Cathedral Activity

A drawing by Peter Breughel the Elder (1559) suggests what the atmosphere inside a medieval cathedral must have been like. People are packed in like sardines. Two friars are preaching, a Mass is being celebrated as well as a marriage; indulgences and livestock are being sold, and a pardoner is hearing confession. Apparently this is an ordinary day, for Breughel shows no elaborate processions or other festive decoration. Everybody is simply "doing his own thing".

Abbot Suger of St. Denis (12th century) describes the crush on a festival day at his cathedral: "Howling men, half-fainting women screaming as if giving birth, pilgrims wishing to see the hallowed relics, so eager that the monks in charge had to flee through the windows, taking the relics with them." Probably the good abbot exaggerates a bit, but he makes clear that medieval churches were hives of religious *activity,* in contrast to ours, which are open for "meditation".

Among other things, the Middle Ages was a period of great and robust preachers, and preaching was a highly specialized art. Preaching friars drew great crowds, much as our politicians organize great rallies. Cathedrals also served as halls for public meetings – whether great gatherings of nobles, popular protests, or heresy trials. After all, it was always the largest building in town. Heresy trials themselves, from the second half of the 13th century especially, were great public spectacles, enhanced with appropriate and popular forms of torture, to strike the fear of God into the faithful and to remind them of the horrors to come in Hell if they should miss Mass or confession or fail to purchase adequate indulgences. With "bell, book, and candle", unbelievers or heretics were separated from Mother Church and declared damned; at best they might get the cat-o'-nine-tails, at worst be burned.

Cathedrals were also used for great public thanksgivings – say, for the city's having been spared the plague – or acts of public penance – if the plague had carried off half the town. Military victories called for pomp and celebration, plagues for sackcloth and solemn fasting.

More prosaically, the cathedral was the normal place for townspeople to meet to discuss private business deals. It was a place where begger and pilgrim alike would sleep on the straw-covered pavement. These pilgrims would journey to the cathedral from miles around, on foot. They would stay for a week and then return. The week in question would usually be that of the patron saint of the cathedral, centering around the saints' day. (Cf. Chaucer's description of these pilgrims in the Prologue of his *Canterbury Tales.*) The cathedral was also a sanctuary for the accused. The latter could not be touched as long as he remained inside.

Sanitary conditions inside the cathedral were abysmal. In Chartres, for example, one notices that the stone floor of the ambulatory (i.e. the walkway around the sides and back of the altar) is uneven. It slopes in various directions, and these slopes form a shallow trough. This sloping is not the result of wear or aging. The trough was designed from the very first to carry off the water which would be dumped by the bucketfuls on the floor in order to wash away the remains left there by the hordes of pilgrims who would spend the night sleeping on the floor. The olfactory qualities of the cathedral can only be left to the imagination. One can readily appreciate the practical function served by the incense, and why it was so prodigiously used.

But above all, the cathedral was the house of God, the Bible of the poor, the shrine of the Sacrament, a gigantic reliquary in the shape of the Cross, the quintessential expression of medieval civilization — of its best and most ingenious qualities, and perhaps too, of its worst.

The Concept of the Gothic

The interests of the early humanists of the Renaissance (Petrarch and others) in classical Greco-Roman culture inspired Italian artists to imitate classical forms. They believed themselves to be reviving the "rational" architecture of the ancients, which the "barbarians" has destroyed, especially the French and Germans. Rappall's theory gave credit to the Germans — "Goths" — for discovering the pointed arch: because they hadn't yet invented the hatchet, they bent together the branches of trees to form roofs. Because the Goths had sacked Rome in 410 A.D., the word took on the connotations of wild, savage, unlearned, extravagant, grotesque, in short, unclassical — and therefore repugnant to the enlightened Renaissance man. Gothic architecture was "tolerated" until the Romantics rediscovered it in the 19th century, construing it as "natural", free, and symbolic of man's soaring, untrammeled spirit. Goethe saw it as the personification of the German character. Henry Adams interpreted the Gothic as "the struggle of (man's) own littleness to grasp the infinite."

The Gothic Principle

Before the Gothic era, arches were constructed in less than ingenious ways. For example, there are records of churches built on top of and around huge mounds of earth, which were later dug out. If all went well, the arches wouldn't collapse. In any case, walls to support such round vaults had to be extremely thick and permitted only small openings for windows.

The Gothic architects developed pointed arches and flying buttresses to support them. These buttresses counteract and support the weight of the vaulted ceiling; the weight of the vault is neutralized by the but-tresses, making it possible to construct walls which are virtually skeletons, almost razor thin in view of the weight they support. The Gothic builders capitalized on the large openings, and instead of blocking them up with stone, filled them with stained glass, adding not only light but splendid color.

The Gothic principle can be summarized this way: every stone that adds weight to the structure must also add to its strength. Pointed arches and flying buttresses made a Gothic structure self-supporting.

The Shape of the Cathedral

The shape of the typical cathedral is that of the cross. Running east to west is a long, narrow, vaulted hall which is intersected by a similar hall running north and south. The east-west hall is thus divided into two unequal parts. The longer part, running west of the intersection, is called the nave (from *navis*, Latin for "ship"; visualize a boat turned upside down). The nave was reserved for the laity, especially for sermons. The shorter part, running east of the intersection, is the chancel or choir, where the monks sang the nine daily services. At the end of the chancel is the high altar and the *cathedra* or bishop's throne, from which the term "cathedral" comes. Often a wall, or at least a screen, separated the chancel from the nave, because of the loud activity going on in the latter. The hall running north and south, and intersecting the nave, is called the transept, or more correctly, transepts, one of them the "north transept", the other the "south transept". Between the buttresses which support the vaulted ceiling are numerous chapels dedicated to various saints; at the various altars each priest would say his daily Mass, and pilgrims would adore the sacred relics. At the west end of the nave, outside, stand two great towers, usually of equal height, but at Chartres one is 344 ft. and the other is 377 ft. (vs. Notre Dame in Paris, whose towers are both 225 ft.) Between the towers are three great doors; the central portal is surmounted by Christ in Majesty, surrounded by beasts representing the four gospels and by a multitude of saints. The great east end of the church, semicircular, is called the chevet, from which radiate yet more chapels.

Relics

The awe with which the medieval churchman venerated relics of the saints can hardly be exaggerated. To men of the time, the beauty of churches was always less important than that of the reliquaries they housed. The latter were of gold or silver and were embellished with precious stones. The real treasure, however, was the relic itself: a piece of rotted cloth, a bit of a fingernail, a splinter of bloodstained wood.

However, the Virgin, believed to have been assumed into heaven, had left no relics to be venerated, and so it often happened that statues of mother-goddesses (pre-Christian but believed to be of supernatural origin) were venerated instead. At Chartres there is preserved a likeness of "Our Lady Underground", the pagan effigy of a Roman goddess worshipped at Chartres in pre-Christian times. It was as if pagans had been worshipping the true Virgin unwittingly, and so Christians later built a church to enshrine the image. This is the origin of the Cathedral of Chartres. The original effigy was destroyed during the Revolution.

Stained Glass

Though almost everything about Chartres seems to require superlatives, there is one feature of the cathedral which towers above all others — the stained glass, and particularly the "Chartres blue". Even on an overcast day, the rich, bright blue of the glass glows as if incandescent. Chartres' glass is remarkable for its stylistic unity. 175 of the windows were produced in the first 30 years of the 13th century, a staggering enterprise in view of the work required for each one. Almost all of the original glass remains.

A word about stained glass in general. Colored glass was used on a small scale as early as the 7th century in Byzantium, but the windows were very small and the designs abstract. Much later, simple designs of sacred symbols and saints were constructed, and by the 10th century in France, more sophisticated "storybook" windows began to appear. It was not until the pointed arch and the flying buttress made possible large openings, however, that the full possibilities of stained glass as a teaching device were realized.

The art of making stained glass was a joint effort of designer, glassmaker, and painter — not to mention the builder, who had to install the window without breaking it. Medieval stained glass is known as "pot-metal glass" because metal shavings were added to the molten glass. Cobalt produced blue glass; copper; green; and ochre, red. A much inferior, slipshod method was simply to paint on clear glass. When the colored glass had cooled, it was cut to match the shapes of the designer's "cartoon". Sometimes lines were painted on the glass (e.g. curly lines might suggest a beard, or facial features might be sketched in). Then the glass was put back into the kiln to fuse the enamel into the glass. Finally, the pieces were assembled into sections, soldered together with strips of lead, and were handed over to the builders to be set into the walls of the cathedral.

At Chartres the windows were arranged according to an elaborate scheme: the aim was to illustrate the whole idea and history of redemption, but in so simple and compelling a manner that the illiterate peasant could understand and believe.

Chartres

Five previous churches – all highly flammable – stood on the site of Chartres. The fifth, Romanesque, did not burn entirely; the western towers and the "Royal Portal" between them still stand. Note the great size of the rose window (44 ft. in diameter); the rose was Mary's flower and emblem and Chartres was her church. According to Henry Adams: "At Chartres one sees everywhere the Virgin, and nowhere any rival . . . " An exaggeration, but it makes the point that more than even Christ, Mary caught the imagination of the medieval mind. Just as chivalric love idealized woman, so medieval religion made the Virgin the apotheosis of its worship.

Ordinarily, the building of a cathedral took at least generations, if not centuries. Notre Dame of Paris took over 200 years to complete. Somehow, the people of Chartres were able to build their cathedral in about 20 years. Everyone pitched in – laborers, stonemasons, carpenters, glassmakers; it was a communal effort in every sense of the term. As a result, Chartres represents a rare architectural unity (except for the unequal towers), and not the stylistic hodgepodge that most cathedrals became.

Some final statistics:

length: 507 ft.
height of the nave: 122 ft.
"Old Tower" (which is actually the newer): 377 ft.
"New Tower" (really the older): 344 ft.
width of nave (widest in France): 52 ft.
area: 68,260 sq. ft.

Suggestions for further reading: The classic (and most thorough) study of Gothic art and medieval religious symbolism is Emile Male's *The Gothic Image. Mont-Saint-Michel and Chartres,* by Henry Adams, is easier to read and gives a genuine "feel" for this fascinating period.